Case for UFOs

By

John J. Ventre

Cover Art by

Richard Lang

www.LangPublication.com

All characters appearing in this book are fictional. All political events depicted or referenced in this book are fictitious. Any resemblance to actual political situations, and or real persons, living or dead, is purely coincidental. Statements and opinions expressed in this book are not in any way representative of Lang Publication (the publisher).

Publication Date: Aug. 25, 2015, 2nd printing Oct. 31, 2020
ISBN: 978-0-9883606-5-5
LANG PUBLICATION
Printed in USA
Word count: 82,494.

Table of Contents

Prologue

"For the time has come for thee to reap;
For the harvest of the earth is ripe"
Revelation 14:14

If you held a contest or convinced a game show to describe a phenomena that appears and disappears, has been around for centuries, shows itself in the shadows of your bedroom at 3 am, enters and possesses your body or mind and returns repeatedly as an uninvited guest; what would a person say it was? My guess would be a malevolent spirit or entity and not scientists or ambassadors from another planet. So then, why all the elaborate camouflage? Thirty percent of Americans experience some form of unexplained event. The bible states that, "Our struggle is not against flesh and blood but against the spiritual forces of evil in the heavenly realms". Do these unknown forces appear to us in the form that we would best receive it; ghosts, angels, aliens, demons or creatures?

I have taken a twenty year journey that I believe is coming to a conclusion. I have never seen a UFO and had no interest in the subject until I was almost 40 years old. I was a B-movie, comicon, horror movie and magazine fan as a kid. I had no interest in ET unless it was a cool movie creature like in Predator or Alien and there was a lot of action in the movie. I started to experience paranormal activity in my early thirties when I moved to Oklahoma weeks after almost getting on doomed Pan Am flight 103 while returning from Europe. This inadvertently led me to wanting to write a sci-fi novel regarding end time prophecy which led me to the UFO question.

Along the way, my opinion has changed numerous times as to the nature of this elusive intrusive subject where the aliens are not human but so similar that the word alien is a misnomer. My involvement with MUFON was nuts and bolts; "They" were ships from outer space. As I learned more about the phenomenon, my opinion changed to, "They" were inter-dimensional. I was searching for the string theory of the unexplained. You can only form your opinion after reading many books with different viewpoints on the topic. My books have gone from religious to anti-religious to the genetic engineering of us to Tribulation. A ramping up of paranormal activity recently and my research into the abduction phenomena has pushed me towards a different conclusion which you will read later in this book which may surprise you.

This subject matter has landed me on the *Anderson Cooper* show along with 27 episodes on seven TV series and 80 lectures on YouTube. I ran into Fran Drescher on the *Anderson Cooper* show in 2012. We were in third grade together in Flushing Queens, NY. I do a UFO talk show on public TV twice a month in Pittsburgh and I was a regular host on *Hangar 1: The UFO Files*; all of which will lead to more TV appearances (I hope).

Many experts in this field have said that the Ufologists are sometimes more interesting than the actual subject matter, I agree. Although I have found more than a few experts in this field to be small minded and self-centered (the scientists and far left liberals), many have been pretty friendly but there is also a very hateful element. The abduction experts are clueless and are only in it to write books. There seems to be a narrow minded hostile prejudice that UFOs have to be from outer space only. Do boats come from beneath the sea? There is also naivety among scientists that the government is incompetent and is not covering up anything. That's probably based on their desire for grant money. Why are "Our Efforts" to achieve space flight viewed differently by scientists and the media than an "ET effort to get here"? Like a monkey in a library, our scientific community seems to suffer from a severe case of consensus "swamp gas". I read Carl Sagan's book, *Demon Haunted World*, and he praised science to the hilt saying that there are no dumb questions but then goes on to debunk every unexplained event and theory in history. What a hypocrite! In the Bible, all scientists would be named Thomas. I actually tore the book in half on my *UFOs over Pittsburgh* TV talk show and said I would use it for kindling. I've never destroyed a book before. We should turn the tables on scientists and analyze UFO reports based on why they are not natural and we would end up with around 40% as unexplained by using science. I firmly believe the UFO question will not and cannot be solved through our science which has a closed universe view sponsored by a fascist men's club that tows the line to protect their grant funding and reputations.

Another common delusional thread among nearly all of the experts is the belief that they will be the "One" who breaks the greatest story never told. Disclosure won't come from any of them but I will tell you as you read on where it will come from (not me even though a retired NSA agent told me it would). Since I am piling it on, it is a complete waste of time to voice your opinion on Facebook forums. They always have haters and antagonists that make it impossible to have an adult conversation. Reading comprehension is also an issue. Some people pick out a word or sentence and make an issue of it while missing the point of the paragraph. I have been savagely attacked by people who want disclosure but don't understand freedom of speech. I've turned my notifications off and only post my conferences and books there.

There are three species on earth that wage war; ants, chimps and humans. We already saw in the movie *Planet of the Apes* that chimps and apes would have to be upgraded in order to take us on. How do you think red ants would do in a war against humans? They obviously wouldn't stand a chance. We would stamp or pesticide them out. We are the red ants in comparison to these intruders who come and go with impunity for thousands of years. But just who are they? Sometimes you can miss the facts but catch the truth!

I have found the UFO question to be the most profound of my life and it has led me to where I need to be and was probably meant to end up. But like Bruce Lee's JKD style of fighting, you must clear your mind of preconceived ideas and boundaries in order to see what is actually confronting you and how to react to it.

Acknowledgement

To the 38 Pennsylvania MUFON field investigators that volunteer against all odds and are in actuality a minority group seeking Affirmative Action. And to the non-human entities that make life interesting if not dangerous for the soul. Only 1/350,000 people investigate UFOs so every one of them is important.

In 1999, I attended my first MUFON Symposium and experienced some very disturbing lucid dreams that lasted for nearly a week. I also discovered I wasn't the only one to have these experiences after a UFO conference. Did I awaken some repressed memory in my mind? Was I followed home by a hybrid or a demon? Did I open a door? Read my conclusion later in this book.

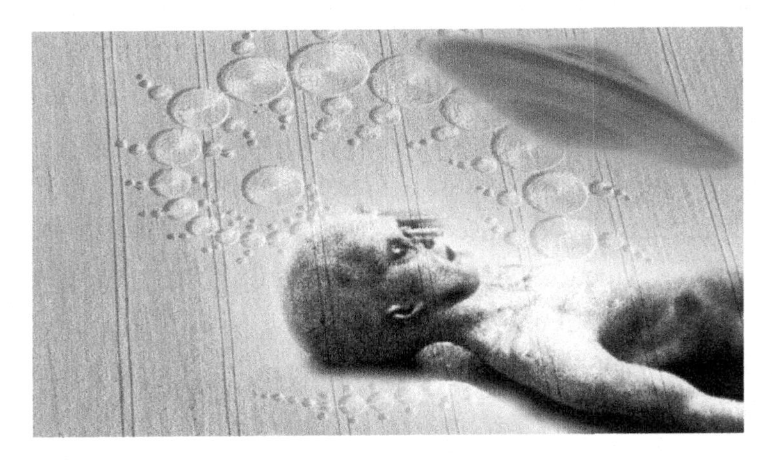

The 1950's *contactee* movement and the *Ancient Aliens* TV series have probably hurt UFO credibility the most. Then again we had the 1996-2006 Ray Santilli *Alien Autopsy* hoax and the current L. Ron Hubbard *Scientology* fraud regarding an alien named *Xenu.* I've met a few people in this field who aren't what they appear to be. No, not aliens or government agents but scammers who obfuscate the truth for others. They have criminal records and/or falsify their work credentials like my former chief investigator Butch Witkowski claiming to have been a homicide detective for 27 years and being a decorated Vietnam Vet or just make up encounters or think every approaching airplane is a morphing UFO. *Coast to Coast AM* continues to have these people on as guests even though they are aware of their falsified backgrounds. It must be really hard to find material to do a nightly show. Some are copy and paste experts and their daily emails contain server bugs and viruses like Lon Strickler who also loves to attack his competition by using fake email names.

I have others in mind but one clear cut personality is Stan Romanek. He basically claimed that every event that has ever happened to every UFO victim has also happened to him. SyFy's TV show, *Fact or Faked,* disproved his alien at the window prop. He wrote books and was a headline speaker at nearly every major UFO Conference. Oh how "we want to believe" and how gullible we are. On YouTube on Feb 9, 2014 you can see Stan on the Peter Slattery show in what appears faking paranormal activity twice. A week later he was arrested for possession of child porn. Similar to Wendelle Stevens's defense in 1983, Stan claims the government planted the evidence. Stevens pleaded guilty. Stan proceeded to open an online GoFundMe site requesting $60k to pay his legal fees even though at the time he had a "paid for" public attorney. I feel sorry for his wife.

James Carrion was correct in calling Stan out as a fraudster in 2010. In 2012, I fell victim to his potential crowd draw and invited him to speak at my Pittsburgh MUFON UFO Conference. He insisted his wife also speak so Pa MUFON sprung for two plane tickets. Stan cancelled their appearance 30 days out because he said he had medical issues. I found out he was actually at a high profile dinner in Bucks County soliciting funds for himself. Stan never did reschedule or refund the $765 in plane costs. If you Google Stan you can read his sorted history and results of his trial conviction which means Stan has to register as a sex offender.

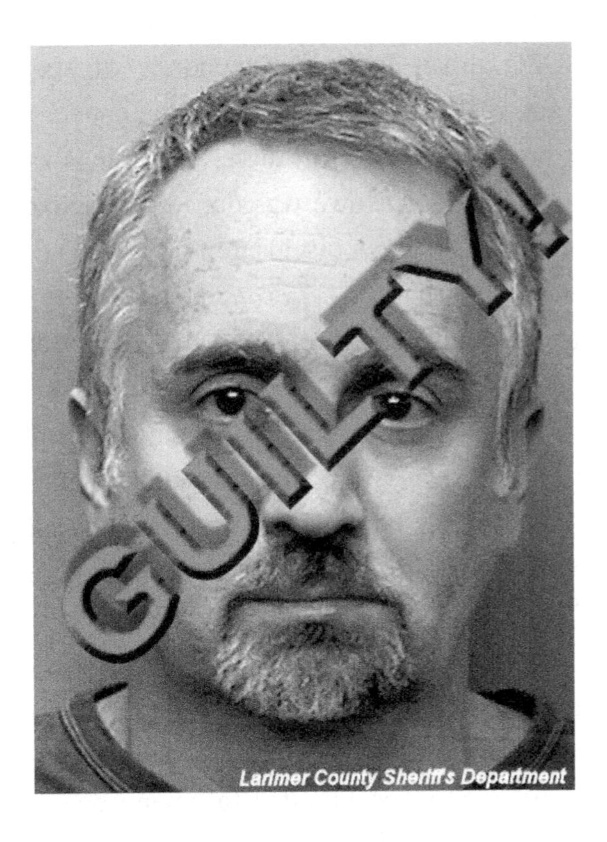

It's a shame that this field, like televised religion, draws in so many with compulsive or psychological issues (Stan was declared competent in March of 2015 to stand trial in June which was postponed to July 2017). Maybe that's all part of the spider web cover story that makes it impossible to unravel. I'm thinking of starting an online site but instead of naming it "Open Minds", which already exists, I'll call it "Simple Minds". We also have David Wilcock and Mike Bara whose Moon and Mars rocks look like rocks but we are told are petrified wheels, aliens, vehicles or buildings. Wilcock is a great story teller who never lets truth get in the way whereas Bara seems bored with his own presentations. And of course Dr. Steven Greer who has a mummified "Atacama" baby alien and he can channel spacecraft at will for a fee. Jaime Maussan promotes everything as if true. Stan Gordon mixes his Kecksburg UFO urban legend with stories of six foot slugs, werewolves and real pterodactyls in the same county where I live and I have never seen any of these. Gullible award winning journalist Linda Moulton Howe was duped by Richard Doty into believing she would be given disclosure for an HBO documentary. She then defended the fake *caret drone* pictures as real and oddly kept asking the audience at our Pittsburgh conference about alligator headed aliens until a number of people walked out.

We also have Ancient Alien guru Erich von Daniken who, in 1970, spent three years in prison for embezzlement (charges dropped in 1982). While in prison, he wrote his book *Return of the Gods*. He claims to be the shepherd of *Ancient Alien theory* but like a wolf in sheep's clothing covertly preaches atheism with a smile. The most famous abductee of all, whose story I believe, had a teenage criminal record for burglary and forgery. Don Schmitt of CUFOS and Roswell fame falsified his credentials. In a 1990 interview, Whitley Strieber admitted to having been a witch and occult follower. "I made choices a long time ago that brought me this experience". One of the main Kecksburg UFO witnesses, Jim Romanski, was convicted of robbing a bank. I guess "stuff happens" but it becomes harder and harder to say these people are 100% credible. These same "Lib-tards" who vehemently support these people recently can out against me for voicing my opinion against white genocide. I used free speech against hate speech but the politically correct cognitive dissonant left can't be reasoned with. They then claimed I had always been an FBI agent protecting MUFON and Bigelow money. In April of 2017, self-proclaimed prophet Sean David Morton and his wife were arrested for civil securities fraud and are in federal prison.

I'm a very good public speaker with twenty two very different presentations. Many lecturers are like a one trick pony with the same presentation from 20 years ago. My biggest disappointment so far with the added TV exposure is that I'm not asked to speak at conferences on the west coast or Europe. Oddly, researchers and historians are asked to lecture but investigators, who have first-hand information, are not. There are zero MUFON investigators on the conference lecture circuit plus, when asked to lecture, we are not paid properly because we don't have an agent. The *Aliencon* and *Comicons* are the worst. They charge $49 a day admission, get huge crowds and want you to lecture for free. The 13th amendment abolished slavery!

"The more you know, the less you understand"

I donated $13k to the Mutual UFO Network during the recession and I am one of five "Inner Circle" major donors. I also came within two Board votes of becoming MUFON's International Director in 2012 even though I said I would not accept a salary and the person they selected did. The two comments aren't related. In 2017, I removed MUFON from my will. Exec Dir. Jan Harzan left MUFON in 2020 due to criminal charges. Was he set up? Who benefits? Will the 3 letter agency heavy TTSA benefit and why trust them? They want to control the UFO narrative and are clearly government influenced.

Publication Note:

When I published *An Alternative History of Mankind*, I had wanted to split it into two books but decided to combine a fictional tale of our history with all of the proof for UFOs. Although *Alternative History* has been very successful, I realized the *Case for UFOs* deserved its own publication so I split *Alternative History* into two books and doubled the amount of factual material in *The Case for UFOs*.

I'd like to thank the ***Lucius Farish Grant*** trust.

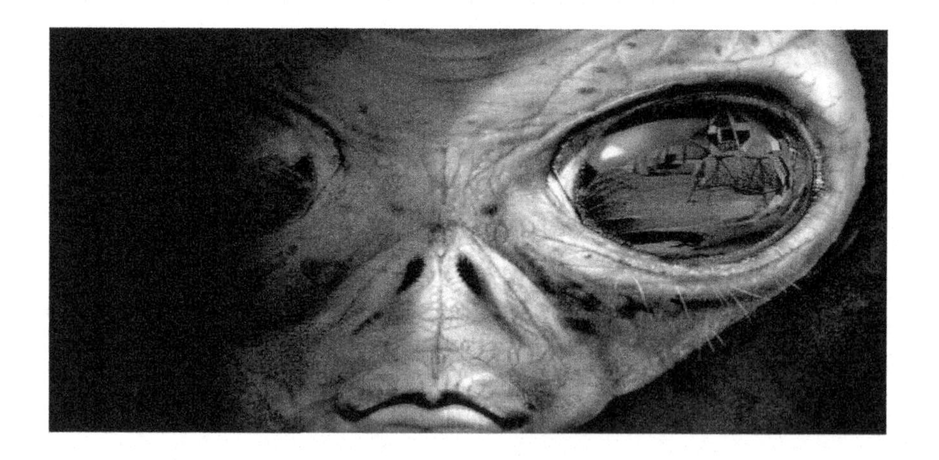

I WRITE THIS BOOK IN DEFIANCE OF THE PENTAGON, CIA AND SCIENTIFIC COMMUNITIES!

"There are two equal and opposite errors that humans can fall. One is to disbelieve in their existence. The other is to believe and feel an excessive and unhealthy interest in them". - - - CS Lewis

Chapter 1

THE CASE FOR UFOs

"If there are no UFOs, then why the secrecy?"

(Courtesy Sandeep Karunakaran)

"Google before you Giggle"- John Ventre

The history of UFOs over earth goes back centuries. It can be traced through every culture and every time period of our so called "evolution". I had heard of rock carvings, Nazca lines and ancient tales. Interestingly, these ancient cultures all speak of acquiring knowledge from star people and Gods. The miracles performed in the time of Moses lead the Egyptians to try and invent the failed science of alchemy. Most cultures also de-evolved into ritual human sacrifices to these Gods. Will history repeat itself? The true recorded history of ancient man was destroyed in 391 AD when the Romans destroyed the library of Alexandria in Egypt. A second repository may lie under the left paw of the sphinx in Egypt.

The more you investigate this field, the more you learn and cannot dismiss the inconvenient facts. What surprised me were the Renaissance paintings and biblical connection to UFOs along with the many government documents and the covert interference regarding UFO research.

Sumerian is our oldest text and Hindu is the oldest religion we know of. Both date back to 6000 BC. The Hindu Mahabharata was written 3500 years ago after being passed down through word of mouth and speaks of flying craft with detailed flight manuals and a detailed nuclear battle in Mohenjo-Daro India (now Pakistan). Skeletons found there are 50 times more radioactive than they should be and sand and rock have been vitrified from high heat.

You should read some of the excerpts from it or purchase my DVD, *UFOs in Art and History.*

In Abydos Egypt, there is a 4600 year old structure that contains a plaque with five modern aircraft and subs depicted. You also have to ask why the older pyramids were nearly perfectly built and in alignment with the compass while the newer imitations were poorly built and are crumbling. In Baalbek Lebanon there are 1200 ton stones that were quarried 50 miles away. Who lifted them? These ancient structures were surely built with advanced technology by non-humans or by the Nephilim who were upgraded hybrid humans. Our modern cranes cannot lift these huge stones.

If you read my book, *An Alternative History of Mankind,* I give many examples of UFO/ET involvement and interference in our history from Egypt to all wars to the present. But what is their origin and agenda?

The Mayans and other South American cultures had the legend of the Viracocha who were a tall white race with elongated skulls that came from the sky and would return again. Kukulcan was said to have come from the stars.

The Black Plague originated in China in 1333 and spread to Europe in 1347. Although it is blamed on fleas and rats, there are more accounts that describe lights in the sky and a foul mist that followed suggesting that a UFO sprayed an infectious biological agent to eradicate earth of humans. For all the "new agers" who believe "They" are here to help, give me one solid example!

At the Palazzo Vecchio in Florence Italy, there hangs a 600 year old painting of the Madonna and Saint Giovanni. In the lower right hand corner, there is a man and his dog looking up at a UFO.

In the upper left hand corner, there is a mother ship with many smaller craft emerging and a man and his dog looking up at them.

On January 24, 1878, John Martin of Dallas Texas saw a strange dark object in the sky that he described as a saucer to the Dennison Daily News who wrote an article entitled, *A Strange Phenomenon*. It was actually Martin and not Kenneth Arnold that coined the flying saucer term.

Prior to 1800, there are only around 60 quality UFO reports on record. There are another 200 in the 1800's and another 100 from 1900-1940. A strange increase in UFO cases started with World War II, almost in tandem with Adolph Hitler. One has to wonder if there wasn't an unholy alliance. Could the same force be behind Herod's first male born infanticide and Hitler's holocaust and todays abductions? The human experiments by the Nazi's on the Jews and the Japanese on the Chinese mirror the human abduction phenomena of today.

(Courtesy Banksy Bristol)

In the 1940's and 1950's, most UFO news was given to the press from our Air Force. Examples are the Battle of LA in 1942, Roswell in 1947 and the UFOs over our Capital in 1952. There was a UFO Officer assigned to all military bases and the position is mentioned in many documents from that time period. In 1948, Project Sign was formed to get an estimate of the situation and concluded UFOs were real and extraterrestrial. Project Grudge followed in 1951 when the Air Force asked that the Navy study UFOs but were forced to accept the assignment. In 1952, the name was changed to Project Blue Book. The C.I.A. got involved in 1953 with the Robertson Panel and their conclusion was to discredit, debunk and infiltrate UFO groups.

In 1954, the airlines industry and the Pentagon agreed to impose military restrictions on commercial pilots that reported UFOs to the media. Pilots would be subject to espionage laws and a $10,000 fine and ten years in prison.

In 1960, The Brookings Institute in Washington, DC conducted a study entitled *Proposed Studies on the Implications of Peaceful Space Activities* with a section entitled *Implications of Extraterrestrial life.* Their conclusion was that there would be profound social consequences and that society could break down. Religious, Scientific and Engineering groups would be devastated by the discovery of superior beings. These findings were presented before the 82nd Congress on April 18, 1961. I would like to comment that they do have superior technology but if they are abducting humans, then they are not morally superior to us! I believe religion would have resurgence. Vice Admiral Hillenkoetter, who was our first C.I.A. Director, called for continued Congressional hearings on UFOs and became a Board member of NICAP.

In 1962, General MacArthur addressed the West Point Military Academy by saying, "One day we may be faced with an ultimate conflict between a united human race and the sinister forces of some other planetary galaxy".

Shortly after Gemini 7 astronauts Frank Borman and James Lovell reported saying and seeing "a bogey, we have several sightings" on December 9, 1965, an acorn shaped object landed in Kecksburg, Pa. The object made a southeast turn near Cleveland and made a controlled minimal crash landing just east of Pittsburgh with minimal impact. Witnesses saw symbols or Cyrillic writing on its base. The U.S. Army showed up in force warning residents that they have orders to shoot to kill and flat bedded an object out of the woods. The military claims they only sent three officers to the scene. A local radio reporter, John Murphy, was told he couldn't air the story he wrote. Murphy died in a hit and run car accident a few years later. To date, no one has identified a satellite that came down that day. A soviet space probe, Cosmos 96, came down 13 hours earlier. A GE Mark 2 spy capsule from Johnson Island near Hawaii lost its orbit 39 hours earlier but no one knows where it landed (see pg 296). The satellites characteristics fully match up with witness testimony. The shape of the crashed object matched the Nazi Bell program from 1945. The Sci-Fi channel sued NASA for the Kecksburg records and won in court. A NASA spokesperson said they examined fragments from Kecksburg which were from a soviet object but NASA claimed the box of records was lost and the air force said it was a meteor.

In October 1966, a UFO was tracked on radar outside of Minot AFB in North Dakota. It activated the missile silo alarms and the 20 ton missile silo door was found opened. Also in 1966, Congressman Gerald Ford asked for and got Congressional hearings on UFOs due to the complaints by Michigan residents.

In March 1967, a UFO shut down 10 missiles at the Echo Flight facility in Montana and a week later did the same at Malmstrom AFB in Montana. Twenty Minute Man missiles were deactivated. Also in 1967, Senator Barry Goldwater requested access to the Blue Room at Wright Patterson AFB. General Curtis LeMay flatly denied him access but did mention a UFO file and above top-secret storage area. Senator Goldwater became a Board member of NICAP.

In 1968, Senator Robert Kennedy stated that he was a card-carrying member of the Amalgamated Flying Saucer Assoc. and expressed his interest in the subject in at least two letters. Also in 1968, an internal Rand document written by George Kocher (UFOs: What to Do? Nov 27 1968 doc # 18154-PR) noted that there would be worldwide panic and that based on the C.I.A. funded Robertson Panel's recommendation, the Government must "deny and ridicule" UFOs and discourage citizens from taking any active interest in the subject. On July 29, 1968, Illinois Senator

Donald Rumsfeld attended a Symposium on UFOs before the 19th Congress House of Representatives. This is the same Donald Rumsfeld who recently said that $2.3 trillion, which was revised down to $300 Billion, has disappeared into black projects. I would challenge you to find Congressional hearings on Bigfoot, ghosts, fairies, elves or other topics of so called "make believe". Walter Cronkite hosted a CBS TV special organized by the C.I.A. to debunk UFOs. That's what the public remembers since they seem to believe everything they see on TV. The University of Colorado received $523K in funding to study UFOs and put Dr Condon in charge. Dr. Condon quickly stated that UFOs were nonsense and an internal memo was leaked where a strategy to trick the public was discussed.

On July 16, 1969, a United States law was passed entitled, *Extra-Terrestrial Exposure Law* (Title 14, Section 1211 of the Code of Federal Regulations). It makes it illegal for the public to come into contact with extra-terrestrials or their vehicles. An individual can be fined up to $5000 and imprisoned for up to one year and be quarantined by NASA without a hearing. In 1991, the law was rescinded after the realization that if someone was prosecuted, it would be confirmation!

From 1968 through 1970, the Air Force Academy in Colorado Springs taught a Physics 370 class to Cadets where Chapter 33 was entitled *Unidentified Flying Objects*. The class discusses the 47,000-year history of UFOs along with prominent cases and comments that, "The phenomenon deserves valid scientific study". Their conclusion was that, "many witnesses have been reliable people and it is doubtful that the phenomenon was entirely psychological. This leaves us with the unpleasant possibility of alien visitors. Data suggests that there are three and maybe four different groups of aliens. It is best to keep an open mind and not take a position on either side of the question". The Physics course was edited and revised in early 1970 and eventually removed in 1971.

MUFON was founded in 1969 after the U.S. Air Force concluded seventeen years of UFO investigations through Project Blue Book. Their conclusion was that UFOs pose no threat to our National Security. Government UFO investigations officially ended and the Physics 370 class were cancelled at the Air Force Academy after 1970. An October 1969 letter from Air Force Brigadier General Bolender stated that UFO investigations that posed a threat to National Security would continue to be investigated by the Air Force and were not part of Project Blue Book. These UFO investigations, as in the past, would be handled in accordance with directive JANAP 146 and Air Force Manual 55-11. MUFON is a private citizen voluntary investigative organization. Dr James McDonald and the American Institute of Aeronautics both recommended the continued study of UFOs.

The Project Blue Book years were marked by the most fascinating spy drama that pitted the C.I.A. sponsored Blue Book and Dr Condon along with J. Allen Hynek against the public and NICAP led by Major Donald Keyhoe, Admiral Hillenkoetter, Captain Ruppelt and later Dr James MacDonald and Leonard Stringfield. NICAP's efforts to get Congressional hearings were constantly thwarted by the secretive C.I.A. and eventually led to the resignation of Ruppelt and Hillenkoetter from NICAP on the eve of possible Congressional hearings and the eventual infiltration of NICAP by C.I.A. agents and NICAP's demise. Even APRO, a Midwest UFO organization, was under surveillance and infiltration by the C.I.A. and they also closed up shop.

On January 27, 1976, Washington, London and Moscow signed the Treaty on Exploration and use of Outer Space. A total of 115 countries have since signed this treaty. It basically says that nuclear weapons cannot be put in space and that all discoveries from space must be shared. Here lies the problem with the back engineering of the Roswell craft.

"In 1987, attitudes began to change. Claims centered on a long term relationship between "Them" and us. They were here to stay; a deal was struck. Abductions were taking place on a scale never before contemplated in exchange for technology. Humanity was sold out pawns used by aliens for genetic material. They were creating human-alien hybrids. Missing children were actually being consumed" (Richard Dolan, UFOs and the National Security State).

In 1992, William Kramer and Charles Bahme copyrighted the *Fire Officers Guide to Disaster Control* which is used in every Fire Dept. in the U.S. This book is a national guide and FEMA approved. Chapter Thirteen discusses "Enemy Attack and UFO Potential. In this chapter we will turn our attention to the very real threat posed by UFOs". The Chapter mirrors the Air Force Cadet class while discussing the 50,000 year history of UFOs, classification systems, recent cases and of course a warning. While citing the Federal Law (previously mentioned), "Near approaches of UFOs can be harmful to humans". Charles Bahme was also a witness to the Feb 1942 *Battle of L.A.* as a teenager.

In 1995, the Clinton's met with Laurance Rockefeller at his ranch in Wyoming and discussed UFOs. Here you can see Hillary carrying Paul Davies book, *Are we Alone*. There were also many big name politicians present or involved who rose to fame after this meeting like John Podesta, Governor Bill Richardson, Secretary Leon Panetta, Al Gore, Congressman Steven Schiff and Webster Hubbell.

In 1999, France's COMETA association (committee for in depth studies; their civilian version of NASA) published *UFOs and Defense*. The report highlights recent cases, hypotheses, implications, UFOs and defense and a conclusion that, "The U.S. holds a position of military superiority over other countries. It is impossible for them to divulge the sources of this research".

We have the technology and are not willing to share even though we signed the Outer Space Treaty. I'm glad that the U.S. has this technology and Iran, China or North Korea doesn't. I'm certain, in a perverted way, that the CIA and Pentagon are actually protecting us from the UFO truth.

President Reagan referenced an armed conflict with extraterrestrials in five separate United Nations speeches because he saw a UFO on two occasions.

In 2002, a Roper poll was conducted. Three out of four claimed that they were psychologically prepared for Government Disclosure and that 88% said it would not affect their religious beliefs. More than half, 56%, believed UFOs were real and 48%

believed that we have been visited. Two thirds believed that there is intelligent life in our universe and 45% believed that we were being monitored; and 21% believed in abductions. A 2008 AOL News poll of 138,507 adults indicated that 93% believed in life elsewhere and 81% believed that earth had been visited.

In 2007, New Mexico Governor Bill Richardson asked for Congressional hearings on what really happened in Roswell. At the 2007 Democrat Presidential candidate's debate, Ohio Rep Dennis Kucinich stated that he had seen a UFO while at Shirley MacLaine's home. Former Arizona Governor Fife Symington also came clean that he saw a UFO in 1997 during the Phoenix Lights incident. Astronauts Buzz Aldrin and Gordon Cooper claim to have seen UFOs. Edgar Mitchell has stated on numerous occasions that he has been privy to information that UFOs and other life forms do exist.

In the past decade, a group of distinguished witnesses gathered four times at the National Press Club in Washington DC and signed affidavits that they were willing to testify before Congress. In 2001 Dr Steven Greer organized 21 military, government and scientific witnesses that told their story. He also identified 350 additional witnesses that were willing to come forward. Their affidavit requested a Congressional inquiry and to utilize this new energy source for good and to stop the weaponization of space.

In 2007 Investigative Journalist Leslie Kean and Producer James Fox organized 19 witnesses; 13 pilots, 5 foreign Generals and former Arizona Governor Fife Symington who testified to what they saw regarding UFOs.

In 2010 Robert Hastings organized seven U.S. Military officers and one enlisted man to testify at the National Press club that UFOs have violated our nuclear facilities. They also produced

120 additional signatures from witnesses on an affidavit that is being ignored by Congress. The Air Force response was that "There have been NO significant cases to warrant an investigation since the conclusion of Project Blue Book in 1969". Somehow they missed our Minuteman missiles being turned off at Malmstrom AFB in 1967 and 2007 even though they do not have a turn off switch. They also missed the same at Nellis AFB in 2003 in the presence of a UFO. Since Project Blue Book ended we have had Bentwaters, the Phoenix Lights, O'Hare airport, Stephenville, the Pennsylvania UFO wave in 2008 and a host of other sightings. CNN and the Tribune Review covered the National Press club story in a positive light. The Washington Post debunked and mocked the officers.

In 2013, The Citizen's Hearing was facilitated by five former Congress people; Lynn Wooley, Carolyn Kilpatrick, Merrill Cook, Darlene Hooley, Roscoe Bartlett along with Senator Mike Gravel and Attorney Daniel Sheehan. Steven Bassett organized the hearings. The setting was a Congressional Hearing where testimony was given and thirty eight witnesses were questioned by the panel. Topics covered included UFO history, the Rockefeller Initiative, RAF Bentwaters, Nuclear bases, documents, Roswell, International cases, pilots and technology.

In 2014, *Hangar 1: The UFO Files* TV show debuted on H2 and moved to the larger History Channel in 2015 and tripled its viewership. It took 45 years to get the files of the Mutual UFO Network on TV to inform the public. When you lay out the timeline of documents from the 1940's through present day, no intelligent human being can believe that the UFO phenomenon is not real. But where do they originate from and for what purpose?

Did you know that on three separate occasions in 1957 by Father Connell, 2001 by Father Balducci and 2008 by Father

Funes, the Vatican made a statement regarding the possibility of extraterrestrial life in space? “God in all his eminence and power has also created life in space. It would be arrogant of us to believe that we are the only intelligent species in the Universe. They are our Brothers and have fallen from grace just as we have”. The Vatican leases time from NASA on the LUCIFER advanced infrared telescope in Tucson and is prepared for contact and disclosure will come from the Vatican and not from any government or individual. I’ll explain more as you read on.

When it comes to eyewitness testimony, experts say that it is unreliable. Seems odd that three people can see a man steal a woman’s purse, call the police, testify in court, have twelve jurors convict even though the purse was never recovered and the three witnesses and twelve jurors can leave the courtroom, look up and see a UFO and not be believed. Eyewitness testimony is the basis for our criminal justice system. I hope we are prepared to free twenty percent of our prisoners if eyewitness testimony is unreliable!

When I’m asked, “Why don’t extraterrestrials make contact with us”, I can’t help but wonder if they are observing us and they see we can’t accept each other because we are white, brown, black and yellow. Then how could we accept them if they are green or gray? When we accept ourselves as one human race, then maybe they will make contact. But who are “They”? There is more to this phenomenon than meets the eye. Why can’t “They” accomplish their goal in thousands of years? Realistically, how much alien abduction does it take to get enough DNA? Why do craft just disappear? You can’t ignore the Bible and fallen angels either. Are we experiencing demons in alien clothing? Are we being deceived, misdirected or taken over?

When confronted with this preponderance of evidence, you have to ask why the U.S. Government refuses to investigate, acknowledge or discuss the existence of UFOs. Is it that they can't or won't? It is obvious that their procedures to debunk and infiltrate and deny are working. What aspect of this secret makes it above top secret? What is the horrible truth that forces our Government to violate the Constitution and misappropriate funds and lie to the public? Are these craft truly extraterrestrial or something else?

When I say UFO, I don't necessarily mean extraterrestrial. I mean unidentified since I do not know where they are from. When I say ET, I mean non-human entity (NHE) which is the correct name for these creatures. With all of that said, if it is more comfortable for you to be a skeptic, at least be an informed skeptic!

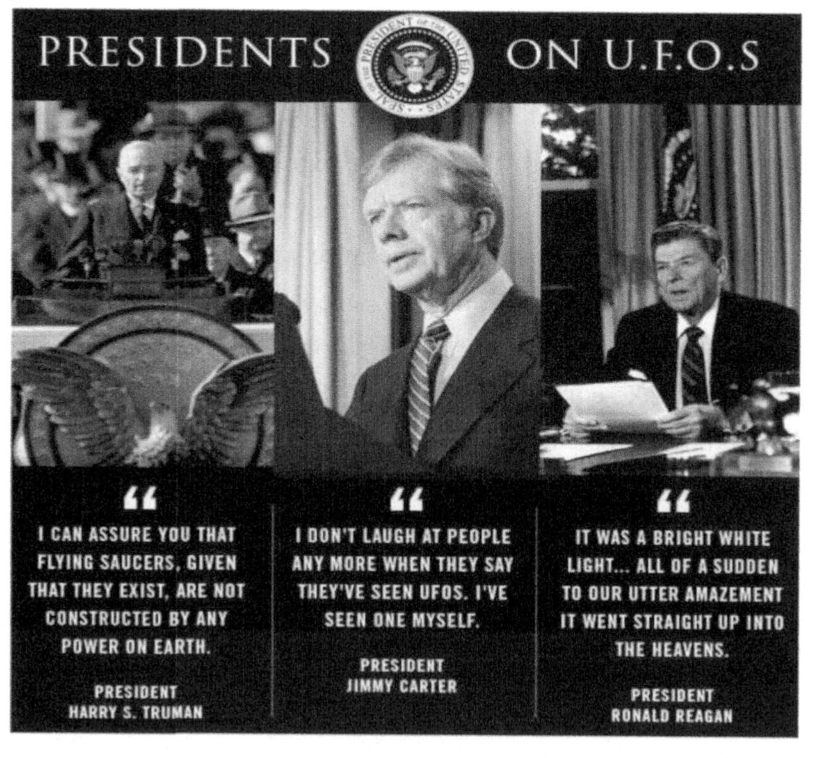

PRESIDENTS ON U.F.O.S
"I CAN ASSURE YOU THAT FLYING SAUCERS, GIVEN THAT THEY EXIST, ARE NOT CONSTRUCTED BY ANY POWER ON EARTH.
PRESIDENT HARRY S. TRUMAN
"I DON'T LAUGH AT PEOPLE ANY MORE WHEN THEY SAY THEY'VE SEEN UFOS. I'VE SEEN ONE MYSELF.
PRESIDENT JIMMY CARTER
"IT WAS A BRIGHT WHITE LIGHT... ALL OF A SUDDEN TO OUR UTTER AMAZEMENT IT WENT STRAIGHT UP INTO THE HEAVENS.
PRESIDENT RONALD REAGAN

Chapter 2

Do You Know? Should You Know?

1956 United Artists film, *UFOs, the True Story*. Captain Ruppelt supplied film footage of two real UFO cases.

"As flies to boys are we to the Gods. They kill us for their sport." – William Shakespeare

There is a moment in everyone's life when you have to decide whether you believe what you have been told about our existence. Humans have an uncomfortable need to explain and justify their origin. Since evolution doesn't add up, where did we come from? Can your soul be taken? Where do all the missing persons actually go? Are we already a hybrid species being infiltrated or a product of creation? Why is this planet so haunted and religion so supernatural?

When I was head of Public Affairs for UPS for PA-WV-VA, my boss from D.C. would always quiz us regarding political facts that we should know. He would invariably end up saying, "Do you know? Should you know?" Over the years, I've acquired some interesting chronological UFO facts that I'd like to share with you. If you are involved in this field, these are facts you should know:

1. There are over 1000 billion galaxies with an average of 200 billion stars each. That's a 2 with 24 zero's (200 billion trillion) for the number of stars in the universe. There are more stars in the Universe than grains of sand on earth. NASA calculates that there are 8.8 billion earthlike planets in the Milky Way Galaxy alone. There are more earths in our Galaxy than people on earth. 1000B x 8.8B = life is abundant in the Universe! But it is a huge leap of faith and assumption to say UFOs come from space. If you see a boat, did it come from under the ocean?

2. Since dinosaurs existed for 150M years and 64M years before humans, are we dealing with intelligent evolved dinosoids in our hollow earth? If you believe in evolution, some dinosaurs stood upright with claws with opposable thumbs for tool making.

3. Intelligent humans (Homo sapiens sapiens) suddenly appeared 30,000 years ago.

4. Samarian is the oldest written language and Hindu is the oldest religion. Both date back to 6000 BC. The Samarian word Astra means terrible airborne weapon. Samarian and the Hindu *Dzyan* and *Mahabharata* text indicate someone was able to fly in Virmana (flying craft) and a terrible nuclear exchange took place approximately 8000 years ago in Mohenjo-Daro India. Skeletal remains found in that area are 50 times more radioactive than they should be.

5. Carvings of 5 aircraft can be found in Abydos Egypt dating to 2600 BC. A helicopter, airplane and submarine are clearly seen.

6. In 1347 BC, Pharaoh Akhenaton is told by a flying disc to build a new capital for Egypt and start a new religion worshipping the disc. His wife, Nefertiti, had an elongated skull.

7. In 593 BC, Ezekiel described seeing and entering a wheel within a wheel with faces that moved with the object. In 1985, Nation of Islam leader Minister Louis Farrakhan claimed to have the same experience.

8. Alexander the Great encountered a UFO in 329 BC which halted his advance into India.

9. In 216 BC, Hannibal sees ships in the sky during the battle of Cannae with men dressed in white on board.

10. Earth is the only planet not named after a Roman God and the only planet that believes in God.

11. Around 50 BC, Roman philosopher Cicero described the sky opening up and spheres appearing.

12. Constantine saw a UFO on October 28 312 AD which looked like the sign of a cross and Constantine won his battle and established Christianity as the official religion.

13. In 776 AD, Saxons attacking Charlemagne's castle saw 2 red flaming shields over the church and withdraw in panic.

14. Airplane trinkets made in gold dating to 500-1000 AD have been found in Central America. They were

displayed at the Smithsonian until it was proven in 1996 by German engineer Peter Belting that they were aerodynamic and flew.

15. Anasazi means Ancient Ones or Ancient Aliens. They believe they originated from inner earth as opposed to extraterrestrial. They mysteriously disappeared around 1300 AD.

16. When the Cherokee settled Tennessee, they encountered white people with large eyes who could only see at night. No Indian tribe ever settled in West Va.

17. In 1347 Florence Italy, low flying cigar shaped craft release a mist and drop diseased animal carcasses causing the Black Plague.

18. Columbus' journal on October 12 1492 documents a UFO prior to landing in North America.

19. February 1, 1554, Nostradamus and 1000 witnesses see a bright burning rod in the sky for 2 hours changing directions and swaying back and forth.

20. The first sci-fi novel was written in 1619 by Johannes Kepler. *Sominium* was about a man taken to the moon by a demon.

21. The first recorded UFO over the mainland U.S. occurred at Charles River Boston, Mass in March of 1639 by Governor John Winthrop.

22. The first reported crop circle was in 1678 in the U.K. and was referred to as the Mowing Devil.

23. Jonathan Swifts 1726 *Gulliver's Travels* got the moons of Mars size and orbit correct. They weren't

discovered until 1877! He also described a gigantic flying circular domed island named Laputa in the north Pacific.

24. George Washington's Journal of 1778 documents meetings with green skinned natives at Valley Forge who give him reconnaissance on British positions.

25. On May 19, 1780, New England was covered by a cloud of darkness although the sky was cloudless and there was no eclipse.

26. Was the 1819 Hudson Valley NY story of Rip Van Winkle based on a true abduction that lasted 20 years?

27. The first known photo of a UFO was taken in New Hampshire in 1870.

28. January 1878, John Martin of Dallas Texas describes a large dark object in the Northern sky as a "Flying Saucer". First time this phrase was ever used.

29. The word "star ship" first appeared in English in the 1882 book by John Newbrough entitled *Oahspe: the New Bible*. The 900 page book was written from visions from the spirit world during automatic writing.

30. The first human mutilation takes place in White Chapel London in 1888. Similar "Phantom Surgeons" commit the cattle mutilations of the 1970's.

31. The first description of Greys was in the 1891 book by Ken Folingby *Meda: A Tale of the Future* and then in 1893 HG Wells book, *Man of the Year Million*. They were transformed humans not ET. In 1901, Wells describes Greys from the Moon in his book, *First Men in the Moon*.

32. The first animal mutilation in the U.S. was in Vernon Kansas in April 1897 when a heifer was seized from the Hamilton ranch in full view of witnesses. The cow was found dismembered the next day on the Lank Thomas farm. The most famous mutilation was in Colorado on September 9 1967 when a horse named Lady was mutilated.

33. The first UFO crash occurred April 19, 1897 in Aurora Texas where an airship struck a windmill. The strange looking pilot is buried in the Aurora cemetery. When MUFON launched an effort to exhume the body in 1973, the headstone was removed.

34. The first alien transmission was received in 1899 by Nikola Tesla.

35. An alienist is a Psychologist.

36. The first space travel movie was released in 1902 by Georges Melies called *A Trip to the Moon.*

37. Did Tesla's1902 wireless transmissions from Waldenclyffe alert aliens to our presence?

38. The 1908 Tunguska Siberia object that exploded took the same flight path or re-entry path that Apollo astronauts use. Was it a failed attempt and not a meteor?

39. In 1917, the Red Baron of Germany reported shooting down a 100' silver saucer over France.

40. In 1917, 50,000 witnesses in Fatima Portugal witnessed 2 large shiny discs dancing in the sky which was as bright as the sun just prior to our "Lady's" apparition and prophecies. The heat from the object dried their rain soaked clothes.

41. Was the 1918 Spanish flu which spread quickly and killed over 50 million people a virus from outer space brought to earth in 1917?

42. In 1918, Aleister Crowley made a satanic contact with a Grey named Lam. Crowley claims to have opened a portal that allowed Greys and demonic entities to enter our world.

43. On March 4, 1918, the largest US naval ship ever to disappear was the USS Cyclops along with its 306 crew members. German records show no record of sinking the 19,360 ton ship and no wreckage was found in the Bermuda Triangle.

44. On August 22, 1924, as Mars passed by earth at its closest point, many radio stations declared radio silence so they could listen for Martian broadcasts.

45. In the fall of 1933, Ghost Rockets (craft) were seen flying over Scandinavia flying low with search lights on the ground. One third of the sightings occurred in hazardous weather and very low to the ground.

46. A UFO crashed in the Black Forest of Freiberg Germany in 1936. This was the impetus for the Nazi secret weapons program, Project Paperclip and the formation of NASA. Were they us from the future?

47. The October 31, 1938 Panic Broadcast of the War of the Worlds by Orson Wells laid the ground work for the policy of non-disclosure of UFOs by the Defense Department today. The 1960 Brookings Institute study on the Implications of Extraterrestrial Contact referenced the Panic Broadcast in its recommendation to not disclose the

truth to the public. The Panic Broadcast was repeated in Chile in 1944 and Ecuador in 1949 with similar results.

48. Hitler's belief in a pure Aryan race of blond hair and blue eyes did not refer to Caucasians. He referenced the Nordic giant Aryan ET race of Aldebaran and the Cryptoterrestrial Aldebaran's living under earth's surface.

49. The 1941 Cape Girardeau Missouri case might have been our first UFO crash and retrieval incident involving a craft with 3 Greys.

50. The February 25, 1942 Battle of LA was the first time our government fired on a UFO, denied their existence and used the weather balloon excuse. There were six civilian deaths that night; three from the shells and three from heart attacks. The Defense Department denied any record of the event. General George Marshall issued a memorandum on March 5, 1942 that a saucer was recovered off the coast and that it was not earthly. The memo was released in 1974. He also ordered the creation of a special Interplanetary Phenomenon Unit. A July 22, 1947 memo refers to the IPU after the Roswell crash and a briefing of Eisenhower and Kennedy. The IPU was deactivated in the late 50's with all records transferred to the AF.

51. The first Foo Fighter was reported by Lt Roman Sabinski on March 25, 1942 off the coast of Holland. They mysteriously seemed to respond to the pilots thoughts. Orbs, Foo Fighters and balls of light are all demonic entities. Lucifer was an angel of light and can masquerade as an angel of light.

52. The 1943 Philadelphia experiment was called Project Rainbow and involved stealth and time travel. It

is linked to the 1983 Montauk Project which harnessed the mind for remote viewing, telepathy and telekinesis.

53. In June of 1944, both Allied and German anti-aircraft guns stopped firing at each other and both fired at an egg shaped craft over Loreto Italy.

54. December of 1945, five bombers from Fort Lauderdale took off and disappeared in clear weather. A large Martin Mariner was sent up to find flight 19. They disappeared also. That's six planes and 27crew that "vanished".

55. In 1945, Hitler ordered the killing of the 62 engineers and prisoners that worked on the Bell Project. When Hans Kammler disappeared in a JU-390, 100 U-boats (subs) also left for Argentina and U-530 and U-977 were captured hauling red mercury which was used in the Bell project. If you spin mercury at 50,000 RPMs and compress it to 250,000 PSI it glows, and defies gravity as it reduces its mass by 89%.

56. Wind test models have proven there is no technical advantage to the saucer shape unless you need to spin an energy source in opposite directions like mercury.

57. Argentina President Juan Peron issued 1000 patents to Nazi scientists.

58. Ufologist Leonard Stringfield saw three tear drop shaped UFOs from the window of his C-46 right before landing in Iowa Jima in 1945.

59. Ufologists say that the A-Bomb got their attention and they got ours but our first bomb test was July 16,

1945 followed by the use of two in Japan in August. As you can see, we had their attention long before that.

60. Hanford Washington is the site of our first nuclear reactor and had four UFO encounters from 1945 to 1952.

61. The first report of UFOs with rows of portholes or windows came August 1, 1946 by Captain Puckett near Tampa Fla.

62. On August 11 1946, 200 Ghost Rockets were tracked on radar over Sweden.

63. Sweden has the only European UFO Memorial at Angelholm Sweden where hockey player Gotsa Carlsson claims to have received natural cures from a May 1946 ET encounter and opened a Pharmaceutical company.

64. June 1947, Einstein and Oppenheimer wrote a draft entitled *Relationships with inhabitants of Celestial Bodies*. The Bulletin of Atomic Scientists created the *Doomsday Clock*.

65. The first human MIB case occurred June 21, 1947 when UFO debris evidence from the Maury Island case was secured by Lieutenant Brown and Captain Davidson and shortly after the 2 officers entered their B-25 for Wright Patterson, the plane crashed killing both men. Three days later, pilot Kenneth Arnold reported 9 saucer shaped objects flying over Mountain Rainier.

66. Roswell occurred July 7, 1947 and said to be a Mogul balloon or test dummies only test dummies were not used until 1952. General Roger Ramey who was at the center of the Roswell incident was never disciplined

for the media attention. He was later promoted to a 4-star General.

67. The day after the Roswell crash, New Mexico Senator Dennis Chavez had a private meeting with President Truman. Chavez then personally called the Roswell media outlets and threatened to pull their broadcasting license if they continued to report the crashed UFO story.

68. Sarah Holcomb, the military typist involved with the Roswell crash, disappeared shortly after and couldn't be located because she did not use her actual name. Her real name was June Crane and she transferred to Wright-Pat in Ohio and then moved to Washington State and died in 1998 but not before giving testimony to Kevin Randle, Tom Carey, Don Schmitt and James Clarkson that the crash was real, small bodies were recovered and material from the crash could not be cut or altered.

69. A July 18, 1947 Air Force memo from Major General George MacDonald to J Edgar Hoover asks the FBI to get involved in UFO investigations. Hoover replies that he would first need access to the recovered disc.

70. A digital enlargement of the memo in General Ramey's hand revealed two phrases; "victims of the wreck" and "in the disk".

71. The July 1947 National Security Act created the CIA, National Security Council, Defense Dept. and Joint Chiefs of Staff weeks after the Roswell incident.

72. The September 1947 Air Technical Intelligence Center report on flying saucers concluded that they are real. Project Sign was then formed to study UFOs.

73. A memo by General Twining on September 23, 1947 stated that UFOs are real. Captain Ruppelt released the *Twining Memo* in 1957.

74. Alfred Ledding designed a flying saucer after the Roswell crash and received a patent after he left Wright Patterson in 1952.

75. The Oak Ridge Tennessee nuclear facility had UFO sightings nearly every year from 1947-66.

76. The Roswell crash, Dead Sea Scroll find and official state of Israel all occurred in 1947.

77. The first fatal UFO crash occurred January 7 1948 in Kentucky involving Captain Thomas Mantell. The crash resulted in no fire and there was no blood at the scene. Mantell's body was quickly removed, never shown to family and buried in a lead casket.

78. On August 5 1948, the Air Technical Intelligence Center of Project Sign concluded that UFOs were interplanetary in origin. Air Force Chief of Staff Hoyt Vandenberg ordered the report burned and suppressed 300 UFO reports and their conclusion due to National Security reasons. When members of Project Sign refused to change their conclusions, the project was dissolved.

79. The Aztec NM crash of March 1948 was a gift to our military as an intact UFO made a controlled landing with nearly no damage after being shot down by our military and 16 alien bodies were recovered. This was a

far more significant find than Roswell if true. The craft and bodies were taken to Hangar 18 at Wright Pat AFB.

80. The first TV show about UFOs was *Captain Video* in 1949.

81. In 1949, Project Grudge replaced Sign and was so named after the Air Force tried to pawn it off on the Navy and was forced to take it back by Congress. Project Grudge became Project Blue Book in May of 1952 after Pentagon Generals complained about Grudges debunking of UFO cases. Captain Ruppelt was then put in charge.

82. James Forrestal was our first Secretary of Defense and was JFK's mentor. He was against keeping the ET issue above top secret and said at a Staff meeting in 1949 that "he was going to the press". He also told an associate Supreme Court Justice that, "Something awful is going to happen to me". Fife Symington's older cousin, Secretary of the Air Force Stuart Symington, met with Forrestal and escorted him to Bethesda Naval Hospital where he was confined for a mental breakdown. Two months earlier he was awarded the Distinguished Service Medal by President Truman. Confined to the sixteenth floor VIP level even though the hospital staff recommended a ground floor room for a man in his supposed mental state. Against Forrestal's wishes, LBJ visited and couldn't change Forrestal's mind so when his brother threatened to check him out, they staged a suicide and threw him out the sixteenth floor window. Forrestal fought back and the window sill had numerous scuff marks on it but a tight noose around his neck tied loosely to a radiator ended his life. His regular guard was off that night and a hospital orderly was heard saying that Forrestal didn't commit suicide.

83. Project Twinkle was established in December 1949 to study the green fireball phenomenon which started in November 1948 over New Mexico. The green fireballs would not steadily drop but changed direction or maintained course. Dr. La Paz said they were artificial. The Project concluded they were natural. I believe NASA was testing copy alloy heat shields like the Kecksburg crash.

84. From March 16-18, 1950, Farmington NM reported hundreds of round silver objects moving across the sky lead by a red saucer. Some engaged in a dogfight. There were many witnesses.

FARMINGTON DAILY TIMES

HUGE 'SAUCER' ARMADA JOLTS FARMINGTON

Jury Gets Bribe Case; Heard Denies Charges

Veracity of Negro Attacked

Crafts Seen By Hudreds

Speed Estimated At 1000 M.P.H. Altitude 20,000 Feet

'Blackout' Game Preceded Slaying Of Pretty Co-ed

Entire Crew Rescued From Exploded Ship

Along The Way

Newsman Writes Letter To Flying Saucer Pilot

Drafting Reply To Commie Charge

85. On May 11, 1950, Paul Trent took 2 photos from 2 angles of a flying saucer which have never been debunked. Even the Condon report said they were authentic. The air force asked for the originals and negatives after they appeared in Life magazine and never returned them.

86. On November 21, 1950, Canada's Project Magnet Wilbert Smith wrote a memo that flying saucers have the highest classification and do exist after meeting with Robert Sarbacher on September 15th. Sarbacher said we were in possession of a craft and aliens that were built like insects.

87. Gordon Cooper saw multiple UFOs over his airbase in West Germany in 1951. He again saw photos of a landed UFO on May 3, 1957 at Edwards AFB.

88. 1951 was the first "falling leaf" flight motion on descent described.

89. On February 2, 1952, the USS Philippine Sea tracked on radar and eye witnesses saw a UFO travelling at 1800 MPH that stopped and reversed direction.

90. On July 2, 1952, a dozen UFOs were filmed over Tremonton Utah by Navy photographer Delbert C. Newhouse. A little more than a minutes worth of color film was taken and the Navy Photo Lab concluded that the objects moved between 470 and 3780 MPH and changed light intensity and were intelligently controlled.

91. UFOs were tracked on radar with military, airline and civilian witnesses on July 19 and 26, 1952 over the nation's capital. They flew between 100 and 7000 MPH.

92. President Truman received quarterly UFO briefings by General Robert Landry. Copies can be accessed at the Truman Library. In a July 20, 1952 interview, Truman said, "We discussed it at every conference with the military. We always had things like that going on; flying saucers." The video is still available on YouTube.

93. On July 28, 1952, Winston Churchill asked for a report on flying saucers. On August 9 1952 the reply from his Air Ministry was that they were in agreement with the Americans that all sightings were identifiable, hoaxes or delusions.

94. On July 29, 1952, President Truman issued an order to shoot down any UFO that couldn't be talked down. That same afternoon, the Air Force held a press conference and stated that UFOs were not a threat to national security yet the same branch of the military always scrambles fighter jets to intercept.

95. After the 1952 UFOs over DC, Captain Ruppelt stated that the temperature inversions registered were not strong enough to be picked up on radar. Captain Ruppelt coined the phrase UFO.

96. The USS FDR became the first carrier to deploy nuclear weapons in 1950 and had UFO encounters in 1952, 53, 56, 58 and 1962.

97. Albert Bender was the first to set up a civilian UFO group called the *International Flying Saucer Bureau* along with the accompanying *Space Review Magazine*. He was the first to have a MIB visit although his was a paranormal event involving aliens. He shut down the highly successful group and magazine in Oct of 1953.

98. In late 1952, the National Security Council asked the CIA to determine if UFOs were a threat to our national security.

99. 1952, Project Stork lead by Battelle Memorial Institute concluded that UFOs were not from a foreign government.

100. During mid-September 1952, Operation Mainbrace near Denmark consisted of 200 ships including six aircraft carriers including the USS FDR and 80,000 men. UFOs buzzed the ships for two weeks. Captain Ruppelt said "photos of the UFOs were excellent".

101. The Dec.1952 Blue Book Report # 8 identified five UFOs spotted by astronomers yet you will find no UFO evidence in astrological studies due to career protection.

102. In 1953, four years prior to the launch of Sputnik, the Air Force started using long range radar and immediately picked up a huge object orbiting at 600 miles out over the equator at 18,000 MPH. In 1960, it was determined to be five times larger than any Soviet satellite and was named the Black Knight.

103. The 1953 Robertson Panel was sponsored by the CIA and concluded to debunk UFOs and strip them of their aura of importance with the public. They went as far as suggesting that book reports by school students should not be accepted for a grade. They also recommended infiltrating civilian UFO groups. The purpose of the CIA is to use psychology and mind control to deceive. Any findings by the CIA are always predetermined before the investigation begins and supported by biased researchers who leave out key information. The CIA is the best in the world at what they do and therefore must never be allowed to operate on U.S. soil. The CIA will protect the best interests of the United States by any means and at all costs; just don't get in their cross hairs! The Robertson Report was released nearly three years later than prescribed by law and indicated that 399 UFO reports were withheld or missing.

104. On May 21, 1953, a craft and a brown skinned occupant were recovered in Kingman Az. Ray Fowler obtained a signed affidavit from the military witness. Four witnesses all gave similar descriptions of the recovery.

105. When Sir Francis Creek discovered the structure of DNA in 1953, he also commented that he thought aliens created humans.

106. In 1953 General Benjamin Chidlaw said, "We have stacks of flying saucer reports. We take them very seriously when you consider how many men and planes we have lost trying to intercept them".

107. On November 23, 1953, an F-89C Scorpion jet was scrambled from Kinross AFB to intercept a UFO. On radar, the 2 merge and the jet and its 4 member crew vanish. The AF told the Moncla family that the plane flew too low and crashed into a lake. The AF then mistakenly told the Moncla family that the plane exploded at high altitude.

108. Major Donald Keyhoe's book *Flying Saucers from Outer Space* contained 51 classified UFO reports. Captain Ruppelt approved the report usage in the book.

109. On February 17, 1954, the Military Air Transport Service met with airlines officials and imposed military restrictions on commercial pilot UFO reporting wherein they were subject to espionage laws and a $10,000 fine and 10 years in prison for discussing UFOs with the media or public. In December 1958, 450 pilots signed a petition opposing the restrictions. In February 1959, Captain Killian went public with his UFO sighting over Pennsylvania and was not prosecuted.

110. In April 1954, SOM1-01 or the special operations manual 1-01 was created to deal with extraterrestrial entities and technology recovery and disposal. It describes two ET species and how to secure, treat and dispose of humanoids. It calls for complete press silence and espionage laws enforced if compromised.

111. All U.S. military bases had a UFO Officer in the 1950's and 60's. Audio tapes from the Oct 7 1965 UFO over Edwards AFB say that the UFO Officer was notified.

112. Muroc (Edwards) AFB was shut down to all air traffic from Feb 19-21 1954. On Feb 20, 1954, President Eisenhower met with Nordic aliens called the Etherians who were able to dematerialize themselves and their five craft; two cigar shaped and three saucer shaped craft. Eisenhower turned down an offer to exchange technology for our nuclear disarmament. There were two more meetings each six months apart at Holloman AFB and the alleged "Greada Treaty" was signed in Feb of 1955 exchanging technology for abductions and an education program. A photo of a UFO at the third Holloman meeting exists. Per Timothy Good, Gerald Light was present with Franklin Allen of Hearst, Edwin Nourse of Brooking Institute, Bishop McIntyre and Air Force witnesses. In 1960, the program name was changed to "Project Aquarius" per Richard Doty.

113. In 1954, the Navy built a secret base in the Bahama's called AUTEC or Atlantic Undersea Test and Evaluation Center. This is the Navy's version of Area 51.

114. Contactee stories emerged in 1954 with George Adamski and his "Venusians".

115. 1954 also marked alien encounters that mirrored the countries culture involved. Americans saw Greys, Brits saw Nordics, French saw goblins and South Americans saw hairy beings.

116. August 10 1954, radio host Frank Edwards was fired from the Mutual Network radio show when he aired Lieutenant Colonial John O'Mara's statement that the Air Force was receiving 700 sightings per week when the official AF statement said that they received 87 cases in four months. Edwards' popular radio show had 13M listeners.

117. A 1954 CIA memo instructed assets in Guatemala to fabricate a story regarding flying saucers as a cover.

118. Area 51 was created in 1955 and placed under the control of the CIA, not the Navy or Air Force. In 1958, President Eisenhower who had allowed Area 51 to operate without Presidential oversight was denied access to and information about the CIA's operations there. The President told the CIA that he will send the first Army from Colorado to dismantle the sight if he did not receive the requested intel. He received his intel but never gained control of Area 51 from the CIA. The Soviet area 51 is Kapustin Yar and was established in 1946.

119. The 1955 Kelly-Hopkinsville case on the Sutton farm was the basis for the 2002 movie *Signs*. The Air Force explanation for the attack by three foot tall goblins that repelled shot-gun blasts was that they were silver painted monkeys that escaped from a circus. Yet the AF 370 manual (see #168) said this was one of the most credible cases. The term little green men originated with this case when the local newspaper said they were green.

120. In 1955 during Operation Deep Freeze, the crew of the USS ice breaker Eastwind saw a craft break through 37 feet of ice and fly off at incredible speeds.

121. In August 1955 in Madagascar, a silent UFO passed 130 feet above tens of thousands of people causing power outages and animals to howl.

122. The Brisbane Australia UFO group was established in 1956 and is the world's oldest UFO organization.

123. In 1956, Captain Ruppelt published *Report on Unidentified Flying Objects*. Ruppelt had headed up Project Blue Book and stated that UFOs were real. Ruppelt verbally said he would join the Board of NICAP in 1957 after Major Keyhoe became its Director but never did. Ruppelt died at 37, six months after being pressured in 1959 into changing the conclusion of his book in a second edition to say that UFOs were not a threat to National Security. Ruppelt also became a critic of NICAP and UFO witnesses. It appears Ruppelt was pressured by the Air Force and his employer, Northrup. Ruppelt's reversal was the opposite and equal reversal to Hynek's where he became a UFO supporter after asking Donald Rumsfeld for the truth regarding UFOs since he had debunked them for the government for years and was verbally undressed by Rumsfeld. Hynek went on to form CUFOs in 1973.

124. In March of 1956, Major Cunningham and Sergeant Lovette were recovering missile debris at Groom Lake when Lovette was lassoed and pulled into a UFO. Missile Control had radar confirmation. Three days later, Lovette's nude body was found 10 miles away drained of blood and missing his eyes, anus, genitalia and tongue;

one of the first human mutilations. Dead birds that picked at the body were found next to the body.

125. In October of 1956, the first workers comp claim was paid to Harry Sturdevant of Trenton NJ who was assaulted by a UFO.

126. In 1956, the first UFO song was released on radio by Buchanan and Goodman called *Flying Saucers*. The first top 40 song was *Purple People Eaters* by Sheb Wooley in 1958.

127. The 1956 Project Palladium created false radar images to trick Soviet and Cuban radar but explained very few UFO sightings.

128. 1957 marked sexual encounters with aliens as Antonio Villas Boas was raped by an oriental alien with red hair. A 200' cigar shaped craft landed in Levelland Texas and witnessed by 2 police and 15 others.

129. America's first C.I.A. Director Roscoe Hillenkoetter joined the Board of NICAP from 1957-62. Senator Barry Goldwater also joined NICAPs Board in 1974.

130. On January 22 1958, CBS pulled the live feed on Major Keyhoe when he said UFOs are under intelligent control.

131. In 1958, the Air Force admitted that bombers were launched against Russia when UFOs were picked up on radar.

132. In 1958, DARPA is created with the goal of engineering advanced technologies.

133. On April 20, 1959, 59 year Morris K Jessup committed suicide one day prior to a scheduled lunch meeting where Jessup planned to reveal breakthroughs in levitation and the Philadelphia experiment.

134. In 1960, Project Ozma was headed up by Dr Frank Drake. Strong intelligent signals were immediately picked up from the Tau Ceti region of space. Project Ozma was immediately shut down and moved to Arecibo Puerto Rico under AF control. Dr Drake went on to head SETI.

135. July 1, 1960, according to Wilbert Smith who headed up the Canadian Project Magnet, a 3000 lb. metallic object from space was recovered on earth. It had been in space for hundreds of years since it was pitted with micrometeorites.

136. Project Environment drafted by CIA and MJ-12 Director Allen Dulles was an assassination directive against anyone who threatened MJ-12. It was used against Pres. Kennedy and no future Pres. will aggressively pursue the UFO question.

137. In 1960, JFK told Air Force officer William Holden aboard AF1 that UFOs were real and that he planned to tell the public.

138. Jacques Vallee became interested in UFOs in 1961 when he observed French astronomers erase a magnetic tape containing eleven UFOs.

139. In November 1961, the Air Force formed Project Moon Dust to recover any foreign space objects including UFOs.

140. In March 1962 Hillenkoetter resigned from the Board of NICAP and decided not to participate in Congressional hearings on UFOs with Major Keyhoe due to pressure from the CIA.

141. In 1962, Kenneth Arnold concluded that the discs that he saw were most likely living creatures in our atmosphere with the ability to change their form.

142. In 1963, the Justice Department was asked if killing an ET would be considered murder. The reply was that it would be ruled the same as cruelty to animals or disorderly conduct.

143. November 1963, President Kennedy issued 2 UFO memo's 11 days prior to his assassination. One requested that all UFO records be placed on his desk by Feb 1964 and the other, National Security Memorandum 271 went to Khrushchev cautioning that a UFO can be mis-identified as a missile and starts a war. JFK also confided in Marilyn Monroe and Dorothy Kilgallen who both committed "suicide". In May of 1947, Kilgallen wrote about a crashed craft in Spitsbergen Norway.

144. On September 15, 1964, Lt Robert Jacobs PHD was filming an Atlas F missile launch from Vandenberg AFB when a UFO flew alongside it and shined 4 beams of light on the missile causing it to plunge into the ocean. The film was reviewed the following day and all were instructed never to discuss it and the film was confiscated.

145. Abductions make up .20% (1 in 500) of UFO cases. IFOs make up at least 80% of cases and hoaxes 10% of cases.

146. The Air Force borrowed the 1964 Socorro film of the UFO ground impressions from Ted Jordon and never returned it. The physical evidence, molten metal on a rock at the landing site, was given to NASA for analysis with the agreement that only half of the substance could be removed. When the rock was returned, it had been scrapped clean.

147. On June 4, 1965, Gemini 4 astronaut James McDivitt photographed a UFO. He never received his pictures back and was told it was the booster rocket which he said he also had in view with the UFO.

148. August 3, 1965, the first of four photos taken by Highway Accident Inspector Rex Heflin showed dust being kicked up in a circular pattern under the UFO. United Press International examined the photos and declared they were real. The original prints were turned over to NORAD for examination. NORAD and the AF denied receiving them and declared the photos a hoax.

149. On August 7 in Venezuela, two Nordics sent a telepathic message to three men that they were here from

Orion to attempt interbreeding experiments while the Greys were hostile to humans.

150. The great north east blackout of November 9, 1965 started in Syracuse when a UFO was spotted by pilot Weldon Ross tapping into power lines which caused the power grid to fail.

151. On December 9, 1965, a U.S. GE Mark 2 spy satellite crash landed in Kecksburg, Pa. See pg 302.

152. On March 16, 1966, J Allen Hynek investigated UFOs over Dexter Michigan. He concluded that they were swamp gas. Congr. Gerald Ford requested a Congressional hearing and got it on April 5 1966.

153. On April 6, 1966, 200 Westfall students in Melbourne Australia witness a gray UFO.

154. On April 17, 1966, a total of 7 police officers in 5 counties chased a UFO from Portage Ohio into Pa. There were 22 civilian witnesses and Pittsburgh airport had it on radar. Two officers quit their jobs after Blue Book said it was a satellite and/or Venus.

155. On June 16, 1966, a UFO hovered over Whiteman AFB for 2 hours and shut down all 150 nuclear missiles.

156. On July 31, 1966, a UFO landed in Presque Island Erie Pa. It was witnessed by 4 adults, 2 children and 2 patrolmen. The 2 adults that stayed in their vehicle after it got stuck in sand on the beach were terrorized by a creature that scratched their car and fled as police approached. A strange substance was found in the foot prints. Air Force investigators destroyed the evidence the following day. Eight additional witnesses came forward

and a UFO landing pad was built by local merchants at a cost of $2600.

157. The initial 1966 Project Blue Book Condon Commission findings were discarded by Dr Condon and he wrote his own findings which caused 19 of the scientists and staff to resign from the project. Only 59 of 12,618 cases were actually investigated over three years at a cost of $523,000 to debunk UFOs; 701 cases were classified unknown.

158. On August 9, 1966 Dr Robert Low, project coordinator, wrote a memo to the Condon Committee outlining how to trick the public into believing the committee is objective while stacking it with non-believers with no expectation of proving UFOs to be real.

159. The January 25, 1967 abduction of Betty Andreasson is one of the few abduction cases of a devout Christian. She thought they were angels initially.

160. The first stealth UFO report occurred on May 13, 1967 when a craft flew 200 feet over NORAD in Colorado Springs and was strongly picked up on radar but was invisible to sight.

161. On March 16 and 24 1967, a UFO shut down 8 nuclear missiles at Malmstrom AFB.

162. Frank Edwards and three other Ufologists died on the morning of June 24, 1967 before the start of the World UFO Conference hosted by Gray Barker in New York City. Edwards had planned to go public against the Condon Commission with UFO evidence. Edwards was the original Art Bell on radio. Barker received a phone

call the previous night telling him that Edwards would die before speaking at the Conference.

163. In July 1967, a UFO started a launch sequence at Minot AFB.

164. The October 4, 1967 UFO crash in Shag Harbour Nova Scotia was the first time Canadian authorities acknowledged a UFO crash. A disabled UFO released yellow foam into the water. Divers from the HMCS could locate nothing. A second UFO joined to repair the first and they escaped.

165. Congressional hearings on UFOs were held on April 5, 1966 and July 29, 1968.

166. The term "*Above Top Secret*" came from Project Saint which referred to a plan for emergency defense measures if UFOs proved hostile to shoot them down. Senator Barry Goldwater used the term in his attempts to gain access to the UFO room at Wright Paterson AFB. General Curtis LeMay denied his request to the blue room but didn't say it didn't exist.

167. On June 16, 1968, U.S. fighters chased and fired at multiple UFOs off the coast of Vietnam and accidently struck the Australian destroyer HMAS Hobart. General George S. Brown who commanded the fleet that struck the Hobart was quoted in 1973 as saying that "UFOs plagued us in Vietnam. We called them helicopters but the North didn't use helicopters until the end of the war". Brown went on to become chairman of the Joint Chiefs of Staff. Some say the UFOs sent our missiles and gunfire back at us.

168. The Air Force taught a UFO class to its cadets from 1968-70 in a Physics 370 class (chapter 33). It stated that UFOs have been visiting earth for as long as 47,000 years and that there are 3 or 4 different species. In 1970, the chapter was shortened from 14 to 7 pages and the 3 or 4 species remark was removed after the public learned of its existence.

169. In 1969, Library of Congress librarian Lynn Catoe read every UFO article stored at the library and published a report for the AF Office of Scientific Research. She concluded that "The literature is closely linked to that metaphysical and similar to demonic possession".

170. In May 1969, Apollo 10 astronauts Stafford, Young and Cernan heard strange music for one hour when they were on radio blackout on the far side of the moon. Hopefully it wasn't rap music from the future……

171. In December of 1969, at the conclusion of Project Blue Book, Projects *Blue Paper and Old New Moon* were put in place to investigate UFOs. The AF Academy chapter on UFOs was removed in 1970.

172. Ronald and Nancy Reagan encountered a UFO while driving to a party at William Holden's house. Lucille Ball and Shirley MacLaine confirmed the story.

173. Exactly 100 years after Jules Verne described our launching the Columbiad spacecraft from Florida and it returning by sling shooting around the moon, the Apollo 13 Columbia did just that as it ran into mechanical difficulties.

174. During the summer of 1971 at Karnes City Texas, a UFO hovered over Uranium mine and depleted a 250 foot area of the uranium ore. A chalky substance was found.

175. The best UFO photo was taken on September 4, 1971 in Costa Rica from a plane surveying a dam.

176. On November 2, 1971, a small UFO landed on a farm in Delphos Kansas. The teen that observed it went temporarily blind. It left a glowing circle on the ground where nothing would grow for over ten years and the soil crystalized and was resistant to liquids. The teen suffered nightmares.

177. In January 1972, a UFO opened the bay door to a missile silo at Malmstrom AFB.

178. In April 1972, an informant told Leonard Stringfield that an elite Army special ops encountered aliens in a Cambodian jungle who were loading the bodies of dead soldiers into bins and moving them to their craft. The ETs had large hairless heads with black wrap around eyes. A fire fight ensued where 4 ETs and 1 US soldier were killed. The soldiers were later interrogated by intelligence officers and this was the basis of the 1987 Predator movie.

179. The Pioneer 10 and 11 and Voyager 1 capsules all had plaques with directions to earth.

180. According to Jackie Gleason's wife, in 1973 President Nixon showed Gleason ET bodies at Homestead AFB and Gleason was never the same.

181. When CIA Director Richard Helms quit the CIA in 1973, he destroyed many of the Project Monarch MK-ULTRA mind control records they had accumulated over the past 30 years.

182. October 17 1973 may have had the most UFO sightings and abductions on record. A UFO wave started on October 11, 1973 in Pascagoula Mississippi and worked its way up the Mississippi river and across Pennsylvania and up the east coast to New Hampshire. A particular species, which resembled the Michelin man, had arrived and were taking soil and human samples. They seem to have had 6 weeks to get in and get out accomplishing their mission.

183. In December 1973 and January 1974, there were large scale disappearances of dogs from small towns across America; 15 at a time.

184. 1974, Governor Ronald Reagan and his pilot see a UFO while flying to Bakersfield California.

185. On August 25, 1974 in Coyame Mexico, a 16' UFO collides with a Cessna 180. The CIA monitors the transmissions. Mexican soldiers go to the scene and deny U.S. help. Four soldiers die after handing the ETs and craft. Mexico allows a U.S. team from Fort Bliss to recover the craft and ETs which are brought to the CDC in Atlanta.

186. An August 22, 1974 DIA Form 1480 signed by Captain Mothe, who was Deputy Director of the Army Medical Intel., said that the DIA is tasked with looking at the paranormal affects associated with UFOs for military significance but would do so unofficially. (*Watchers II*)

187. On November 9, 1974, 3 teens reported that a red flying object landed in a silt pond in Carbondale Pa. An underwater glow lasted 9 hours as divers were unable to lift an object but then found an old railroad lantern. The pond was partially drained after spectators were cleared for 12 hours and no object found. Some claim an object had been flat bedded out of the area. The police chief threatened staff to stick to the hoax story and he refused to release 35mm film of the incident.

188. The 1940's MK-ULTRA CIA project to alter human behavior became public in 1975. Human subjects were given mind altering drugs without their consent. LSD was created by the CIA. Behavioral effects of different vibratory frequencies were tested (Velostat can block transmissions). Operation-Often looked into the use of paranormal assassination by demonic forces.

189. Researcher Robert Temple published that the Dogan tribe of Mali knew all about the Sirius star system and its double star and hidden dwarf and that Saturn had rings. All their info proved correct.

190. General Stubblebine was the PSI Tech Director for remote viewing until its cancellation in 1995 and stated that there is operating machinery above and below the surface of Mars. $20 million were spent on this project.

191. On November 7, 1975, a UFO changed the targeting info on a nuclear warhead at Malmstrom AFB.

192. A November 11, 1975 NORAD document stated: Since 28 Oct 75 numerous reports of suspicious objects have been received at NORAD. Reliable military personnel at Loring, Wurtsmith, Malmstrom, Minot and Falconbridge have visually sighted suspicious objects.

Air Guard helicopters, SAC helicopters and NORAD F-106s have failed to produce positive ID.

193. On August 20, 1976, four artists (2 twins) set out on a camping-canoe trip in Allagash Maine and were abducted by a walnut shaped UFO with insect-like creatures inside. Sperm samples were taken. Two of the men took polygraphs and passed.

194. On September 18, 1976, an Iranian pilot tried to fire his AIM-9 warhead at a UFO over Tehran, his control panel went dead.

195. NASA scientist and photo analyst George Leonard published his 1976 book *Somebody Else is on the Moon* and claimed that photos showed structures on the moon. Engineers Vito Saccheri and Lester Howes visited NASA in Houston and viewed the photos which showed bridges, pyramids, pipelines and a rectangular structure.

196. In 1977, President Jimmy Carter twice asked the Vatican for their UFO files. The Vatican denied the request twice but did allow Jesuit Attorney Daniel Sheehan to view them. In June of 1977, President Carter was seen sobbing at his desk in the Oval Office after attending a UFO briefing.

197. In 1977, NASA was asked by Congress to consider resuming UFO investigations but they declined due to the fact that nothing would be gained.

198. The Aug 1977 *UFOs and Related Subjects* report prepared for the USAF Office of Scientific Research concluded that "UFOs are strikingly familiar to demonic possession and psychic phenomena" after analyzing over

1600 books and articles in the Library of Congress on UFOs.

199. In 1977 in Colares Brazil, UFOs scan citizens with a radioactive beam of light that resulted in 10 deaths, 54 burns, 54 temporary paralysis, 23 puncture wounds, 34 vision problems, 41 vomiting, 55 migraine headaches, 74 experiencing temperature changes, 36 prolonged illnesses, 30 people levitated and 18 abductions. Light beams would engulf and pursue people. The 8 different craft were silent. Animals reacted violently. Most occupants were 3 feet tall while some were human size. There were 56 military personnel and 48 doctors involved. Eleven vehicle engines died when the craft flew over.

200. In many UFO instances, The U.S. has asked the Brits if they have a new craft. During WWII, both the Americans and Germans thought the Foo Fighters were a secret weapon. This would eliminate misidentification of secret craft as an explanation.

201. On January 18, 1978, an alien was shot by an MP at Fort Dix army base NJ and it managed to flee only to die on a runway at adjoining McGuire AFB.

202. The release of 1000's of C.I.A. UFO documents in 1978 exposed the fact that Major Keyhoe, Captain Ruppelt and Admiral Hillenkoetter and others were replaced on NICAP's Board by CIA agents in the late 60's. They paid themselves salaries and expenses that bankrupted the UFO organization in 1980 that did so much in the 60's to offset the lies of Project Blue Book. It was also determined that there were another 257 CIA UFO documents and 18 NSA UFO documents withheld.

On October 29, 1979, a federal appeals court gave the NSA a special dispensation exempting it from FOIA. CIA records were then moved to the NSA and private contractors. (See chapter 17).

203. Oct 21, 1978, Melbourne Australia pilot Fred Valentich radioed in that he saw a shiny elongated object with four lights and that, "It is not an aircraft". His plane then disappeared and no debris field was found. The original audio tape was destroyed but was reconstructed by witnesses in the Tower. There were 15 UFO reports that day.

204. UFO hearings were held at the U.N. on November 28 1978 at the request of Grenada Prime Minister Eric Gairy. UN draft decision 33/426 requested an agency be established to investigate UFOs. Three months later, a military coup in Grenada ousted Gairy and ended his Grenada UFO initiative (CIA?).

205. Ian Watson published *Miracle Visitors* in 1978 and was the first to describe UFO consciousness or the Oz effect of altered states.

206. On January 18, 1979, the British House of Lords conducted a debate on UFOs.

207. An October 14, 1976 FBI memo states that, "mutilations of cattle are only the forerunner of mutilations of human beings". Between 1975 and 1979, there were over 10,000 cattle mutilations. Besides surgical removal of organs, the carcasses are found deliberately in plain sight with all blood drained and predators avoid them.

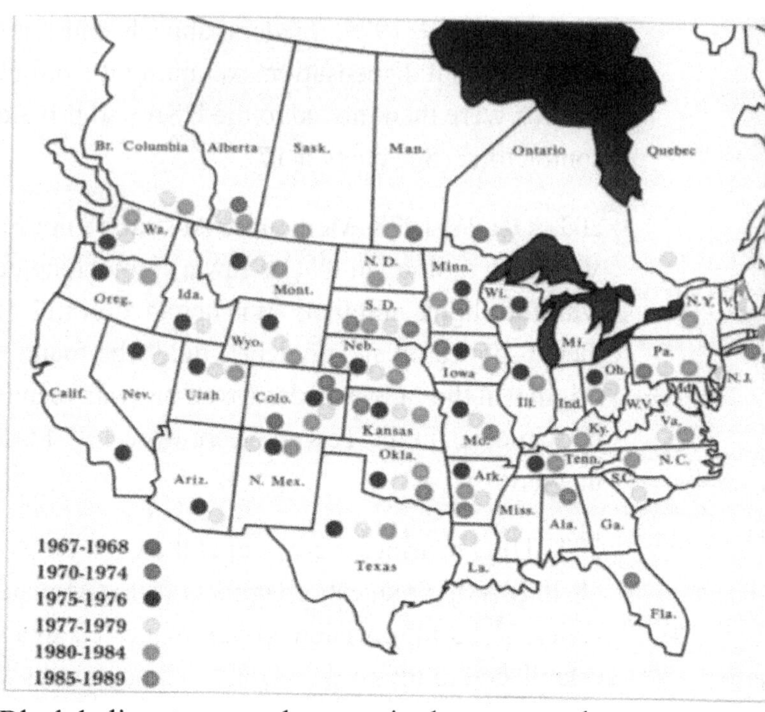

Black helicopters are also seen in the area yet the government surely has the resources to fund their own research. Many are dropped within monitoring status of NORAD. The Gomez ranch near Dulce lost over 50 cattle. The cattle were being marked with a potassium-magnesium substance that could be seen with a black light at night. Are the helicopters actually built by ETs with ET pilots or are they a branch of our Military called the Night Stalkers who appease ancient deities in exchange for supernatural weapons? Or do “They” need genetic material to reconstruct themselves on this planet? Cattle DNA are only 80% similar to human DNA. Does this also explain the 4000 people a year in the U.S. that just disappears or is it the E.P.A. and a covert para-military team monitoring for radiation which was established in 1970? Since 1957, 100 families near the Nevada test sites routinely are monitored for radiation at

U.N.L.V. Either the government is causing the mutilations or won't investigate because they can't.

208. In the summer of 1979, a UFO dove and hit Warren Minnesota Deputy Val Johnson's patrol car. He and the car were found 300 yards from the scene and his watch and the car clock were running 14 minutes behind. The car is on display at the local museum.

209. June 14, 1980, 30 UFOs are reported over Chile, Uruguay, Brazil, Argentina and Paraguay.

210. The Dec 1980 Cash-Landrum Texas incident and the Bentwaters U.K. UFO occurred within days of each other. The blacktop pavement where the Cash-Landrum car was located had to be replaced due to radioactivity. Betty Cash died exactly 18 years later on the same day as her December encounter with what was most probably an experimental nuclear powered Wasp II US military craft that was malfunctioning and being escorted by military Chinook helicopters. The Bentwaters radiation also measured 10 times higher than normal.

211. Margaret Thatcher made this statement regarding the Bentwaters case, "You have to get your facts straight, there are some things you just cannot tell the people". Some say the case was a military test of holograms and virtual reality technology.

212. Beginning in the 1980's, the missing fetus syndrome started showing up in conjunction with abductions.

213. The largest number of UFO witnesses was in China on August 24, 1981 by over one million Chinese of a spiral shaped craft.

214. On March 8, 1982 the Supreme Court decided not to hear a case where the NSA was holding 135 UFO documents marked Top Secret.

215. On October 4, 1982 in the Ukraine, a UFO started the launch sequence on nuclear missiles for 15 seconds before returning to stand by.

216. The Overton Principle refers to certain concepts that are outside of public acceptability and cannot be disclosed.

217. In April of 1983, journalist Linda Moulton Howe met with Air Force special agent Richard Doty at Kirkland AFB. Doty showed Howe a Presidential briefing paper on UFOs in an attempt to flush out Howe's sources in regards to her *Strange Harvest* documentary. Linda fell hook line and sinker for the bait.

218. The first time authorities acknowledged a UFO over a nuclear reactor was during the Hudson Valley wave in 1984 when a 300' UFO hovered over reactor # 3 on July 24 1984 at the Indian Point nuclear reactor.

219. On March 21, 1985, the Hudson Valley FAA reported that arrests were made by State Police of persons flying in an illegal formation as the FAA responded to UFO reports by numerous witnesses. No arrests actually took place as the FAA participated in the cover-up. There were over 5000 witnesses over four years to these sightings.

220. President Reagans diary dated June 11, 1985 noted that we had a space capacity for 300 crew yet we only had 5 space shuttles that held 8 each = 40. In 2001, 16 year old Gary McKinnon hacks into military computers

and finds project Solar Warden which states that the U.S. has a space fleet consisting of 8 mother ships and 43 smaller craft and 300 personnel.

221. The Pentagons 1985 budget listed the Aurora project which is a Mach 6 (4567 mph) SR-72 scramjet and is the likely source of the load booms that are heard.

222. In January 1986, a 7' wide red orb crashed into the hilltop of Height 611 in Russia. Lead balls and a black chemical laced film is discovered imbedded in the impact area.

223. Immediately after the April 26, 1986 Chernobyl disaster, a UFO was spotted emitting 2 red rays that reduced radiation levels by 70% and prevented a nuclear explosion.

224. May 20, 1986, 20 UFOs are tracked on radar over Sao Paolo Brazil.

225. November 1986- Japan Airlines flight 1628 over Alaska confirmed a mile long UFO by ground and air radar and is seen by pilots and confirmed by the FAA.

226. The Gulf Breeze Florida UFO wave started in November of 1987 and had hundreds of witnesses and centered on photos taken by Ed Walters in December of 1987. In 1990, a UFO model was found in the former home of Walters and used to discredit him; only the model was made from blueprints Ed developed in September of 1989 after the wave and photos were taken. Someone went through Walters's trash at his new home and created the model and hide it at his former home next to a damaged water line that the new owners would discover.

227. On March 4, 1988, a UFO landed on frozen Lake Erie and broke through the ice. A half dozen smaller triangular craft emerged and were witnessed by 2 coast guard officers and residents of East Lake Ohio. The coast guard filed a report but was not allowed by NASA to investigate further.

228. In 1988, alien abduction insurance was first issued by Florida based UFO Abduction Insurance Co for $19.95. The Heaven's Gate cult also had a $1M policy on each of its members against alien abduction, pregnancy and death.

229. Three ARV- alien reproduction vehicle (back engineered saucer) were spotted on November 12, 1988 in a Lockheed hangar at the Norton AFB air show.

230. In 1989, Bob Lazar described propulsion Element 115 at Area 51. He said it was given to us by ETs. In 2004 Element 115, Ununpentium, was officially discovered with the same properties. It is rumored that some of the bases activity has moved to the Dugway Proving Ground at Michael AFB in Utah which is surrounded by deadly biological testing fields.

231. On March 14, 1989, MUFON investigator Don Ratsch recorded STS-29 say that they had an alien space craft under observance.

232. On November 30, 1989, multiple witnesses saw Linda Cortile Napolitano abducted from the 12th floor of her lower Manhattan apartment and floated to a craft along with 3 ETs on a blue ray. Witnesses included United Nations Secretary General Javier Perez de Cuellar and his security guards. Budd Hopkins, who investigated the case, concluded that the ETs portray themselves as

benevolent environmentalists but are here for a hybrid breeding program to benefit themselves although they are not inherently evil or benign.

233. Thirty employees of the British Aerospace Marconi company which worked on SDI technology died mysterious deaths in the 1980's.

234. The March 31, 1990 Belgium UFOs were picked up by 5 different radar tracks, chased by F-16's and also consisted of eye witnesses verifying that the craft accelerated to over 2000 MPH in a second and turned at over 40 G's at low altitude which would kill humans.

235. On May 4, 1990, Mikhail Gorbachev said, "The UFO problem is real and we should approach it seriously and study it". A month earlier, the Soviets announced the formation of the Soviet Ufological Commission.

236. On January 24, 1991, a UFO was tracked on radar in the Persian Gulf by 3 U.S. and 2 British ships that all five fired at once at the UFO and shot it down.

237. In 1991, Danny Casolaro uncovered evidence that the Octopus organization was developing advanced biological viruses at the underground Dulce NM base. He believed UFOs were a cover story for the advanced weapons. Casolaro committed suicide by slashing his wrists.

238. In November 1991, Gorbachev dissolved the KGB whose *Blue Folder* UFO files became public. More than 40 cases confirmed the UFO reality.

239. Even after the December 1991 collapse of the Soviet Union, U.S. military and black project spending continued to climb due to the UFO threat.

240. In 1992, Congress ordered NASA to search the Universe for radio signals. This started Project SETI which was abandoned in 1993 due to cost and became a private venture. Most scientists support SETI's ridiculous search for radio signals but reject MUFONs investigation of sightings.

241. The 1992 *MIT Conference on Abductions* established that regressive hypnosis does work.

242. During Black project testing, all video cameras are turned off. All footage taken at Area 51 and from satellites is of real UFOs.

243. John Mack's introduction to alien abduction came in 1990 through a meeting with Budd Hopkins. In 1992, Dr Mack was asked to evaluate Air Force and Police Officers who had UFO sightings and it became a life's passion for him. Mack was hit by a car in London and killed in 2004. John had an Eastern philosophical spin to his work and a distain for materialism and the out of harmony destruction of the environment. John wrote that the abduction was a forced consciousness expansion by showing us we have no control which destroys our ego. The abduction brings us closer to our spiritual roots while the alien longs to experience our emotions. The aliens are subtler and permeate our culture from the bottom up. John believed the hybrid program was at the center of the abductions and was not evil but about the preservation of life on earth.

244. At the May 1992 Bilderbergers meeting, Henry Kissinger said "If Americans were told an outside threat threatened our existence, people will pledge with world leaders to deliver them from this evil. Individual rights will be relinquished".

245. In 1994, Project Delta examined 473 cases over the past 2500 years and concluded that UFOs have not changed significantly over the years.

246. The 1994 *Alexander UFO Religious Crisis Survey* concluded that religious institutions would not collapse as the Brookings Institute concluded in 1960 and that humans are not as fragile as their leaders believe.

247. Sept 16, 1994, 62 children see a UFO and two aliens in Zimbabwe and draw similar pictures.

248. The first alien implant was analyzed on January 6, 1995 from the earlobe of Betty Dagenais who died in 1989 and willed that her earlobe be autopsied. She was told in 1986 by her alien abductors that she would die if she tried to have her implant removed.

249. In 1995, 48 year old New Mexico Congressman Steven Schiff partitioned the General Accounting Office

for the Roswell crash memos. Their reply was that the memos had been improperly destroyed. These memos were permanent records. Congressman Schiff passed away from fast acting cancer three years later.

250. In 1995, Laurance Rockefeller supported the *Unidentified Flying Objects Briefing Document – The Best Available Evidence* and sent a copy to the White House.

30 Rockefeller Plaza
New York, N.Y. 10112

Room 5600

(212) 649-5600

November 1, 1995

11-1-95
JHG.
Staff
John

Dear Jack,

Attached are: (1) A draft letter to the President which Laurance has been discussing with Mrs. Clinton and her staff; and, (2) A draft report on the "best evidence" about UFOs.

Laurance thinks that it is perhaps timely to send a letter to the President. We think the "best evidence" report, although we haven't reviewed it in detail or analyzed it, is a good piece of work.

Laurance would like to discuss these items by telephone, perhaps on Thursday, November 2 between 11:30 and 12:30, if this is convenient for you.

Sincerely,

Henry (signed in absence)

Henry L. Diamond

Doctor John H. Gibbons
Assistant to the President for
Science and Technology
Old Executive Office Building
Room 424
Washington, D.C. 20500

Enclosures
Via Federal Express

Rockefeller paid for regular meetings of the Starlight Coalition, a group made up of former intelligence and military men interested in UFOs. Rockefeller funded a plan to establish contact with aliens by signaling them with powerful halogen lamps. Rockefeller held a UFO conference at his ranch in Wyoming in August 1995 which was attended by the Clintons. The attached letter proves the Clintons were present.

251. The Collins Elite is a branch of the C.I.A. that investigates the paranormal and UFOs. They concluded that there are no UFOs. The NSA version of the Collins Elite is the JASON Society, named after the quest for the fleece or "truth".

252. Varginha Brazil, January 20, 1996, red eyed foul smelling humanoids with small horns are discovered and captured and killed by locals. Fire officer Corporal Marco Eli Chereze (23) dies on February 15 after handling the body of one of the creatures which is turned over to the U.S. for examination. The bacteria likely created the Ebola virus.

253. In 1996, Long Island UFO Network founder John Ford accused Suffolk County Republican John Powell of covering up a UFO crash and of being dishonest. Powell was friends with Gov. Pataki and helped get him elected. Ford was arrested for planting extremely low level radioactive radium laced toothpaste in Powell's home which Ford denied and he was committed to Bellevue Mental Hospital where he remains today. Ford acquired radioactive radium to test his radiation detectors for the UFO investigation. Ford was held on his knees with a gun to his head by Suffolk County police officers as his dogs were beaten in an attempt to gain a confession from Ford.

Powell was eventually found guilty of racketeering. Powell had allowed illegal toxic dumping where the UFO or military craft crashed. Powell was afraid the UFO investigation would reveal his illegal dumping and orchestrated the Ford arrest. The person who set up and entrapped Ford was a police informant with a criminal record. Ford had pleaded insanity out of fear of losing his pension as a Suffolk County Court Officer if convicted of a crime. Powell served less time for toxic dumping than Ford for making a threat with a non-toxic substance that he had in his vehicle for weeks.

254. This case is less about Ford being an Ufologist than about where the UFO investigation took Ford; to the site of an illegal toxic waste dumping scheme by a high profile politician. Ford became collateral damage of an illegal cover up.

255. According to NASA's Kepler telescope, there are more earthlike planets in the Universe than dollars in our national debt.

256. Were the flares dropped by the Army in Phoenix March 13, 1997 a cover-up diversion for the large triangular UFO that was seen two hours earlier? The only problem is that a FOIA to Luke AFB regarding flares dropped came back from the Air Force that no flares were launched. No training flares have ever been launched before or after this incident in this location. Gov. Symington debunked the sightings at a press conference and waited 10 years before disclosing that he actually saw the large triangle.

257. In 1997, Lord Hill-Norton stated that UFOs were of satanic origin and he helped form the *UFO Concern Group* which issued their findings.

258. A UFO was shown on CNN over Baghdad on December 16, 1998 and was hit by Iraqi forces and captured and brought to the Qalaate-Julundi research facility. Some say this was the real reason for the Iraqi invasion in 2003.

259. On August 2, 2002, Todd Sees went for an ATV ride in Montour Ridge Pa and went missing. He was found the next day completely emaciated of blood wearing just his underwear. A boot was found a mile away in the top of a tree. Three farmers reported a UFO in the area. Family members were not allowed to see the body and it remains a police cold case today.

260. In 2004, Nevada Gov. Bill Richardson asked for files related to the Roswell crash.

261. The Vatican's Chief Astronomer Reverend Gabriel Funes in 2008 reiterated Father Balducci's 2001 comment that if there is life in space, they are our brothers and most likely have fallen from grace just like us and need to be redeemed. In 1957, Father Connell made the same statement. Conferences were held at the Vatican on Extraterrestrial Life on Nov. 6-11, 2009 with 30 scientists including SETI and Feb. 12, 2020with Jesuit priests.

262. A simple breakdown of close encounters are; a CE1 is a strange low level light in sky; a CE2 is a craft that leaves trace evidence; a CE3 is an entity; a CE4 is an abduction; a CE5 is a human initiated contact like SETI that invokes a response, a CE6 is death, a CE7 is a human-alien hybrid. CE1-3 was based on Hynek's 1972

book, *The UFO Experience*. We need a new level separating physical from altered state abduction.

263. It is now believed that if you experience a CE 2 or 3, you have already been abducted or are about to be.

264. All abductees have opened a door by showing interest in the unexplained through horoscopes, tarot cards, psychics, Ouija boards, evolution and/or New Age beliefs, the occult, mysticism and eastern philosophy, secret societies, witchcraft, Ufology and science fiction.

265. Why does the message abductees receive only try to discredit Jesus Christ and not the prophets of other religions? Christians oppose a one world government, religion and ruler.

266. Some people have the Oz factor which is the ability to communicate by telepathy.

267. The U.N. lists UFO as a codified term in its encyclopedia.

268. Rods are life forms similar to what Kenneth Arnold believes he saw.

269. Alfred Webre coined the term Exopolitics.

270. In 1994, MUFON N.C. Ufologist George Fawcett created a list of 25 characteristics that repeat during UFO cases. Number 6 listed boron as a trace element. Boron was highlighted in lab reports as elevated during the 2008 Denise Murter investigation in Bucks County Pa.

271. The TR-3B is the alleged Astra craft that the Air Force developed after the 1976 Stealth Fighter and is a

triangular craft that defies gravity. Its description matches many of the 2008 Bucks County sightings reports.

272. The National Press Club has hosted public hearings on UFOs in 2001, 2007, 2010 and 2013 where Generals, pilots, scientists, officers and a Governor signed affidavits to testify in front of Congress on UFOs.

273. The November 11, 2006 O'Hare airport UFO was seen by 12 employees and recorded conversations with the Tower exist discussing the incident even though the FAA and United Airlines denied the incident and claimed a hole-punch cloud caused the incident. Hole-punch clouds occur at 20,000 feet and can only form when air temperature is below 32 degrees. Air temperatures during the O'Hare Airport incident were 53 degrees and the hole formed just hundreds of feet in elevation.

274. 2007-12, The Pentagon paid $22M a year for the *Advanced Aviation Treat ID Program* to investigate UFOs.

275. 2008 started with the Stephensville UFO sightings over President Bush's Crawford Texas ranch confirmed by radar and the year ended with over 200 sightings in Bucks County Pa that resulted in radar and trace evidence. In both cases, the FAA tried to block the investigation.

276. In 2008, the U.S. Air Force decided it would no longer accept UFO reports and refers the caller to NORAD who is not subject to FOIA's.

277. In a 2008 interview with James Oberg of NASA, he said that Air Force personnel would routinely pose as NASA agents on UFO investigations. Is this the source of

many MIB encounters? UFOs have been seen over cemeteries. Some say MIBs are reanimated corpses.

278. The 2008 *Peters ET Religious Crisis Survey* concluded that the seven major religions would not collapse if ET visited earth.

279. When my TV debut occurred in 2008 on *UFOs over Earth*, my mom watched *Desperate Housewives* instead!

280. In June 2010, the U.K. decided to close its UFO desk and retain reports for only 30 days in order to avoid FOIA's.

281. NASA decided it will not release pictures from space for 6 months until after they are analyzed or scrubbed as many former NASA employees charge.

282. Half of all Defense Satellites face outward.

283. Many Asian and South American countries have official UFO reporting centers.

284. On July 7, 2010, China's Xiaoshan airport shut down and delayed 18 flights and 2000 passengers due to a UFO.

285. In 2011, an exorcism was performed on an alien by the name of Hexabor Ur.

286. On Sept. 11, 2010, China's Baotau airport shut down for one hour due to a UFO. June 10, 2013 China Air 757 is struck by something. A similar nose strike and damage is documented Oct 27, 2017 of Delta FL 8935 carrying OKC NBA team.

287. Pilots report only 5% of their UFO sightings to the FAA and say that UFOs usually approach when dark out. Pilots see UFOs as often as they strike birds. Only .4% (point four) of the 6000 cases MUFON receives yearly is from pilots. Obviously, pilots are discouraged from reporting UFOs.

288. According to Russian UFO files, 50% of UFOs occur in Oceans and 15% occur in Lakes.

289. The FEMA approved Fire Officers Guide to Disaster Control has a chapter (13) on UFOs.

290. Of the 6000 cases MUFON receives each year, 3.6% are reported by military or law enforcement.

291. The Air Force Space program has been funded higher than NASA since 1982. The AFSP receives $8.8B a year and this is where the "real" space program occurs.

292. The U.S. and U.K. approach UFOs through their Department of Defense or Ministry of Defence whereas many other countries look at it as an air safety issue and investigate UFOs through their FAA or as research as in the French studies.

293. Radar is not configured to pick up anything that doesn't look similar to a plane. If it is too big, hovers, travels too fast or has no transponder the FAA system will paint it as weather.

294. Magnetism for propulsion doesn't work because it is strongest at the equator and weakest at the poles.

295. UFOs that exceed the sound barrier do not cause sonic booms and some appear to be concentrations of energy that can change size and shape.

296. What if governments are not hiding UFO secrets but their lack of knowledge of them?

297. There will be no disclosure if some ET's are complicit with a branch of our government and don't want disclosure. How can you trust disclosure from a government that has been working with aliens?

298. French pilots are required by law to report UFOs. The French police investigate UFOs and will arrest you if you perpetrate a hoax. The GEIPAN in France trains pilots on how to report UFOs.

299. Since gravity bends light, zero point energy may move faster than the speed of light.

300. UFOs are based at the poles because they prefer the weather, we have trouble flying in intense polar storms and the intense radiation from the Van Allen belt at our equator is not present at the poles.

301. The internet is as dangerous as the printing press was 400 years ago . . . to the truth.

302. Men want to see the craft, weapons and decide whether they can take "them" in a fight. Women are interested in telepathy, the message and emotions of contact!

303. What if the Universe is a hologram; a reflection of the Milky Way Galaxy and not really expanding or even there?

304. It's not the UFO that is the problem, it's the people.

305. All birds and animals on earth are in tune with nature. They flee prior to an earthquake, tsunami etc. All

except humans who are not in tune because we are not from here.

306. Have you ever tasted beer made from crop circle barley? A cereologist studies crop circles.

307. Alpha Centauri is only 4.3 light years away. A species travelling at half the speed of light can get to earth in less than 9 years.

308. The medical billing code for injury by spaceship is E845.0.

309. We've named the unexplained to be paranormal, but we have never explained it.

310. It has to be realized that earth is on the outer edge of the Milky Way galaxy and a perfect way station and launch point for missions beyond our galaxy.

311. The Star of Bethlehem has never been identified by astronomers.

312. In order to study religion, you do not have to first prove the existence of God.

313. Disclosure must come from the religious community because Jews, Christians and Muslims view ET as demonic but only Christians can stop these entities through the name of Jesus.

314. God, the Devil and Angels are de facto extraterrestrials (to us).

315. Jesus said to Thomas, "the Fate of the Universe depends upon these three words: Caulacau, Saulasau,

Zeesar". The words do not have any meaning in any known language (on earth).

316. Death is the ultimate abduction.

317. U.S. national security would be threatened by open discussion of the UFO secrets it holds.

318. Although the Kenneth Arnold sighting took place on June 24th, many Ufologists have also died that day including Frank Scully, Frank Edwards along with Edward Bryant and Richard Church all at the same World UFO conference, Robert Charroux and Jackie Gleason.

319. U.S. missing persons reports have gone up by six times since 1980 with 90,000 people never found. In 1980, there were only seven demonologists in the U.S. and six were priests. Exorcism has increased from a handful prior to 1990 to over 1300 a year today. Around this same time, the alien abduction changed from entities in uniform on ships to Greys lurking in the corner of your bedroom after midnight.

320. Brazil has the greatest concentration of injury encounters with UFOs.

321. March 20 is Alien Abduction Day. . . . . . .

322. Aug 3, 2016 marked the first time a private company was granted permission to land on the moon by the DOD and State Dept. Fla based Moon Express will make the 2017 landing.

323. Although Bigfoot has been seen with some UFO cases. The primate version of Bigfoot is most likely a Neanderthal that has survived and possibly evolved or mated with other primates like apes.

324. There are 1071 operational satellites in space. We seem to be waiting for number 1072 but what if "It" does not originate from space?

325. Most cattle mutilations, military bases and best UFO cases are along the 37th parallel. Is that evidence for aliens or military covert operations?

326. The U.S. government can no longer say that they do not investigate UFOs since the end of Project Blue Book because they admitted that they funded Robert Bigelow with $22M from the defense department to fund MUFON investigations from 2007-12. They admitted on Dec 16, 2017 that we have an Advanced Aviation Threat ID Program. They have yet to explain what the Navy pilot videos are of a Tic-Tac object that has been labeled unidentified…

327. In December 2019, SETI announced that we will discover alien life by 2029 and President Trump formed the sixth branch of the military; the *Space Force*. Haven't we had that since 1980?

328. UFO disclosure is planned for June 27, 2021 by the Pentagon.

"It's sad that the UFO crowd has come to this – seemingly giving up on proving their own case and hoping that the feds will do their work for them. That's both an unconvincing argument and a mentally lazy one" - SETI

Here are some possible explanations for the UFO phenomena. Are we dealing with super technology or the supernatural?

Extraterrestrial hypothesis (**ETH**), proposed by Major Keyhoe after the Thomas Mantell incident, theorizes that aliens travel here from other planets. Keyhoe shifted the burden of proof to the government. But the distances are vast and they have never been seen approaching from deep space even though statistically there must be life in space. The theory of evolution makes the chances of a genetic match zero. There are over 1000 sightings per month. Wouldn't that indicate a massive fleet is here? Yet there are radar, photo and government documents. In 1963, Carl Sagan theorized that we would be visited every 10,000 years by a new species. Why are SETI and NASA silent? Are they placebos?

Ancient Astronaut (**AA**) - We've misidentified angels and God and the bible. ET's have been here from our beginning and genetically upgraded us from hominids and actively participate in our history. Ancient structures, rock carvings and cave paintings along with the Hindu Mahabharata seem to support this. Ancient Alien falls under **ETH.**

Prison-Zoo Earth- Aliens look like us and originally used earth like a Devils Island or Botany Bay for the unwanted or we are being contained here for our own good. Zoo earth maintains that species are dropped off and negate evolution. They don't invade because they herd their cattle. Prison-Zoo earth falls under **ETH**.

Interdimensional or Ultraterrestrial hypotheses (UTH) theorizes there are eleven dimensions and that they exist on a different plane or parallel universe but are indigenous to earth and have always co-existed with us. Our Quantum physics attempts to explain them. They may create the perception of a UFO by manipulating matter or energy. Jesus said, "*My Kingdom is not of this world*"- John 18:36.

Demonic- ETs are Fallen Angels and exist in a malevolent dimension and have found a way to enter ours and are deliberately disguised as ET. The fact that they hide, operate at night and avoid open contact may support this. If Fallen Angels can materialize craft, then this is what we are experiencing. God gave Lucifer two thirds of the Universe and he is the prince of the air (UFOs) and was an angel of light (orbs). Their goal is to draw us away from belief in Christ, corrupt our DNA and ultimately deceive us. Real ET's experience the same abductions and preternatural oppression and infestation as we do which truly makes the ET our space brothers. They have also mated with us in the past and produced the Nephilim. Altered state CE4 and demonic possession are one in the same. Demonic falls under **UTH**.

Cryptoterrestrial **(CTH)** or hollow earth proposed by Mac Tonnies- They co-exists with us on this planet either in inner earth or under the oceans. Biologically could this explain abductions for a DNA match by Atlanteans, evolved reptiles or dinosaurs? But again, how do you explain the Grey unisex look and unworkable large head to slim hip proportions for a natural birth, if they are birthed?

Extratemporal time travel where they are us returning for a look or in need of something or to fix an event. This is a biological way an exchange of DNA could work during abductions and would explain their ability to prophesize future events (nuclear war, environment, Fatima). But how do you explain the Grey unisex look and unworkable large head to slim hip proportions for a natural birth, if they are birthed? Is the Grey a worker or android?

Hoax- Which makes up about 10% of cases.

Natural phenomena hypothesis- science can explain everything.

Psychological- Carl Jung believed that some UFOs are a projection of our mind in response to our beliefs but that some UFOs show signs of intelligent guidance by quasi human pilots. Others say magnetic fields and drugs can cause UFO hallucinations. There is a mass delusion or collective schizophrenia where we have replaced séances and mediums with UFOs. J Allen Hynek believed we might be projecting these sightings with our mind and telekinesis.

Military- the Air Force or Navy uses UFOs as a cover story for our own advanced military craft. A UFO was back engineered from recovered Nazi technology (1936 Black Forest crash) through Project Paperclip and some of the subsequent crashes were our test flights (Roswell). We test our new weapons in foreign countries like the 1977 Colares Brazil case. The 1984 Hudson Valley sightings and 1997 Phoenix lights sightings were of our craft which make up *Project Solar Warden*. The military is involved in cattle mutilations and abductions (***MILabs***) and abductees are brought to underground bases. Disinformation and staged events like the Richard Doty hoax of gullible Linda Moulton Howe for example along with MK-Ultra, Collins Elite and Operation Often. The CIA debunking of UFOs was deliberate to keep scientists and the media from investigating. What if the government doesn't use computers for the alien question but still files paper reports? You can't hack paper. . . . .

Programmers- The pending release of PC game *No Man's Sky*- in which a supercomputer generated trillions of inhabited worlds after being given the guidelines for its universe by human programmers- raises questions as to whether a more advanced civilization could create our reality with exponentially more powerful computers. Over the past 5 years, mainstream physicists have begun to explore whether our "universe" could be a hologram, and prominent figures like *Space X* CEO Elon Musk have been fascinated with the possibility. In this theory, the "Big Bang" was

basically the program itself initiating or turning on, and it has been evolving with the guidelines given to it ever since. This would be not unlike *The Matrix* movies starring Keanu Reeves, in which an alternate reality is "projected" for us. This could explain why UFOs seemingly pop in and out of our reality and exhibit flight characteristics not consistent with known physics: it's the programmers checking in on the simulation at various places and times, much like a child lifting the lid off of an ant colony. It could also explain why so many given access to the "truth" of UFOs and extraterrestrials refuse to talk about it: beyond any security clearances or oaths, the reality that we do not actually exist- but are simply a manifestation of an artificial program- is too upsetting to share, because it would invalidate our entire existence. (Courtesy James Krug).
None or a **C**ombination of all of the above?

How would you rank these when the only source of data comes from the UFO and what they want us to see? Is it a faulty premise to even believe the UFO is from space? Each theory has its own extensive convincing kaleidoscope history but none have enough empirical evidence. They all can't be correct. My guess is, like the cases we investigate; only around 10% are real while 90% are deliberate C.I.A. or entity disinformation or misdirection. But which 10% is real? Are we dealing with super tech or the supernatural? Are inter-dimensional and demonic the same?

In April of 2017, nineteen of my Pa MUFON Investigators discussed these possibilities and voted on each category. Two investigators abstained due to lack of evidence. ETH received the most first place votes, Ancient Alien the most second place votes and Military the most third place votes. There were 98 total points and Ancient Alien received 26, ETH 25, Military 15, UTH 13, Combo 11, Demonic 4, Prison 2, Psychological and Programmers 1 each: Hoax, CTH, Extratemporal and Natural zero votes. My question is how well read were the investigators on all possibilities? Were they influenced by TV and movies that stress ETs are from space?

Abductions

This is the area of Ufology that raises the most disturbing questions for me and causes me to question the expert opinions on this entire topic. There appears to be a covert deceptive "fifth column" at work. Although most UFO sightings take place at 10 pm, most alien abductions take place at 3 am to predominantly females at puberty and again in their early twenties. These ETs would qualify as predators under Megan's Law. Where's the national map (not addresses) where these offenders have struck? ETs are advanced enough to be able to communicate but don't. They use telepathy, deception and altered states and choose to kidnap rape and possess victims. Abductees suffer post-traumatic stress and are never the same. There is no choice. If DNA was needed, wouldn't they focus on athletes and scholars?

Fred Saluga and I do a bi-monthly UFO talk show in Pittsburgh. On the very first episode, Fred asked the abduction expert, "Why have they been abducting people for 1000 years if they just need a sample"? This got me thinking. I need to explain this behavior. "They" have taken enough samples to repopulate earth. Experts say there is a hybridization program. In my mind, the last hybridization program involved Fallen Angels and the Nephilim. The 1973 abduction wave was clearly ET explorers and scientists that were here for human, plant and soil samples and completed their mission in a five week period but the clandestine abductions that mirror paranormal reports are not ET but Fallen Angels and demonic.

There is nothing good about abductions. Aliens are not here to help us and have shared zero technology with us. It seems to me that new age thinkers are being easily duped in this area. They willingly cooperate with their kidnappers believing they will be given the knowledge of the Universe. They are making the ET message be what they want it to be, not what it is. The 1956 movie, *Invasion of the Body Snatchers* is much closer to the truth than the 1951 movie *The Day the Earth Stood Still.*

There is an abduction group out there called FREE. It is a group of high level PHD psychologists (12), Ufologists and astronauts like the late Dr. Edgar Mitchell. They say their group is neutral in coming to their conclusions but the entire group is loaded with delusional new age experts who believe "They" are here to help us and have prevented a nuclear war. Their survey concluded 85% of abductions are positive. I said they should expose their kids to it if that's what they believe. I also questioned why dogs react so violently to "Them"? Maybe because animal instincts can't get tricked like thinking humans. I got into an extremely heated debate online with one of the group's founders when I said abductions are evil. He questioned whether I should be "allowed" to say that. Really? Humanity is in trouble when "They" arrive and these gullible left wing new agers are the experts who are consulted and advise to let "Them" in like a Trojan horse. I take a much more guarded hawkish view. We better have our guard up and not trust but verify if it is even possible to verify their intentions.

Instead of regressive hypnosis, you might be better served to contact the *International Association of Exorcists*, which is sponsored by the Catholic Church, rather than contact the Mutual UFO Network to communicate with these so called 3 am ETs. Interesting that 3 am is the opposite of when Jesus was crucified; at

3 pm. And "They" use 3 which mocks the Holy Trinity! We are dealing with two types of contact; ET and Malevolent inter-dimensional entities. Angels and demons can and do materialize in our realm!

Position Statement by John Ventre:

"UFOs are real but are unexplainable. Maybe if we weren't trying to shoot them down we would be closer to an answer, but until disclosure is made this will remain an observational science. Although some appear to be neutral, you cannot ignore the statements of abductees and pilots. We may have been in contact with them for as long as 47,000 years. Some say we may be codependent on each other; us for progress as they pull us forward and them for genetic material. I cannot support a theory of evolution that has missing links and assumes but can't demonstrate that life can be created from matter and advance over time rather than decay. I also firmly believe in God and a spirit world. There is also the possibility that they occupy part of our minds through telepathy or consciousness since many people feel a detachment between their minds and bodies but believe there is intervention from a guardian angel or demonic entity at times and events are pre-determined. We absolutely have free will which is the whole point. It seems as though this has something to do with everything; I believe it goes way beyond "interplanetary" as an explanation. I believe there is a connection between all paranormal including religion, dimensions and UFOs. Maybe we're just spirits on a human experience.

It is also obvious that the U.S. Air Force and C.I.A. have deliberately deceived the public in violation of the law and may be in communication with them. I also believe that our Defense Department is acting in our own best interests in this perverted act of protecting us and obtaining technology. The real Sword of Damocles that hangs over us is the scientific community's failure to investigate this phenomena and the media's failure to report on it seriously. They inadvertently created a situation where the public no longer trusts the media or military or scientific communities. Ufology has raised my consciousness and I no longer fear the unknown. I hope that humans are a unique and precious species in the Universe and not a resource for exploitation. I think the real threat of disclosure will be loyalty. Like a "Zeta" (Stockholm) Syndrome, many will side with the superior being, not their own kind. The same left wing liberals that love Obama and hate America are primed for treason with the invaders. Liberalism is a mental illness. This is why my final conclusion is that the late night Grey abduction experience is demonic and is trying to pull us away from Christ and salvation and towards *Childhood's End.* Everything that can be imagined exist somewhere in God's universe. Ultimately, it all exists as a test of our character and soul.

What to do?

Many of my peers in Ufology have recently come out with their conclusion that Congress should study UFOs and appoint a small group to investigate the matter. I disagree. We have already gone down that path with the Robertson Panel, Project Blue Book and the Condon Committee. Every time the C.I.A. or the Air Force has gotten involved with this issue, there has been a whitewash of the truth and an effort to debunk and discredit witnesses. Why would we want to repeat the same mistake but expect different results? Can we really expect a government agency to conduct an objective study when there are huge technological and institutional paradigms at stake? I say Congress needs to fund an independent 501c3 non-profit group to conduct world class analysis with

Congressional budgetary oversight by the General Accounting Office. The only such group in existence to perform this monumental task is the Mutual UFO Network. Congress foolishly spends multi millions of dollars each year studying topics such as the psychology of ducks, the reproduction of flies and bridges to nowhere. There would need to be cross functional reviews from other disciplines such as theology and psychology since science has been a dead end so far and often start with their conclusion already in mind. Private labs would also have to be contracted. The abduction phenomenon requires faith and not science.

I unfortunately expect SETI to one day soon announce that they have found a repeatable verifiable signal that confirms there is intelligent life in space. They will also say that it is so far away that "They" cannot get here. This will perpetuate the myth that "They" are not already here and 90% of the public and mass media will believe it. SETI and NASA are disinformation agencies regarding ETs.

Disclosure will not come from the U.S. Government. It will come from the Vatican. This would be a convenient cover for the U.S. Government who has benefited from the back engineering of retrieved ET technology and disclosure would also spur faith in religion when it is spun correctly. I am sure that both already know the truth. The U.S. can never make the announcement because it goes too deep for too long. I also believe one reason we give foreign aid to almost every country is so they will contact us on a UFO crash. If you research overseas cases, nearly every time they say "the Americans came in and took over the investigation". Based on what authority or agreement?

I hope you are now questioning everything you've been taught and are asking yourself, "What is the String Theory that explains everything?" The String Theory for how we became us would be in this order:

1. Creation because it is the easiest and most accepted answer for everything. An all-powerful Being answers all questions and doubts.
2. Alien intervention because it fills in the evolutionary missing links but we still need to produce the alien and or craft to the public.
3. And lastly, Evolution because it has too many holes. Or is there a multi creation theory?

But more importantly, how can we truly advance as a species until we know how we got here? How can we decide on our purpose until we know what the purpose of us is? If a superior Being created us, then we should all be in harmony with nature and non-violence and human equality. If we were genetically engineered then we should continue that engineering by enhancing our DNA to reach our pinnacle of perfection. I don't think I want to be a new species. We would no longer be in the image of our creator and wouldn't this in essence avert Satan's destruction? If we evolved with no God then we should continue the Darwinian survival of the fittest pursuit of money and technology and be the best sinners possible since we are just animals and the end justifies the means with no ethics or morality. We should protect our planets resources from overpopulation by eugenically eliminating the weaker strains of humans from the genetic pool. Without God, everything is permissible. Hasn't evolution taught us to not believe in God but to put our faith in the infallibility of science and the coming ETs? This duplicity is our single most important question.

Chapter 3

UFO Photos & Documents

Los Angeles, February 25, 1942, 02:25 PM-Alarm sirens installed in the event of a Japanese air raid is started as flying objects are seen and announced in the sky. A blackout is declared and the anxious and even terrified inhabitants follow the instructions by turning all the lights off. 03:16 PM Anti-aircraft guns open fire on the unidentified flying objects coming from the ocean, and projector beams are searching the sky. Witnesses observe small objects flying at high altitude, of red or silver-plated color, moving in formation at high speed, and untouched by the AAA salvos. This large object was unhurt by many AAA projectiles, according to the reports. Photograph from the *Battle of Los Angeles*.

May 11, 1950-This is one of the most famous UFO pictures ever taken. Photographed by Paul Trent, and first witnessed by his wife. They were published in a local newspaper in McMinnville, Oregon shortly thereafter. Soon, the Trent photos were published in Life magazine edition of June 26, 1950. The rest is history. These photos have been deemed authentic for over 50 years.

Washington, D. C. 1952. During the dawn of Ufology in the United States, unidentified flying objects made themselves known to the leaders of the free world, buzzing over the White House, the Capitol building, and the Pentagon. Seemingly the unknown objects were defying the very governmental agencies sworn to protect the United States from foreign powers. Washington National Airport and Andrews Air Force Base picked up a number of UFOs on their radar screens on July 19, 1952, beginning a wave of sightings still unexplained to this day.

I just like this one......

1956-Rosetta/Natal, South Africa, July 17. Photograph was taken by a well-respected member of South African society. Her husband was a major in the South African Air Force, and Elizabeth worked for Air Force Intelligence. Seven photographs were taken in all. There were also two witnesses to the taking of the photos. Taken in the foothills of the Drakensburg Mountains, and so-dubbed the Drakensberg photos. If these are real, they are extremely impressive. She never changed her story. She died in 1994, at the age of 83.

1965-Santa Ana, California. August 3. Photo taken by highway traffic engineer Rex Heflin while driving near the Santa Ana freeway. Heflin did not report his sighting, but the photographs were published by the Santa Ana Register on 09-20-65. This turned into a very controversial case with photos confiscated, and disagreements between different Ufologists about the photograph's authenticity.

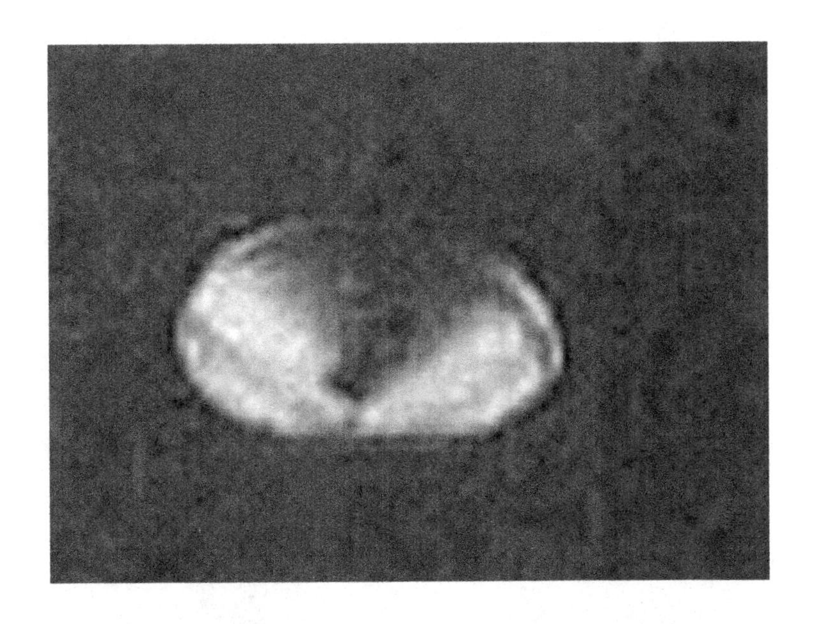

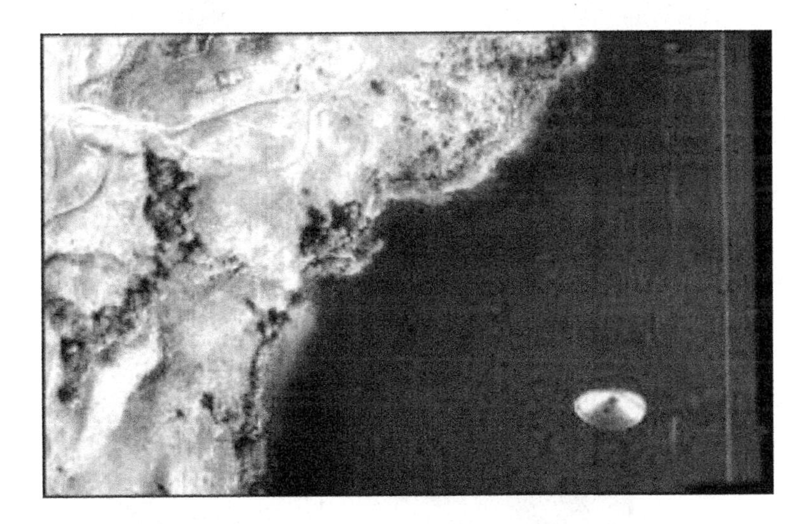

September 4, 1971-An official mapping aircraft of the Costa Rican government took this photograph. The aircraft was flying at 10,000 feet over Lago de Cote. An investigation could not identify the object as a "known" aircraft. Debunkers took some stabs at it, but it is still recognized as authentic by most investigators. No "earthly" explanation has ever been given to explain the object.

1972, Apollo 16, Moon mission dates: April 16-27, CDR: John W. Young, CMP: Kenneth Mattingly, LMP: Charles Duke. Importance of mission: Explored the Moon's rocky central highlands. NASA archives (photo No AS16-114-18423) Mission Apollo 16 on the Moon. Astronaut Charles Duke photographed collecting lunar sample at Station 1. The UFO is seen at just right of top center. No explanation has been given for the object.

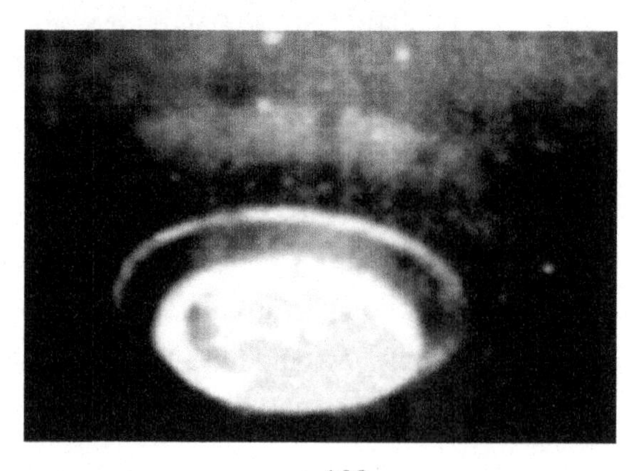

1987-Gulf Breeze, Florida. When the news of the flurry of sightings spread beyond the close-knit community of Gulf Breeze, soon the whole world was involved. Both pro and con were well represented. Shortly after Walters' photos hit the local newspaper, more UFO photographers came forward with their stories or sightings fortified with the proof; more images, both still and moving, and a war of words began. Walters became everything from a community leader to a con man, depending on who you listened to. This is only one of many photographs from Gulf Breeze.

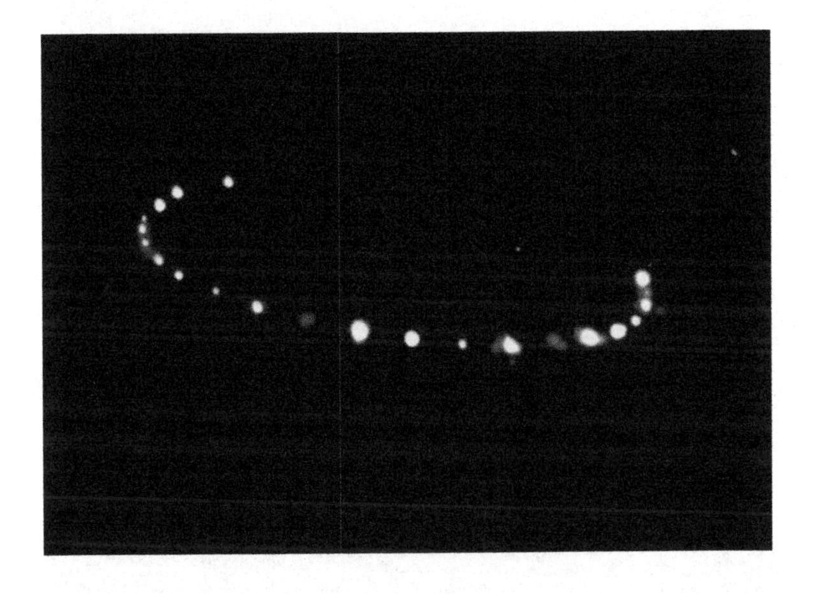

May 26, 1988 picture taken by pilot Randy Etting and corroborated by a second photo taken by a State Trooper along I-84 in Waterbury Connecticut. The object has been determined to be solid and approximately 1000 feet in width.

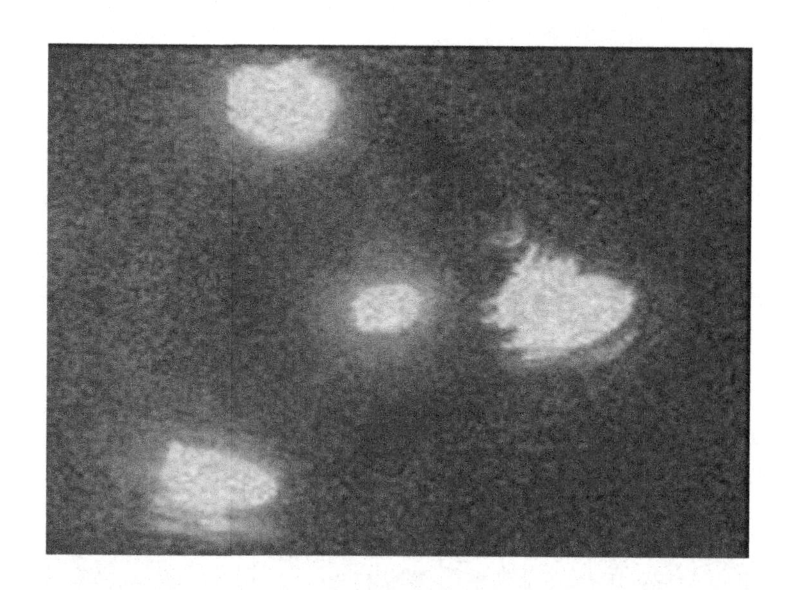

Petit Rechain, Belgium, 1990. One of the most famous UFO pictures ever taken. The photographer, to my knowledge, still remains unnamed. Taken on an April night during a well-known "wave," the photo very clearly shows a triangle-shaped object with lights. One of the best proofs of UFOs we have, especially of a triangle. Original photo was too dark to show object outline, and had to be lightened. Occurred during the wave beginning in 1989.

Phoenix, Arizona, 1997. One of the most publicized UFO events in history was accompanied with many photographs of a giant UFO. First observed in a hexagram pattern at about 7:30 PM over the Superstition Mountains area east of Phoenix, the characteristic 8+1 formation of amber orbs was next seen in two separate arc patterns with "trailing lights" over the Gila River area at about 9:50 and again at 10:00 at the southern edge of Phoenix, where they were seen by thousands and videotaped by a handful who had camcorders close enough at hand to catch the fleeting minutes of their displays. Many other photographs and video film have been taken over the city of Phoenix.

Courtesy of B J Booth Webmaster www.ufocasebook.com

If UFOs are not real, then why are there so many "Agency" memos discussing them? I would challenge you to find the memos discussing a Bigfoot invasion or ghost attack.

HEADQUARTERS, ARMY AIR FORCES
WASHINGTON

AFPIR-CC

5 SEP 1947

Director
Federal Bureau of Investigation
Department of Justice
Washington 25, D. C.

Dear Sir:

Attention: Liaison Section

In answer to a verbal request of your Mr. S. W. Reynolds, a complete survey of research activities discloses that the Army Air Forces has no project with the characteristics similar to those which have been associated with the Flying Discs.

Yours sincerely,

Geo F Schulgen

GEO. F. SCHULGEN
Brigadier General, U.S.A.
Deputy, Ass't. Chief of Air Staff-2

62- 83894-87

Sept 1947 Air Force response to FBI

United States Department of Justice
Federal Bureau of Investigation
Washington, D. C.

IN REPLY, PLEASE REFER TO
FILE No. ________

September 27, 1947

Major General George C. McDonald
Assistant Chief Air Staff - 2
The Pentagon
Washington, D. C.

Dear General McDonald:

The Federal Bureau of Investigation has been requested by your office to assist in the investigation of reported sightings of flying discs.

My attention has been called to instructions disseminated by the Air Forces relative to this matter. I have been advised that these instructions indicate that the Air Forces would interview responsible observers while the FBI would investigate incidents of discs found on the ground, thereby relieving the Air Forces of running down incidents which in many cases turned out to be "ash can covers, toilet seats and whatnot."

In view of the apparent understanding by the Air Forces of the position of the Federal Bureau of Investigation in this matter, I cannot permit the personnel and time of this organization to be dissipated in this manner.

I am advising the Field Divisions of the Federal Bureau of Investigation to discontinue all investigative activity regarding the reported sightings of flying discs, and am instructing them to refer all complaints received to the appropriate Air Force representative in their area.

Sincerely yours,

J. Edgar Hoover

John Edgar Hoover
Director

Sept 1947 FBI response to Air Force request on UFOs

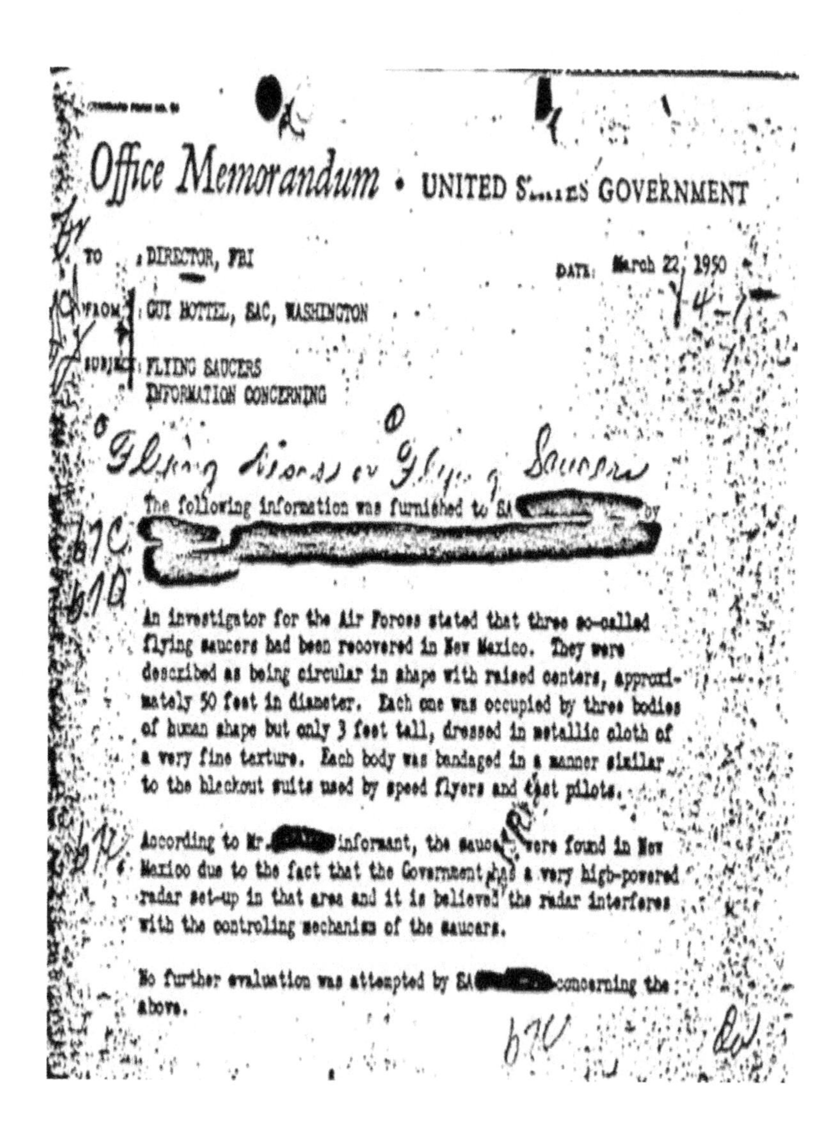
Office Memorandum • UNITED STATES GOVERNMENT

TO : DIRECTOR, FBI

DATE: March 22, 1950

FROM : GUY HOTTEL, SAC, WASHINGTON

SUBJECT: FLYING SAUCERS
INFORMATION CONCERNING

Flying Discs or Flying Saucers

The following information was furnished to SA [redacted] by [redacted]

An investigator for the Air Forces stated that three so-called flying saucers had been recovered in New Mexico. They were described as being circular in shape with raised centers, approximately 50 feet in diameter. Each one was occupied by three bodies of human shape but only 3 feet tall, dressed in metallic cloth of a very fine texture. Each body was bandaged in a manner similar to the blackout suits used by speed flyers and test pilots.

According to Mr. [redacted] informant, the saucers were found in New Mexico due to the fact that the Government has a very high-powered radar set-up in that area and it is believed the radar interferes with the controling mechanism of the saucers.

No further evaluation was attempted by SA [redacted] concerning the above.

1950 Roswell FBI memo released in 2011

Memorandum for Mr. Ladd

[redacted] also discussed this matter with [redacted] of MID. [redacted] indicated that it was his attitude that inasmuch as it has been established that the flying disks are not the result of any Army or Navy experiments, the matter is of interest to the FBI. He stated that he was of the opinion that the Bureau, if at all possible, should accede to General Schulgen's request.

SWR:AJB

ADDENDUM

I would recommend that we advise the Army that the Bureau does not believe it should go into these investigations, it being noted that a great bulk of those alleged discs reported found have been pranks. It is not believed that the Bureau would accomplish anything by going into these investigations.

DML

I think we should do this
7-15

I would do it but before agreeing to it we must insist upon full access to discs recovered. For instance in the La. case the Army grabbed it & would not let us have it for cursory examination.

- 2 -

Edgar Hoover FBI UFO handwritten memo response

ER - 3 - 2809

CENTRAL INTELLIGENCE AGENCY

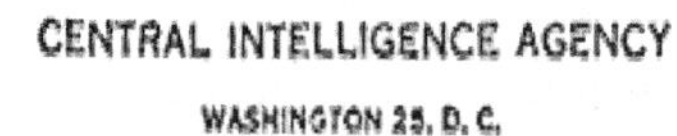

WASHINGTON 25, D. C.

1950

OFFICE OF THE DIRECTOR

MEMORANDUM TO: Director, Psychological Strategy Board

SUBJECT: Flying Saucers

1. I am today transmitting to the National Security Council a proposal (TAB A) in which it is concluded that the problems connected with unidentified flying objects appear to have implications for psychological warfare as well as for intelligence and operations.

2. The background for this view is presented in some detail in TAB B.

3. I suggest that we discuss at an early board meeting the possible offensive or defensive utilization of these phenomena for psychological warfare purposes.

Walter B. Smith
Director

Enclosure

1950 CIA UFO memo

DEC 2 1952

MEMORANDUM FOR: Director of Central Intelligence

THRU : Deputy Director for Intelligence

SUBJECT : Unidentified Flying Objects

1. On 20 August, the DCI, after a briefing by OSI on the above subject, directed the preparation of an NSCID for submission to the Council stating the need for investigation and directing agencies concerned to cooperate in such investigations.

2. In attempting to draft such a directive and the supporting staff studies, it became apparent to DD/I, Acting AD/SI and AD/IC that the problem was largely a research and development problem, and it was decided by DD/I to attempt to initiate action through RADB. A conference was held between DI/USAF, Chairman of RADB, DD/I, Acting AD/SI and AD/IC at which time it was decided that Dr. Whitman, Chairman of RADB, would investigate the possibility of undertaking research and development studies through Air Force agencies.

3. On approximately 6 November, we were advised by Chairman, RADB, that inquiries in the Air Staff did not disclose "undue concern" over this matter, but that it had been referred to the Air Defense Command for consideration. No further word has been received from RADB.

4. Recent reports reaching CIA indicated that further action was desirable and another briefing by the cognizant A-2 and ATIC personnel was held on 25 November. At this time, the reports of incidents convince us that there is something going on that must have immediate attention. The details of some of these incidents have been discussed by AD/SI with DDCI. Sightings of unexplained objects at great altitudes and travelling at high speeds in the vicinity of major U.S. defense installations are of such nature that they are not attributable to natural phenomena or known types of aerial vehicles.

5. OSI is proceeding to the establishment of a consulting group of sufficient competence and stature to review this matter and convince the responsible authorities in the community that immediate research and development on this subject must be undertaken. This can be done expeditiously under the aegis of CSNIS.

Dec 1952 CIA UFO memo

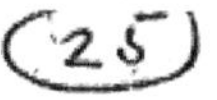

ER - 3 - 2872

OCT 2 1952

MEMORANDUM TO: Director of Central Intelligence

THROUGH: Deputy Director (Intelligence)

FROM: Assistant Director, Office of Scientific Intelligence

SUBJECT: Flying Saucers

1. PROBLEM--To determine: (a) Whether or not there are national security implications in the problem of "unidentified flying objects"; (b) whether or not adequate study and research is currently being directed to this problem in its relation to such national security implications; and (c) what further investigation and research should be instituted, by whom, and under what aegis.

2. FACTS AND DISCUSSION--OSI has investigated the work currently being performed on "flying saucers" and found that the Air Technical Intelligence Center, DI, USAF, Wright-Patterson Air Force Base, is the only group devoting appreciable effort and study to this subject, that ATIC is concentrating on a case-by-case explanation of each report, and that this effort is not adequate to correlate, evaluate, and resolve the situation on an over-all basis. The current problem is discussed in detail in TAB A.

3. CONCLUSIONS--"Flying saucers" pose two elements of danger which have national security implications. The first involves mass psychological considerations and the second concerns the vulnerability of the United States to air attack. Both factors are amplified in TAB A.

4. ACTION RECOMMENDED--(a) That the Director of Central Intelligence advise the National Security Council of the implications of the "flying saucer" problem and request that research be initiated. TAB B is a draft memorandum to the NSC, for the DCI's signature. (b) That the DCI discuss this subject with the Psychological Strategy Board. A memorandum to the Director, Psychological Strategy Board, is attached for signature as TAB C. (c) That CIA, with the cooperation of PSB and other interested departments and agencies, develop and recommend for adoption by the NSC a

Oct 1952 CIA UFO memo

DEPARTMENT OF THE AIR FORCE
STAFF MESSAGE DIVISION

OUTGOING ~~CLASSIFIED MESSAGE~~

CONFIDENTIAL
SECURITY INFORMATION
PRIORITY

PARAPHRASE NOT REQUIRED. NOTIFY
CRYPTOCENTER BEFORE DECLASSIFYING
CRYPTOPRECAUTION APPLIES

HQ USAF, AFOIN-2A3
Capt Time 71016

MULTIPLE ADDRESS

TO : CGAIRDEFCOM ENT AFB COLO
CG AMC WRIGHT-PATTERSON AFB OHIO
CG TAC LANGLEY AFB VA

NR : AFOIN 53722 16 Jul 52 (DTG 160554Z)

The following cable from 7th dis OSI (10) MACDILL AFB FLA is quoted for your information. Quote - Eight unidentified luminous circular objects flying in formation, vicinity Langley AFB Va sighted by Capt Frank Koepke, Pilot Pan American Airways while on New York - San Juan flight. Objects sighted 14 July 52, at approx 2100 hrs. Witnesses by W B Nash, co-pilot and Bill Frontenbery, engineer. Crew members stated circular objects turned to avoid collision with airliner. Estimated speed 1-thousand miles per hour. Crew members being interviewed by OSI at Miami, Fla.

ORIGINATOR : OIN

DISTRIBUTION: ARMY, NAVY, CIA, AFSA, JCS, OOP, OSD

CAF OUT : 53722

RBS/nlb

July 1952, 8 UFOs avoid collision with a plane.

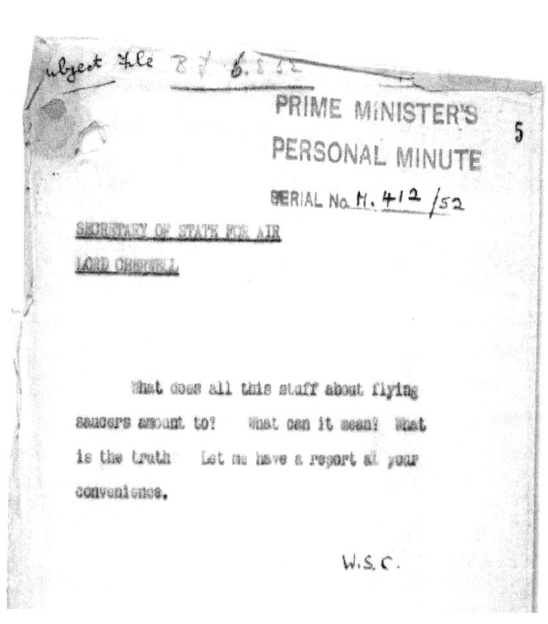

PRIME MINISTER'S PERSONAL MINUTE

5

SERIAL No. M. 412/52

SECRETARY OF STATE FOR AIR

LORD CHERWELL

What does all this stuff about flying saucers amount to? What can it mean? What is the truth Let me have a report at your convenience.

W.S.C.

FIG. 15 Following a 'flap' of UFO sightings over Washington DC, British Prime Minister Winston Churchill asked the Secretary of State for Air: 'What does all this stuff about flying saucers amount to?' PREM 11/855

1952 Winston Churchill memo

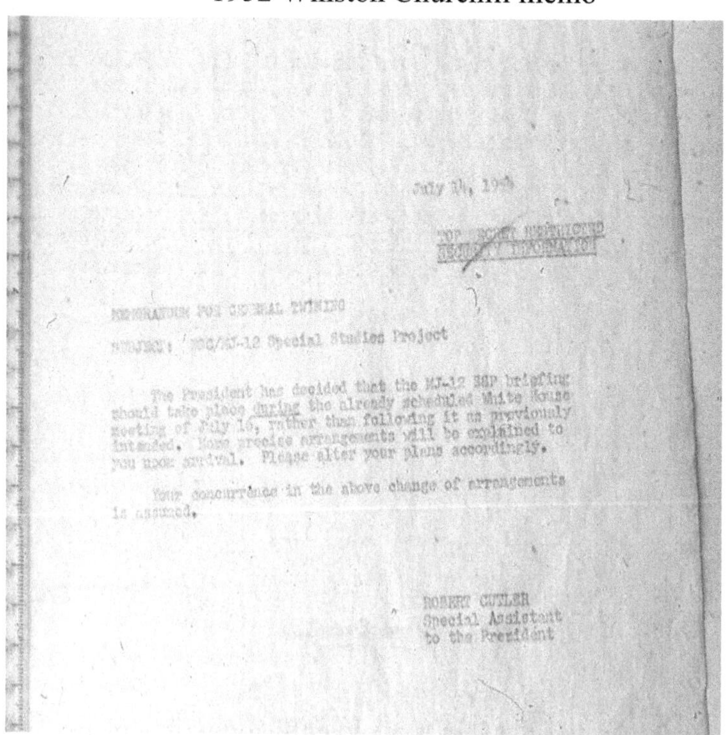

July 14, 19[illegible]

TOP SECRET RESTRICTED SECURITY INFORMATION

MEMORANDUM FOR GENERAL TWINING

SUBJECT: NSC/MJ-12 Special Studies Project

The President has decided that the MJ-12 SSP briefing should take place during the already scheduled White House meeting of July 16, rather than following it as previously intended. More precise arrangements will be explained to you upon arrival. Please alter your plans accordingly.

Your concurrence in the above change of arrangements is assumed.

ROBERT CUTLER
Special Assistant
to the President

1954 Cutler Twining memo

TOP SECRET

November 12, 1963

MEMORANDUM FOR
The Director, Central Intelligence Agency

SUBJECT: Classification review of all UFO intelligence files affecting National Security

As I had discussed with you previously, I have initiated and have instructed James Webb to develop a program with the Soviet Union in joint space and lunar exploration. It would be very helpful if you would have the high threat cases reviewed with the purpose of identification of bona fide as opposed to classified CIA and USAF sources. It is important that we make a clear distinction between the knowns and unknowns in the event the Soviets try to mistake our extended cooperation as a cover for intelligence gathering of their defence and space programs.

When this data has been sorted out, I would like you to arrange a program of data sharing with NASA where Unknowns are a factor. This will help NASA mission directors in their defensive responsibilities.

I would like an interim report on the data review no later than February 1, 1964.

/S/ John F. Kennedy

1963 JFK UFO memo- 10 days prior to his assassination.

Excerpt: 1969 BOLENDER MEMO

4. As early as 1953, the Robertson Panel concluded "that the evidence presented on Unidentified Flying Objects shows no indication that these phenomena constitute a direct physical threat to national security" (Atch 9). In spite of this finding, the Air Force continued to maintain aspecial reporting system. There is still, however, no evidence that Project Blue Book reports have served any intelligence function (Atch 8). Moreover, **reports of unidentified flying objects which could affect national security are made in accordance with JANAP 146 or Air Force Manual 55-11, and are not part of the Blue Book system** (Atch 10). The Air Force experience therefore confirms the impression of the University of Colorado researchers "that the defense function could be performed withing the framework established for intelligence and surveillance operations without the continuance of a special unit such as Project Blue Book."

5. The conclusion which follows is that Project Blue Book does not merit future expenditures of resources. Accordingly, we recommend that it be terminated and that the actions which follow from this decision, such as cancelling Air Force Regulation 80-17 and not renewing the consultant contract, be initiated. Termination of Project Blue Book would have no adverse effect on Air Force operations or research programs. It would free manpower for useful purposes, eliminate the need for a scientific consultant and relieve base commanders of a minor responsibility and an administrative burden.

6. Termination of Project Blue Book would leave no official federal office to receive reports of UFOs. However, as already stated, **reports of UFOs which could affect national security would continue to be handled through the standard Air Force procedures designed for this purpose**. Presumably, local police departments respond to reports which fall within their responsibilities. Similarly, as to scientific research, the Colorado researchers conclude that, although they do not see "any fruitful lines of advance from the study of UFO reports, we believe that any scientist with adequate training and credentials who does come

up with a clearly defined, specific proposal for study should be supported." We see no reason why the normal channels and criteria for the funding of scientific research should not be adequate for UFO-related research.

-General Bolender Blue Book memo

458 *Fire Officer's Guide to Disaster Control*

Guard Against Complacency

It is easy for those of us in North America to consider the possibility of enemy attack as being quite remote. While it is true that this continent has not been visited with the death and destruction accompanying past wars, we have found in each generation that wars are all too common and could indeed at some future date involve our country. Certainly many portions of North America are within easy range of enemy nuclear submarines and we could at the least expected time be suddenly involved in a conflict.

The Persian Gulf War served as an example of how quickly the United States can find itself in military conflict. Hence, there is always a need to guard against the complacency that has evolved as our country has enjoyed relative insulation from previous wars.

THE UFO THREAT—A FACT

In this chapter we will now turn our attention to the very real threat posed by Unidentified Flying Objects (UFOs), whether they exist or not. The well-documented and highly publicized *War of the Worlds* radio drama by Orson Welles shows how even a perceived existence to alien creatures can cause very real disaster-like conditions and panic among a given populace. In addition, if the apparent visits by alien beings and their space vehicles should pose any type of threat, it will, as always, be the fire service that is called upon to provide the first line of life-saving defense and disaster mitigation.

On April 23, 1991, radio station KSHE in St. Louis, Missouri, was fined $25,000 by the Federal Communications Commission for broadcasting a mock warning of a nuclear attack during the Persian Gulf War. The seriousness with which the FCC treated this case is indicative of the very real panic that can be created from even illusionary or fictional phenomena. Certainly if these unexplainable events become more prevalent, the possibility of panic could be even greater; and again, the fire department will be the agency called upon to handle the situation.(35) Hence, as we near the year 2000 and move beyond, any comprehensive disaster plan should address the potential for panic and other deleterious effects that might befall a populated area when unexplainable phenomena occur. We will see, as we continue our discussion in this chapter, that widespread blackouts, communication disruptions, and other potentially disastrous conditions have been linked directly to UFO sightings. Hence, fire service leaders who want to ensure that their disaster planning is complete will not neglect an appendix to outline those things that could be done in preparation for the occurrence of such phenomena.

Throughout this book, many of the references to actual events are based on the experiences of both of the authors. However, in this area of UFOs and their potential, we are relying largely on the research and experiences of Charles Bahme. Chuck has made a considerable study of this subject and

Enemy Attack and UFO Potential 459

UFOS—EMERGENCY ACTION

In view of the fact that many UFOlogists believe that we are fast approaching a time when overt landings of UFOs will become less remarkable, and in the absence of our knowing whether their visits are friendly or hostile, it would not be remiss to give some thought to the part that fire departments might play in the event of the unexpected arrival of UFOs in their communities. For example, what would be your course of action as an incident commander at the scene of a school ground where a UFO has crashed into the boiler room, rupturing a fuel line, and ignition has occurred in the spilling oil, endangering the occupants of the craft who are trapped in the wreckage? If your rescue attempts are successful, and two of the five small alien creatures are injured but still alive, how do you dispose of the dead and treat the survivors? How would the presence of children on the school grounds affect your actions? What persons and agencies would be notified?

The authors have never read any advice on these matters. The following admonition was printed on the inside front jacket of Frank Edward's book on flying saucers:

WARNING

"Near approaches of UFOs can be harmful to human beings. Do not stand under a UFO that is hovering at low altitude. Do not touch or attempt to touch a UFO that has landed. In either case the safe thing to do is to get away from there very quickly and let the military take over. There is a possibility of radiation danger and there are known cases where persons have been burned by rays emanating from UFOs. Don't take chances with UFOs!"

In view of the federal law (cited earlier) empowering NASA's administrator to impound, without a hearing, anyone who touches a UFO or its occupants, it would be inadvisable to make personal contact unless you are willing to submit to NASA's quarantine requirements, should the law be invoked.

Besides the possible physical effects of approaching a UFO, e.g., burns, radiation, etc., there may be psychological effects produced by force fields that could induce a hypnotic state in the viewer, loss of consciousness, memory relapse, and submission to the occupants. Jacques Vallee, author of *The Invisible College* cautions that we should consider psychic effects, such as space-time distortions experienced by percipients of craft-like devices which appear to fade away—dematerialize—and then reappear, of alien, strange voices or thoughts that may effect involuntary changes in the manner in which witnesses may react in such circumstances.(72)

Perhaps the above warnings of Edwards and Vallee are a little too cautious and apprehensive to adopt as a general pattern of conduct in every situation. In the absence of overt acts indicating hostility, there may be no danger in approaching a landing (or landed) UFO with a positive, solicitous

FEMA approved Fire Officers Guide Chapter 13.

GERALD R. FORD
FIFTH DISTRICT, MICHIGAN

MICHIGAN OFFICE:
425 CHERRY STREET SE
GRAND RAPIDS

Congress of the United States
Office of the Minority Leader
House of Representatives
Washington, D.C.

April 1, 1966

Loveland, Col., 80537

Dear

Thank you for your recent communication endorsing my proposal that Congress investigate the rash of reported sightings of unidentified flying objects in southern Michigan and in other parts of the country.

It is proper for the Federal government to look into a matter which is causing alarm to the people of our nation as these sightings have, and it is for this reason that I have called for the investigation.

Such an inquiry is necessary and wholesome because of the incidents that have occurred and I assure you that I will continue to press for this investigation. I want you to know that your specific comments were helpful to me in this respect, and that your remarks do not go unheeded. I am aware of other reports such as the UFO Evidence which pose questions that, like the most recent sightings, cannot be answered by a few "pat" solutions.

Kindest personal regards.

Sincerely,

Gerald R. Ford

Gerald R. Ford, M.C.

[No. 55]

UNIDENTIFIED FLYING OBJECTS

HEARING

BY

COMMITTEE ON ARMED SERVICES

OF THE

HOUSE OF REPRESENTATIVES

EIGHTY-NINTH CONGRESS

SECOND SESSION

APRIL 5, 1966

[Pages of all documents printed in behalf of the activities of the House Committee on Armed Services are numbered cumulatively to permit a comprehensive index at the end of the Congress. Page numbers lower than those in this document refer to other subjects.]

U.S. GOVERNMENT PRINTING OFFICE
WASHINGTON : 1966

59-068 O

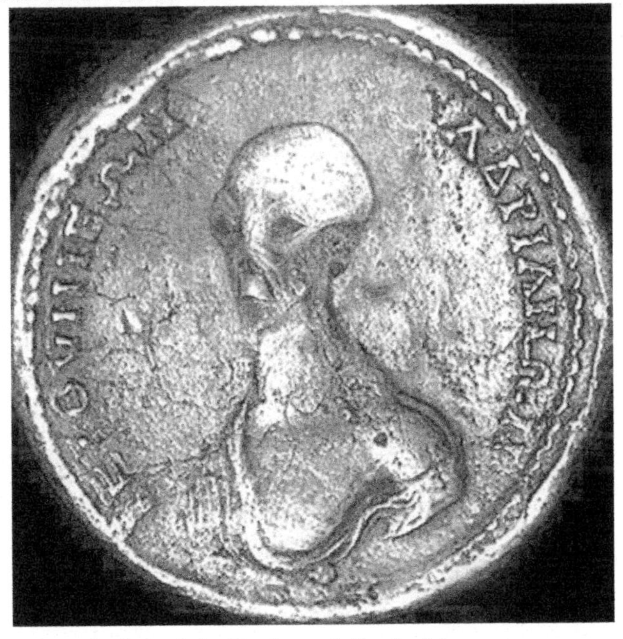

A “hobo nickel” altered for hobby art. . . . .

SYMPOSIUM ON UNIDENTIFIED FLYING OBJECTS

MONDAY, JULY 29, 1968

HOUSE OF REPRESENTATIVES,
COMMITTEE ON SCIENCE AND ASTRONAUTICS,
Washington, D.C.

The committee met, pursuant to notice, at 10:05 a.m., in room 2318, Rayburn House Office Building, Hon. J. Edward Roush (chairman of the symposium) presiding.

Mr. ROUSH. The committee will be in order.

Today the House Committee on Science and Astronautics conducts a very special session, a symposium on the subject of unidentified flying objects; the name of which is a reminder to us of our ignorance on this subject and a challenge to acquire more knowledge thereof.

We approach the question of unidentified flying objects as purely a scientific problem, one of unanswered questions. Certainly the rigid and exacting discipline of science should be marshaled to explore the nature of phenomena which reliable citizens continue to report.

A significant part of the problem has been that the sightings reported have not been accompanied by so-called hardware or materials that could be investigated and analyzed. So we are left with hypotheses about the nature of UFO's. These hypotheses range from the conclusion that they are purely psychological phenomena, that is, some kind of hallucinatory phenomena; to that of some kind of natural physical phenomena; to that of advanced technological machinery manned by some kind of intelligence, that is, the extraterrestrial hypotheses.

With the range in mind, then, we have invited six outstanding scientists to address us today, men who deal with the physical, the psychological, the sociological, and the technological data relevant to the issues involved. We welcome them and look forward to their remarks. Additionally we have requested several other scientists to make their presentations in the form of papers to be added to these when published by the committee.

We take no stand on these matters. Indeed, we are here today to listen to their assessment of the nature of the problem: to any tentative conclusions or suggestions they might offer, so that our judgments and our actions might be based on reliable and expert information. We are here to listen and to learn.

Events of the last half century certainly verify the American philosopher, John Dewey's conclusion that "Every great advance in science has issued from a new audacity of imagination." With an open and inquiring attitude, then, we now turn to our speakers for the day.

(Chapter 33 of "Introductory Space Science" Physics 370 1968 - 1970

INTRODUCTORY SPACE SCIENCE - VOLUME II
DEPARTMENT OF PHYSICS - USAF
Edited by: Major Donald G. Carpenter
Co-Editor: Lt. Colonel Edward R. Therkelson

CHAPTER XXXIII
UNIDENTIFIED FLYING OBJECTS

33.2 OPERATIONAL DOMAINS - TEMPORAL AND SPATIAL

What we will do here is to present evidence that UFO's are a global phenomenon which may have persisted for many thousands of years.

33.6 CONCLUSION

From available information, the UFO phenomenon appears to have been global in nature for almost 50,000 years. The majority of known witnesses have been reliable people who have seen easily-explained natural phenomena, and there appears to be no overall positive correlation with population density. The entire phenomenon could be psychological in nature but that is quite doubtful. However, psychological factors probably do enter the data picture as "noise." The phenomenon could also be entirely due to known and unknown phenomena (with some psychological "noise" added in) but that too is questionable in view of some of the available data.

This leaves us with the unpleasant possibility of alien visitors to our planet, or at least of alien controlled UFO's.

*This course was revised after Project Blue Book ended in 1969 but was taught to our Air Force cadets at Colorado Springs. The original version read that, "Data suggests that there are three and maybe four different groups of aliens"

The RAND Corporation
RAND DOCUMENT
UFOs: What to Do?
George Kocher
27 November 1968

DO NOT QUOTE OR CITE IN EXTERNAL RAND PUBLICATIONS OR CORRESPONDENCE

By 1952 the number of reports coming in was so large that the CIA was concerned that an actual attack on the country might not be immediately recognized. A panel of scientists was then convened in January 1953 to study the available evidence and see what conclusion could be reached about UFOs. After seven days of hearing evidence and discussing the matter it was concluded that there was only circumstantial evidence of the extraterrestrial hypothesis. The CIA recommended that, since the UFOs apparently posed no threat, the Air Force should debunk UFO reports and try generally to discourage public interest in them, in the hope that they would go away.

Certainly the conclusions drawn by NICAP from reports in their file are startling and, if valid worthy of considerable scientific effort. It would be much more convincing if data could be collected worldwide and if the most interesting reports could be intensively and completely investigated. I believe current reports justify the expanded data collection and analysis effort.

DEPARTMENT OF THE AIR FORCE
HEADQUARTERS 81ST COMBAT SUPPORT GROUP (USAFE)
APO NEW YORK 09755

REPLY TO ATTN OF: CD 13 Jan 81

SUBJECT: Unexplained Lights

TO: RAF/CC

1. Early in the morning of 27 Dec 80 (approximately 0300L), two USAF security police patrolmen saw unusual lights outside the back gate at RAF Woodbridge. Thinking an aircraft might have crashed or been forced down, they called for permission to go outside the gate to investigate. The on-duty flight chief responded and allowed three patrolmen to proceed on foot. The individuals reported seeing a strange glowing object in the forest. The object was described as being metalic in appearance and triangular in shape, approximately two to three meters across the base and approximately two meters high. It illuminated the entire forest with a white light. The object itself had a pulsing red light on top and a bank(s) of blue lights underneath. The object was hovering or on legs. As the patrolmen approached the object, it maneuvered through the trees and disappeared. At this time the animals on a nearby farm went into a frenzy. The object was briefly sighted approximately an hour later near the back gate.

2. The next day, three depressions 1 1/2" deep and 7" in diameter were found where the object had been sighted on the ground. The following night (29 Dec 80) the area was checked for radiation. Beta/gamma readings of 0.1 milliroentgens were recorded with peak readings in the three depressions and near the center of the triangle formed by the depressions. A nearby tree had moderate (.05-.07) readings on the side of the tree toward the depressions.

3. Later in the night a red sun-like light was seen through the trees. It moved about and pulsed. At one point it appeared to throw off glowing particles and then broke into five separate white objects and then disappeared. Immediately thereafter, three star-like objects were noticed in the sky, two objects to the north and one to the south, all of which were about 10^0 off the horizon. The objects moved rapidly in sharp angular movements and displayed red, green and blue lights. The objects to the north appeared to be elliptical through an 8-12 power lens. They then turned to full circles. The objects to the north remained in the sky for an hour or more. The object to the south was visible for two or three hours and beamed down a stream of light from time to time. Numerous individuals, including the undersigned, witnessed the activities in paragraphs 2 and 3.

CHARLES I. HALT, Lt Col, USAF
Deputy Base Commander

1981 Col. Halt Rendlesham Forest memo.

UNCLASSIFIED

PAGE:0053

INQUIRE=DOC17D
ITEM NO=00502993
ENVELOPE
CDSN = LGX487 MCN = 92107/10876 TOR = 921070814
RTTUZYUW RUEKJCS6879 1070816-UUUU--RUEALGX.
ZNR UUUUU
HEADER
R 160816Z APR 92
FM JOINT STAFF WASHINGTON DC
INFO RUEALGX/SAFE
R 160758Z APR 92
FM FBIS OKINAWA JA
TO AIG 4581
RUCIAEA/FASTC/TAI WRIGHT PATTERSON AFB OH
ACCT FBOW-EWDK
BT
CONTROLS
UNCLAS 1L

SERIAL: OW1604075892

BODY
COUNTRY: PRC
SUBJ: UFO RESEARCH ORGANIZATION TO HOLD CONFERENCE IN BEIJING

SOURCE: BEIJING XINHUA IN ENGLISH 0717 GMT 16 APR 92
TEXT:

((TEXT)) BEIJING, APRIL 16 (XINHUA) -- THE CHINA UFO RESEARCH ORGANIZATION (CURO) WILL HOLD A NATIONAL CONFERENCE NEXT MONTH IN BEIJING.

WANG CHANGTING, ACTING CHAIRMAN OF THE CURO, SAID THAT SEARCHING FOR CREATURES THAT MIGHT BE LIVING IN OTHER SOLAR SYSTEMS IS ONE OF THE THEMES OF THE "1992 INTERNATIONAL SPACE YEAR".

MORE THAN 100 CHINESE AND OVERSEAS RESEARCHERS WILL BE PRESENT, MAKING THE ACTIVITY THE LARGEST OF ITS KIND EVER HELD IN CHINA.

UNIDENTIFIED FLYING OBJECTS, ALSO KNOWN AS FLYING SAUCERS, BECAME A HOT TOPIC IN CHINA IN THE LATE 1970S. THERE HAVE BEEN OVER 5,000 SIGHTINGS OF UNEXPLAINED AERIAL PHENOMENA IN CHINA.

THE FIRST REPORT OF UFOS CAME FROM AMERICA, AND THERE HAVE BEEN 400,000 REPORTS OF SIGHTINGS WORLDWIDE.

IN 1978 THE UNITED NATIONS CALLED ON THE GOVERNMENTS OF ALL COUNTRIES BE ON FULL ALERT FOR SIGHTINGS AND ESTABLISH UFO INVESTIGATION BODIES.

CHINA SET UP ITS OWN UFO INVESTIGATION BODY, CURO, IN 1978, AND IT IS NOW A MEMBER OF THE CHINA ASSOCIATION FOR SCIENCE AND TECHNOLOGY, LARGELY SUPPORTED BY THE GOVERNMENT.

ADMIN
(ENDALL) 160717 [redacted] 21604.00 [redacted] 16/07592 APR
BT

UNCLASSIFIED

Approved for Release
Date AUG 1997

15

1992 memo from China that states that the U.N. called on all countries to establish UFO investigative bodies.

Chapter 4
UFO QUOTES

"**F**irst they ignore you. Then they laugh at you. Then they fight you. Then you win" . . . . . **Gandhi**

"The day will arrive when the governments of earth will finally admit we are not alone, that humans have come face-to-face with other life forms from the cosmos. Anyone still on the fence about the existence of UFOs must contend with the testimonies of these respected and honored men." **Clark McClellend** - NASA

"Germany may have recovered a flying saucer as early as 1939". **General James H. Doolittle** went to Sweden in 1946 to inspect a flying saucer that had crashed in Spitsbergen.

"Regarding the air raid over Los Angeles it was learned by **Army G2 that Rear Admiral Anderson**...recovered an unidentified airplane off the coast of California...with no bearing on conventional explanation. This Headquarters has come to the determination that the mystery airplanes are in fact not earthly and, according to secret intelligence sources, they are in all probability of interplanetary origin." **General George C. Marshall** top-secret memo to the President, March 5, 1942

"...Coming to grips with the reality that our planet is not the only one harboring intelligent life the universe."
Franklin D. Roosevelt, President Memo on White House stationary to 'The Special Committee on Non-Terrestrial Science & Technology'. Concerning the Cape Girardeau UFO crash of 1941, Roosevelt went on to state that we will, "take every advantage of such wonders that have come to us" after we have won the war. Feb 22, 1944

"Before we could do any more, the Army, after conferring with (U.S.) officials, ordered the investigation stopped."
Dr. Paul Santorini, on UFOs over Greece in 1946

"...Submit an agreement providing for the peaceful absorption of celestial races(s) in such a manner that our culture would remain intact with guarantee that their presence not be revealed." "One must consider the fact that misidentification of these space craft for an intercontinental missile in a re-entry phase of flight could lead to accidental nuclear war with horrible consequences."
Dr. J. Robert Oppenheimer, Director of Advanced Studies, Princeton.

Professor **Albert Einstein**, Princeton draft of joint memo from Oppenheimer/Einstein, June 1947. "As I understand it, Marshall rebuffed the idea of Oppenheimer discussing this with the President. I talked to Gordon and he agreed." 'VB' (Vannevar Bush?)

RAAF CAPTURES FLYING SAUCER ON RANCH IN ROSWELL REGION

"No Details of Flying Disk are revealed"

Roswell Daily Record

RAAF Captures Flying Saucer On Ranch in Roswell Region

Claims Army Is Stacking Courts Martial

House Passes Tax Slash by Large Margin

Security Council Paves Way to Talks On Arms Reductions

No Details of Flying Disk Are Revealed

Ex-King Carol Weds Mme. Lupescu

ome of Soviet Satellites May Attend Paris Meeting

Miners and Operators Sign Highest Wage Pact in History

oswellians Have Differing Opinions On Flying Saucers

American League

"The many rumors regarding the flying disk became a reality yesterday when the intelligence office of the 509th Bomb Group of the Eighth Air Force, Roswell Army Air Field, was fortunate enough to gain possession of a disk through the cooperation of one of the local ranchers and the sheriff's office of Chaves County."
"Roswell Daily Record" July 8, 1947

(Referring to crash retrieval in New Mexico desert in July of 1947 and its subsequent security classification) "I must insist upon full access to discs recovered... The Army grabbed one and would not let us have it for cursory examination."
J. Edgar Hoover, FBI Director, 1947

"We soon established that they were not missiles. But, before we could do any more, the Army, after conferring with foreign officials, ordered the investigation stopped. Foreign scientists flew to Greece for secret talks with me... A world blanket of secrecy surrounded the UFO question because the authorities were unwilling to admit the existence of a force against which we had no possibility of defense." **Dr. Paul Santorini**, Greek physicist and engineer credited with developing the proximity fuse for the Hiroshima atomic bomb; two patents for US Nike missile guidance system, and a cent metric radar system.

"The phenomenon reported is something real and not visionary or fictitious." **General Nathan Twining**, Chairman, Joint Chiefs of Staff Sept. 23, 1947

"The first UFO came down in 1941 into the ocean west of San Diego and was retrieved by the Navy. The Navy has held a leadership position in UFO matters ever since. There was another crash in 1946, as well as two other crashes in 1947 besides Roswell."**Dr. Michael Wolf, Colonel USAF**

Dr. Michael Wolf: scientific consultant to the President and the National Security Council on extraterrestrial matters; member of Majestic Twelve (MJ-12), UFO secrecy management agency's (Special Studies Group) and has been in charge of its lead agency, the Alphacom Team. Previously Dr. Wolf served as an Air Force Colonel, pilot, flight surgeon and counter-intelligence officer for the CIA and NSA. He has an MD in Neurology, a Ph.D. in Theoretical Physics, a ScD in Computer Science, a JD in Law, an M.S. in EM influence on organisms, and a B.S. in biogenetics.

"It appears to be metallic object... tremendous in size... directly ahead and slightly above... I am trying to close for a better look." (His last radio broadcast made in fatal pursuit of unidentified flying object) Pilot Captain **Thomas Mantell**; January 7, 1948

"Army intelligence has recently said that the matter of 'Unidentified Aircraft' or 'Unidentified Aerial Phenomena,' otherwise known as 'Flying Discs,' 'Flying Saucers,' and "Balls of Fire,' is considered top secret by intelligence officers of both the Army and Air Forces." **FBI memo on UFOs1949**

Memo regarding a disk found in the Mojave Desert in January 1950: "On this land a flying disk has been found intact, with eighteen three-foot tall human-like occupants, all dead in it but not burned." **New Orleans FBI Branch to Direct**or, FBI March 31, 1950

"I can assure you that flying saucers, given that they exist, are not constructed by any power on earth."
President Harry S. Truman, Press conference, Washington DC, April 4, 1950

"The matter is the most highly classified subject in the United States Government, rating higher even than the H-bomb. Flying saucers exist. Their modus operandi is unknown but a small group headed by Dr. Vannevar Bush is making concentrated effort. The entire matter is considered by the United States authorities to be of tremendous significance."
Wilbert Smith in a formerly classified Canadian government memorandum. Nov 21, 1950

Donald Slayton a Mercury astronaut revealed in an interview he had seen UFOs in 1951: "I was testing a P-51 fighter in Minneapolis when I spotted this object. I was at about 10,000 feet on a nice, bright, sunny afternoon. I thought the object was a kite, and then I realized that no kite is going to fly that high. As I got closer it looked like a weather balloon, gray and about three feet in diameter. But as soon as I got behind the darn thing it didn't look like a balloon anymore. It looked like a saucer, a disk. About the same time, I realized that it was suddenly going away from me -- and there I was, running at about 300 miles per hour. I tracked it for a little way, and then all of a sudden the damn thing just took off. It pulled about a 45 degree climbing turn and accelerated and just flat disappeared." **Donald "Deke" Slayon, NASA Mercury Astronaut**

"For six hours...there were at least ten unidentifiable objects moving above Washington. They were not ordinary aircraft." **Harry. G Barnes**, Senior Air Traffic Controller for the CAA 1952

"In view of the wide interest within the Agency, outside knowledge of Agency interest in Flying Saucers carries the risk of making the problem even more serious in the public mind than it already is." **CIA memo 1952**

"The least improbable explanation is that these things UFO's are artificial and controlled. My opinion for some time has been that they have an extraterrestrial origin. **Dr. Maurice Bilot**, one of the world's leading aerodynamicists and mathematical physicists. Life, April 7, 1952

"At this time the reports of incidents convince us that there is something going on that must have immediate attention. Sightings of unexplained objects at high altitudes and traveling at high speeds in the vicinity of major U.S. defense installations are of such nature that they are not attributable to natural phenomena or known types of vehicles." **H. Marshall Chadwell**, Assistant Director of Scientific Intelligence, CIA; December 2, 1952

"There are many reasons to believe that they (UFOs) do exist: there is so much evidence from reliable witnesses."

Prince Phillip, Duke of Edinburgh (Sunday Dispatch, London, Mar. 28, 1954)

"More than 10,000 sightings have been reported, the majority of which cannot be accounted for by any 'scientific' explanation... I am convinced that these objects do exist and that they are not manufactured by any nation on this Earth." **Air Chief Marshal Lord Dowding**, Commander-in-Chief of RAF Fighter Command, London Sunday Dispatch July 11, 1954

"Of course flying saucers are real -- and they are interplanetary." **Air Chief Marshall Lord Dowding**, former head of Royal Air Force during World War II; August 1954

"...It is as impossible to confirm UFOs in the present as it will be to deny them in the future." **Dr. Wernher von Braun**

"(UFOs) are conceived and directed by intelligent beings. They probably do not originate in our solar system." Years later he was quoted as saying, "We cannot take the credit for our record advancement in certain scientific fields alone. We have been helped." When asked by whom, he replied, “The people of other worlds." **Dr. Herman Oberth**, father of modern rocketry 1954

"It is my thesis that flying saucers are real and that they are space ships from another solar system. I think that they possibly are manned by intelligent observers who are members of a race that may have been investigating our earth for centuries. I think that they possibly have been sent out to conduct systematic, long-range investigations, first of men, animals, vegetation, and more recently of atomic centers, armaments and centers of armament production."

"These objects are conceived and directed by intelligent beings of a very high order. They probably do not originate in our solar system, perhaps not even in our galaxy." **Dr. Hermann Oberth** Army Ballistic Missile Agency and later NASA, 1954

"The problem of 'flying discs' has polarized the attention of the whole world, but it's serious and it deserves to be treated seriously. Almost all the governments of the great powers are interested in it, dealing with it in a serious and confidential manner, due to its military interest." **Brigadier General João Adil Oliveira**, Chief of the Air Force General Staff Information Service, Brazil, "Briefing to the Army War College" in Rio de Janeiro on Nov. 2, 1954

Washington, July 28th, 1995 - **Congressman Steve Schiff** released the General Accounting Office report detailing the results of a records audit related to events surrounding a crash near Roswell, New Mexico in 1947. The 20-page report is the result of information requests to Congressman Schiff and the difficulty he had getting answers from the Department of Defense. Schiff said important documents, which may have shed more light on what happened at Roswell, are missing. *"The GAO report states that the outgoing messages from Roswell Army Air Field (RAAF) for this period of time were destroyed without proper authority. It is my understanding that these outgoing messages were permanent records, which should never have been destroyed. The GAO could not identify who destroyed the messages...or why."*
Congressman Steve Schiff

"In the firm belief that the American public deserves a better explanation than that thus far given by the Air Force, I strongly recommend that there be a committee investigation of the UFO phenomena. I think we owe it to the people to establish credibility regarding UFOs, and to produce the greatest possible enlightenment of the subject." **President Gerald Ford**

"In my opinion, the UFO problem...constitutes an area of extraordinary scientific interest." **Dr. James McDonald**, Professor of Atmospheric Sciences, UFOS: A Scientific Debate

"Well, Slim, (McClelland's knick name by Astronaut friends), I was flying a P-51 Mustang at about 12,000 feet over Minneapolis in 1951. I thought it was a simple kite. As I flew closer to it I looked at it and thought it was a weather balloon. But as I got behind it I could tell it wasn't a balloon. It looked like a disc." NASA astronaut **Donald "Deke" Slayton** to Clarke McClelland

"Maximum security exists concerning the subject of UFOs." **CIA Director Allen Dulles** 1955 (later, member of the Warren Commission)

"I have discussed this matter with the affected agencies of the government, and they are of the opinion that it is not wise to publicize this matter at this time." **Senator Richard Russell**, head of Senate Armed Services Committee regarding his sighting of a UFO during a 1955 trip to the Soviet Union.

"Because of the developments of science, all the countries on earth will have to unite to survive and to make a common front against attack by people from other planets. The politics of the future will be cosmic, or interplanetary." **Gen. Douglas MacArthur**, former Five Star General of the Army, (New York Times, Oct 8, 1955).

"While flying with several other USAF pilots over Germany in 1957, we sighted numerous radiant flying discs above us. We couldn't tell how high they were. We couldn't get anywhere near their altitude." "While working with a camera crew supervising flight testing of advanced aircraft at Edward's Air Force Base, California, the camera crew filmed the landing of a strange disc object that flew in over their heads and landed on a dry lake nearby. A camera crewman approached the saucer; it rose up above the area and flew off at a speed faster than any known aircraft." **NASA astronaut**, L. **Gordon Cooper**

"Reliable reports indicate there are objects coming into our atmosphere at very high speeds and controlled by thinking intelligences." **Navy Admiral Delmar Fahrney** public statement, 1957

"We have stacks of reports about flying saucers. We take them seriously when you consider we have lost many men and planes trying to intercept them." **General Benjamin Chidlaw** - US Eastern Air Defense, Air Defense Command

"It is impossible to deny any more the existence of flying saucers at the present time. The flying saucer is not a ghost from another dimension... It is a fact confirmed by material evidence. There are thousands of documents, photos, and sighting reports demonstrating its existence. For instance, when I went to the Air Force High command to discuss the flying saucers I called for ten witnesses - military (AF officers) and civilians - to report their evidence about the presence of flying saucers in the skies of Rio Grande do Sul, and over Gravataí AFB [Air Force Base]; some of them had seen UFOs with the naked eye, others with high powered optical instruments. For more than two hours the phenomenon was present in the sky, impressing the selected audience: officers, engineers, technicians, etc." **Brigadier General João Adil Oliveira** Brazil, Feb. 28, 1958

"Congressional investigations are still being held on the problem of unidentified flying objects and the problem is one in which there is quite a bit of interest. Since most of the material presented to the Committees is classified, the hearings are never printed." **Congressman William H. Ayres** 1958

"Saucers exist; I saw two. They were intelligently flown or operated (evasive tactics, formation flight, hovering). They were mechanisms, not United States weapons, nor Russian. I presume they are extraterrestrial." **Lt. Colonel Richard Headrick** radar bombing expert, 1959

"I've talked with people of military and government credentials and position and heard their stories, and their desire to tell their stories openly to the public. And that got my attention very, very rapidly...the first hand experiences of these credible witnesses that, now in advanced years are anxious to tell their story. We can't deny that, and the evidence points to the fact that Roswell was a real incident, and that indeed an alien craft did crash, and that material was recovered from that crash site..." **NASA Astronaut Dr. Edgar Mitchell**, Apollo 14 Mission veteran.

Dr. Brian O'Leary, on 18th September 1994 made the following declarations publicly at the International Forum on New Science in Fort Collins, Colorado. Dr O'Leary said, "For nearly 50 years, the secrecy apparatus within the United States Government has kept from the public UFO and alien contact information." He flatly stated that. "We have contact with alien cultures..." As for the non-disclosure of these facts, Dr O'Leary said, "The suppression of UFO and other extraterrestrial intelligence information for at least 47 years is probably being orchestrated by an elite band of men in the CIA, NSA, DIA and their like. This small group appears able to keep these already-hard-to-believe secrets very well. Those who have investigated this hydra-headed beast believe that the Cosmic Watergate of UFO, alien, mind-control, genetic engineering, free-energy, anti-gravity propulsion and other secrets will make Watergate or Iran-Gate...appear to be kindergarten exercises." **Brian O'Leary - NASA Astronaut**

"We find ourselves faced by powers which are far stronger than we had hitherto assumed, and whose base is at present unknown to us. More I cannot say at present. We are now engaged in entering into closer contact with those powers, and in six or nine months' time it may be possible to speak with some precision on the matter." **Dr. Werner von Braun** (on the deflection from orbit of a United States satellite, 1959)

"Unknown objects are operating under intelligent control... It is imperative that we learn where UFO's come from and what their purpose is. Behind the scenes, high-ranking Air Force officers are soberly concerned about UFOs. Through official secrecy and ridicule, many citizens are led to believe that unidentified flying objects are nonsense. To hide the facts the Air Force has silenced its personnel." **Admiral Roscoe H. Hillenkoetter**, 1st Director, CIA Feb 18, 1960

"It is time for the truth to be brought out in open Congressional hearings. Behind the scenes high-ranking Air Force officers are soberly concerned about the UFOs. But through official secrecy and ridicule, many citizens are led to believe the unknown flying objects are nonsense." **Admiral Roscoe H. Hillenkoetter**, 1st Director, CIA (Statement in NICAP news release, Feb 27, 1960.)

"The overall effectiveness about the actual Soviet response and alert status is not documented to the point where U.S. intelligence can provide a true picture of how Soviet air defenses perceive unidentified flying objects. 80% of the sighting reports investigated by the Air Force's project Blue Book were explainable and posed no immediate threat to national security. The remaining cases have been classified for security reasons and are under review. While the possibility remains true U.F.O. cases are of non-terrestrial origin, U.S. Intelligence is of the opinion that they do not constitute a physical threat to national defense. For reasons of security, I cannot divulge pertinent data on some of the more sensitive aspects of MJ-12 activities, which have been deemed properly classified under the 1954 Atomic Energy Act." **Allen W. Dulles, CIA Director** Nov 5, 1961, top-secret operations review concerning the MJ-12 project, referencing Presidential National Security Memorandum of June 28, 1961 "It has been speculated that of all groups scientists and engineers might be the most devastated by the discovery of relatively superior creatures, since these professions are most clearly associated with the mastery of nature, rather than with the understanding and expression of man." **Brookings Institute for NASA** 4/18/61

"At no time, when the astronauts were in space were they alone: there was a constant surveillance by UFOs." **Astronaut Scott Carpenter-**Carpenter photographed a UFO while in orbit May 24, 1962. NASA still has not released the photograph.

"You now face a new world - a world of change. The thrust into outer space of the satellite, spheres and missiles marked the

beginning of another epoch in the long story of mankind - the chapter of the space age. We speak in strange terms: of harnessing the cosmic energy ...of the primary target in war, no longer limited to the armed forces of an enemy, but instead to include his civil populations; of ultimate conflict between a united human race and the sinister forces of some other planetary galaxy..."
Gen. Douglas MacArthur, former Five Star General of the Army, (Address to the United States Military Academy at West Point, May 12, 1962.)

Major Robert White reported a UFO during his fifty-eight-mile high flight of an X-15. "I have no idea what it could be. It was grayish in color and about thirty to forty feet away." According to a Time Magazine article, Major White exclaimed over the radio: "There ARE things out there! There absolutely is!"
Major Robert White, USAF X-15 Test Pilot July 17, 1962

"Based upon unreliable and unscientific surmises as data, the Air Force develops elaborate statistical findings which seem impressive to the uninitiated public unschooled in the fallacies of the statistical method. One must conclude that the highly publicized Air Force pronouncements based upon unsound statistics serve merely to misrepresent the true character of the UFO phenomena.
Yale Scientific Magazine (Yale University) Volume XXXVII, Number 7, April 1963

"[I am] disturbed by the way in which the CIA has been diverted from its original assignment. [It has] become a government all of its own and all secret. They don't have to account to anybody." **President Harry S. Truman** Washington Post, December 22, 1963

"I made discreet enquiries through the Canadian Embassy staff in Washington who were able to obtain for me the following information:

a. The matter is the most highly classified subject in the United States Government, rating higher even than the H-bomb.

b. Flying saucers exist.

c. Their modus operandi is unknown but concentrated effort is being made by a small group headed by Doctor Vannevar Bush.

d. The entire matter is considered by the United States authorities to be of tremendous significance.

Wilbur B. Smith, TOP SECRET Memo; Department of Transport, Intra-departmental Correspondence, OTTAWA, Ontario, Nov 21, 1950 (downgraded to CONFIDENTIAL 15/9/69)

"As a member of the House Committee on Science and Astronautics, I, of course, have had contact with high Air Force officers and have had opportunity to hear their comments on and off the record on the subject of unidentified flying objects. Despite being confronted with seemingly unimpeachable evidence that such phenomena exist, these officers give little credence to the many reports on the matter. When pressed on specific details the experts refuse to answer on grounds that they are involved in the nation's security and cannot be discussed publicly ...I will continue to seek a definite answer to this most important question."
Congressman Joseph E. Karth (D. Minn.) - Aug 24, 1960

"I feel that the Air Force has not been giving out all the available information on the Unidentified Flying Objects. You cannot disregard so many unimpeachable sources."
John McCormack, Speaker of the House of Representatives of the United States; Jan 1965

"Many of the reports that cannot be explained have come from intelligent and technically well-qualified individuals whose integrity cannot be doubted." **Major General E.B. LeBaily**, USAF Director of Information (Sept 28, 1965 letter to USAF Scientific Advisory Board)

"In the firm belief that the American public deserves a better explanation than that thus far given by the Air Force, I strongly recommend that there is a committee investigation [of the UFO phenomenon]." **Congressman Gerald Ford**, 1966 [later President]

"The trick would be to describe the project so that, to the public, it would appear a totally objective study, but to the scientific community would present the image of a group of nonbelievers trying their best to be objective but having an almost zero expectation of finding a saucer."
Robert Low, University of Colorado senior administrator, former intelligence officer, and assistant director of the Condon Committee, in a confidential 1966 memo suggesting the approach of the Condon UFO study

"My study of past official Air Force investigations (Project Blue Book) leads me to describe them as completely superficial. Officially released 'explanations' of important UFO sightings have been almost absurdly erroneous."

James McDonald, speech to American Meteorological Society 1966

"I have begun to feel that there is a tendency in 20th Century science to forget that there will be a 21st Century science, and indeed a 30th Century science, from which vantage points our knowledge of the universe may appear quite different than it does to us. We suffer, perhaps, from temporal provincialism, a form of arrogance that has always irritated posterity." **J. Allen Hynek**, letter to Science magazine, Aug. 1, 1966

"When the team was ten miles from the landing site, static disrupted radio contact with them. Five to eight minutes later the glow diminished, and the UFO took off. Another UFO was visually sighted and confirmed by radar." **Classified report by an Air Force Strike Team at Minot AFB,** 1966

"UFOs sighted in Indonesia are identical with those sighted in other countries. Sometimes they pose a problem for our air defense and once we were obliged to open fire on them."
Air Marshall Roesmin Nurjadin, Commander-in-Chief of the Indonesian Air Force, in a letter to **Yusuke J. Matsumura** dated May 5, 1967, reprinted in Good.

"Much evidence tells us UFOs have been tracked by radar; so, UFOs are real and they may come from outer space... UFO photographs and various materials show scientifically that there are more advanced people piloting the saucers and mother ships."
General Kanshi Ishikawa, Chief of Staff of Japan's Air Self-Defense Force; Commander of the 2nd Air Wing, Chitose Air Base. 1967

"I have absolutely no idea where the UFO's come from or how they are operated, but after ten years of research, I know they are something from our side our atmosphere. **Dr. James E. McDonald**, Professor of Atmospheric physics University of Arizona, 1967

"My own present opinion, based on two years of careful study, is that UFOs are probably extraterrestrial devices engaged in something that might very tentatively be termed 'surveillance'. I believe no other problem within your jurisdiction is of comparable scientific and national importance. These are strong words, and I intend them to be. I now regard the [extraterrestrial hypothesis] as the one most likely to prove correct."
Dr. James McDonald, testimony to the United States Congress 1968

"The type of UFO reports that are most intriguing are close-range sightings of machine-like objects of unconventional nature and unconventional performance characteristics, seen at low altitudes, and sometimes even on the ground. The general public is entirely unaware of the large number of such reports that are coming from credible witnesses... When one starts searching for such cases, their numbers are quite astonishing. Also, such sightings appear to be occurring all over the globe."
Dr. James E. McDonald, Senior Physicist, Institute of Atmospheric Physics testimony to the U.S. House of Representatives, "Symposium on Unidentified Flying Objects," Hearings before the Committee on Science and Astronautics, July 29, 1968.

"*Mission Control, please be informed...there is a Santa Claus*."

NASA astronaut, James Lovell flying with **Frank Borman** and **William Anders**, emerging from the dark side of the moon during their historic first lunar orbit mission, Apollo-8, in December, 1968. ("Santa Claus" was the mission code name used if sighting a 'strange object' such as a UFO)

Both **Neil Armstrong and Edwin "Buzz" Aldrin** saw UFOs shortly after that historic landing on the Moon in Apollo 11 on 21 July 1969. One of the astronauts' referred to a "light" in or on a crater during the television transmission, followed by a request from mission control for further information. Nothing more was heard.

According to a NASA employee **Otto Binder**, unnamed radio hams with their own VHF receiving facilities bypassed NASA's broadcasting outlets picked up the following exchange:

NASA: What's there? Mission Control calling Apollo 11...

Apollo11: These "Babies" are huge, Sir! Enormous! OH MY GOD! You wouldn't believe it! I'm telling you there are other spacecraft out there, Lined up on the far side of the crater edge! They're on the Moon watching us!

A professor engaged in a discussion with Neil Armstrong during a NASA symposium:

Professor: "What REALLY happened out there with Apollo 11?"

Armstrong: "It was incredible. Of course we had always known there was a possibility. The fact is we were warned off! (by the aliens). There was never any question then of a space station or a moon city."

Professor: "How do you mean 'warned off'?

Armstrong: "I can't go into details, except to say that their ships were far superior to ours both in size and technology - Boy, were they big and menacing!"

"**Neil Armst**rong relayed the message to Mission Control that two large, mysterious objects were watching them after having landed near the moon module. But this message was never heard by the public -- because NASA censored it." Buzz Aldrin took color movie film of the UFOs from inside the module, and continued filming them after he and Armstrong went outside. Armstrong confirmed that the story was true but refused to go into further detail, beyond admitting that the CIA was behind the cover-up." **Dr. Vladimir Azhazha**, Physicist; Professor of Mathematics, Moscow University

"...Highly secret government UFO investigations are going on that we don't know about." **Senator Barry Goldwater**

"We all know that UFOs are real. All we need to ask is where they come from."
Captain Edgar D. Mitchell, Apollo 14 Astronaut, 1971

"I've been convinced for a long time that the flying saucers are real and interplanetary. In other words, we are being watched by beings from outer space." **Albert M. Chop**, Deputy Public Relations Director, NASA former USAF spokesman for Project Blue Book.

"If I become President, I'll make every piece of information this country has about UFO sightings available to the public and scientists. I am convinced that UFOs exist because I have seen one." **President Jimmy Carter** during his Presidential campaign

"I've said publicly I thought they were somebody else, some other civilization." **Eugene Cernan**, Commander, Apollo 17 Mission Los Angeles Times, 1973

"Sometimes we actually got lucky enough to score a hit with a missile before the UFO could take any evasive action, which an army air defense battalion did with an antiaircraft missile near Ramstein Air Force Base in Germany in May 1974. The spacecraft managed to crash-land in a valley. The craft was retrieved and flown back to Nellis Air Force Base in Nevada."
Col. Phillip J. Corso (retired), Ramstein AFB, Germany, May 1974 "The Day After Roswell"

"I was in a plane last week when I looked out the window and saw this white light. It was zigzagging around. I went up to the pilot and said, "Have you ever seen anything like that?" He was shocked and he said, "Nope." And I said to him: "Let's follow it!" "We followed it for several minutes. It was a bright white light." "We followed it to Bakersfield, and all of a sudden to our utter amazement it went straight up into the heavens." "When I got off the plane I told Nancy all about it. But we didn't file a report on the object because for a long time they considered you a nut if you saw a UFO..." **Ronald Reagan** 1974

"The flying saucer situation is not all imaginary . . . Something is flying around." July 1947 FBI/Army Intelligence Report

(declassified by the United States Freedom of Information Act in 1976)

"Everything is in a process of investigation in the United States and in Spain, as well as in the rest of the world... (Speaking as an individual) I believe that UFOs are spaceships or extraterrestrial craft. The nations of the world are currently working together in the investigation of the UFO phenomenon. There is an international exchange of data. Maybe when this group of nations acquire more precise and definite information, it will be possible to release the news to the world."
General Carlos Castro Cavero, General in the Spanish Air Force and former Commander of Spain's Third Aerial Region; interview with J. J. Benitez, La Gaceta del Norte, Balboa, Spain, June 27, 1976.

Gordon L. Cooper, one of America's original seven Mercury Astronauts, personally saw and his men filmed UFOs so he has been outspoken about the need for an open inquiry into UFOs. In 1978, he sent the following letter to the United Nations:

"I believe that these extraterrestrial vehicles and their crews are visiting this planet from other planets, which are a little more technically advanced than we are on Earth. I feel that we need to have a top level, coordinated program to scientifically collect and analyze data from all over the Earth. We may first have to show them that we have learned how to resolve our problems by peaceful means rather than warfare, before we are accepted as fully qualified universal team members. I should point out that I am not an experienced UFO professional researcher - I have not yet had the privilege of flying a UFO or of meeting the crew of one. However, I do feel that I am somewhat qualified to discuss them, since I have been into the fringes of the vast areas of which they travel. Also, I did have occasion in 1951 to have two days of observation of many flights of them, of different sizes flying in fighter formation, generally from west to east over Europe. They were at a higher altitude than we could reach with our jet fighters."

"I do believe UFOs exist and that the truly unexplained ones are from some other technically advanced civilization." **Gordon Cooper, Mercury 7 Astronaut NASA**, USAF Pilot, Nov. 27, 1978

"I think that Walter Schirra aboard Mercury 8 was the first of the astronauts to use the code name 'Santa Claus' to indicate the presence of flying saucers next to space capsules. However, his announcements were barely noticed by the general public". **Maurice Chatelain** (former) Chief - NASA Communications Systems

"UFOs defy worldly logic... The human mind cannot begin to comprehend UFO characteristics: their propulsion, their sudden appearance, their disappearance, their great speeds, their silence, their maneuver, their apparent anti-gravity, their changing shapes." **Earl of Kimberly**, House of Lords Debate on Unidentified Flying Objects, HANSARD (Lords), vol. 397, no. 23, Jan. 18, 1979.

"Many men have seen those [UFOs] and have not been mistaken. Who are we to doubt their word? Only a few weeks ago a Palermo policeman photographed one and four Italian Navy officers saw a 300-foot long fiery craft rising from the sea and disappearing into the sky... Why should these men of law enforcement and defense lie?" **Lord Rankeillour**, Member of the House of Lords (Ibid)

"The evidence that there are objects which have been seen in our atmosphere... that cannot be accounted for either as man-made objects or as any physical force or effect known to our scientists, seems to me to be overwhelming... Persons whose credentials seem to me unimpeachable have vouched for a very large number of sightings. It is striking that so many have been trained observers, such as police officers and airline or military pilots. Their observations have in many instances... been supported either by technical means such as radar or, even more convincingly, by... interference with electrical apparatus of one sort or another..." **Lord Hill-Norton** (GCB), Chief of Defense Staff, Ministry of Defense, Great Britain (1971-73); Chairman, Military Committee of NATO (1974-77); Admiral of the Fleet; Member of House of Lords (Ibid)

"It followed us during half of our orbit. We observed it on the light side, and when we entered the shadow side it disappeared completely. It was an engineered structure, made from some type of metal, approximately 40 meters long with inner hulls. The object was narrow here and wider here, and inside there were openings. Some places had projections like small wings. The object stayed very close to us. We photographed it, and our photos showed it to be 23 to 28 meters away."- **Cosmonaut Victor Afanasyev** commenting on a UFO sighting that occurred while en route to the Solyut 6 space station in April of 1979

"We have indeed been contacted by extraterrestrial beings, and the US government in collusion with other national powers of the Earth is determined to keep this information away from the general public. *The purpose of the inter-nation conspiracy concerning the reality of UFOs is to maintain a workable stability amongst the nations of the world, and for them in turn to retain institutional control over their respective populations."*

"Thus for governments to admit that there are beings from outer space with mentalities and technological capabilities obviously far superior to ours, could, once fully perceived by the average person, erode the foundations of the Earth's traditional power structure. Political and legal systems, religions, economic and social institutions could all soon become meaningless in the eyes of the public. The national oligarchic establishments, even civilization as we know it, could collapse into anarchy. *Such extreme conclusions are not necessarily valid*, but they probably accurately reflect the fears of the ruling classes of most major nations whose leaders, particularly those in the intelligence business, have always advocated excessive government secrecy as being necessary to preserve national security..." **Victor Marchetti**, former Executive Assistant to the deputy director of the CIA, 1979.

"It is true that I was denied access to a facility at Wright-Patterson Air Force Base in Dayton, Ohio, because I never got in. I can't tell you what was inside. We both know about the rumors (concerning a captured UFO and crew members). I have never seen what I would call a UFO, but I have intelligent friends who have." **Barry Goldwater** - US Senator, US Air Force General and candidate for President, quoted from his letter dated April 11, 1979.

"Armstrong had indeed reported seeing two UFOs on the rim of a crater. The encounter was common knowledge in NASA but nobody has talked about it until now." "...All Apollo and Gemini flights were followed, both at a distance and sometimes also quite closely, by space vehicles of extraterrestrial origin. Every time it occurred, the astronauts informed Mission Control, who then ordered absolute silence." **Maurice Chatelain** (former) Chief - NASA Communications Systems, 1979

"Neil Armstrong relayed the message to Mission Control that two large, mysterious objects were watching them after having landed near the moon module. But his message was never heard by the public - because NASA censored it." **Dr. Vladmimir Azahzha**, Soviet physicist and mathematics professor.

"In this field [Ufology], prejudice will take you farther from the truth than ignorance..." **Bang Wen-Gwang**, Chinese Academy of Sciences, Beijing Astronomical Research Society, 1981

"I still do not know why the high order of classification has been given and why the denial of the existence of these objects [has been perpetuated]." **Dr. Robert Sarbacher** (on his involvement with secret government programs dealing with UFOs), Nov. 29, 1983

"I know other astronauts share my feelings.... And we know the government is sitting on hard evidence of UFOs. I had a good friend at Roswell, a fellow officer. He had to be careful about what he said. He made it clear to me that what crashed was a craft of alien origin, and members of the crew were recovered. It wasn't a weather balloon, like the Air Force cover story." "Every day in the U.S.A., our radar instruments capture objects of form and composition unknown to us."

"For many years I have lived with a secret, in a secrecy imposed on all specialists and astronauts. I can now reveal that every day, in the USA, our radar instruments capture objects of form and composition unknown to us. And there are thousands of witness reports and a quantity of documents to prove this, but nobody wants to make them public." **Colonel L. Gordon Cooper**, Mercury/Astronaut, address to the UN in 1985

"As far as my Air Staff is concerned, we believe implicitly that the unexplained UFOs are from some civilization beyond our planet." Air Commodore **David Thorne**, Director General of Operations letter to Timothy Good, Oct. 24, 1985

"Most scientists have never had the occasion to confront evidence concerning the UFO phenomenon. To a scientist, the main source of hard information (other than his own experiments' observations) is provided by the scientific journals. With rare exceptions, scientific journals do not publish reports of UFO observations. The decision not to publish is made by the editor acting on the advice of reviewers. This process is self-reinforcing: the apparent lack of data confirms the view that there is nothing to the UFO phenomenon, and this view (prejudice) works against the presentation of relevant data." **Peter A. Sturrock**, "An Analysis of the Condon Report on the Colorado UFO Project," Journal of Scientific Exploration, Vol.1, No.1, 1987

“I wish to bring to your attention a very real and dangerous situation that threatens not only us, the world, but our very existence as a race. No longer can the United States be in the position, which it found itself in 1947. This was realized in January 1950 when President Truman made a decision to go ahead with a defense program exceeding in scope and cost of the Manhattan Project.” **Dr. Edward Teller**, memo to President Reagan

"In our obsession with antagonisms of the moment, we often forget how much unites all the members of humanity. I occasionally think how quickly our differences, worldwide, would vanish if we were facing an alien threat from outside this world." Former **President Ronald Reagan, while sharing the stage with former Russian leader, Mikhail Gorbachev**, 1988

"His Excellency recognizes the importance of the [UFO] matter, to the extent that within the Ministry of Aeronautics there exists a Bureau in charge of studying the matter, receiving, analyzing and archiving chronologically the phenomena observed in Brazilian airspace that comes to the attention of this Ministry." Air Force **Colonel Sergio Candiota da Silva**, Assistant to the Minister of Aeronautics Dec. 19, 1988

"The phenomenon of UFOs does exist, and it must be treated seriously." **Mikhail Gorbachev**, former USSR leader. Reply to workers in the Urals. 'Soviet Youth' May 4, 1990

"I believe it is a reasonable time to take the UFO problem seriously as a reality... I hope that this Symposium will contribute to peace on earth from the point of view of outer space, and take the first step toward the international cooperation in the field of UFOs. From the point of view of 'people' in outer space, all human beings on earth are the same people, regardless of whether they are American, Russian, Japanese, or whoever." **Toshiki Kaifu**, Prime Minister, Japan Letter to Mayor Shiotani, June 24, 1990

"Skeptics, who flatly deny the existence of any unexplained phenomenon in the name of 'rationalism,' are among the primary contributors to the rejection of science by the public. People are not stupid and they know very well when they have seen something out of the ordinary. When a so-called 'expert' tells them the object must have been the moon or a mirage, he is really teaching the public that science is impotent or unwilling to pursue the study of the unknown." **Dr. Jacques Vallee**, astrophysicist, computer scientist 1990

"We're not dealing with mental projections or hallucinations on the part of the witness but with a real physical phenomenon. Reports of anomalous aerial objects (AAO) appearing in the atmosphere continue to be made by pilots of almost every airline and air force of the world, in addition to private and experimental test pilots. This paper presents a review of 56 reports of AAO in which electromagnetic effects (E-M) take place on-board the aircraft when the phenomenon is located nearby - but not before it appeared or after it had departed.

"Reported E-M effects included radio interference or total failure, radar contact with and without simultaneous visual contact, magnetic and/or gyro-compass deviations, automatic direction finder failure or interference, engine stopping or interruption, dimming cabin lights, transponder failure, and military aircraft weapon system failure." **Dr. Richard Haines**, Chief of Space Human Factors Office, Ames NASA Research Center International UFO Symposium Proceedings, 1992

Jacques Vallee reveals from his diaries how the government has deliberately misled the scientific world, the media and the public regarding their information on UFOs and paranormal research:

"I have followed this rule of silence for the last thirty years, but I have finally decided that I had no right to keep them (diaries) private anymore... They provide a primary source about a crucial fact in the recent historical record: the appearance of new classes of phenomena that highlighted the reality of the paranormal. These phenomena were deliberately denied or distorted by those in authority within the government and the military. Science never had fair and complete access to the most important files.

"The thirteen years covered here, from 1957 to 1969, saw some of the most exciting events in technological history... Behind the grand parade of the visible breakthroughs in science, however, more private mysteries were also taking place: all over the world people had begun to observe what they described as controlled devices in the sky. They were shaped like saucers or spheres. They seemed to violate every known principle in our physics.

"Governments took notice, organizing task forces, encouraging secret briefings and study groups, funding classified research and all the time denying before the public that any of the phenomena might be real. The major revelation of these Diaries may be the demonstration of how the scientific community was misled by the government, how the best data were kept hidden, and how the public record was shamelessly manipulated." **Dr. Jacques Vallee**, astrophysicist, computer scientist 1992

In a published article in April 1995, Chatelain dropped the bombshell revelation that, "...the Apollo Moon Mission found 'several mysterious geometric structures of unnatural origin' on the Moon".**Maurice Chatelain** - former NASA Director of Communications

"...If the United States Air Force did recover alien bodies, they didn't tell me about it either, and I want to know."
Bill Clinton, President - United States of America, Oct. 1995.

"I know other astronauts share my feelings...we know the government is sitting on hard evidence of UFOs."
Col. Gordon Cooper, Mercury/Gemini Astronaut, Jan 14, 1997

"...The General Staff of the Polish Army have had a special division which gathered and evaluated all information about UFO sightings and close encounters with aliens since the early 1980s".
Col. Zdzislaw Czekierda, Spokesman, General Staff - Polish Army, 1997

Hare said she saw a NASA technician air brush a UFO out of a space satellite photo and "that it was done routinely".
Donna Hare - photo labs, Johnson Space Center - Houston, TX. 1998

"I've talked with people of stature - of military and government credentials and position - and heard their stories, and their desire to tell their stories openly to the public. And that got my attention very, very rapidly... the first hand experiences of these credible witnesses, now in advanced years and anxious to tell their story. We can't deny that, and the evidence points to the fact that Roswell was a real incident, and that indeed an alien craft did crash, and that material was recovered from that crash site."
Dr. Edgar Mitchell, Apollo 14 astronaut from a taped interview in 1998.

"If you suppress the truth it becomes your enemy...if you expose the truth it becomes your weapon. I had the evidence that a crash did happen. I ask [you] this: 'were you there with me? Did you have the clearances?' They can't answer these questions. They simply criticize with no evidence."

Colonel Philip Corso - National Security Advisor Eisenhower Administration; former head of the Foreign Technology Desk, United States Army Research and Development; 1998 video interview, shortly before his death.

"Sometimes we actually got lucky enough to score a hit with a missile before the UFO could take any evasive action, which an army air defense battalion did with an antiaircraft missile near Ramstein Air Force Base in Germany in May 1974. The spacecraft managed to crash-land in a valley. The craft was retrieved and flown back to Nellis Air Force Base in Nevada."
Col. Phillip J. Corso, U.S. Army from "The Day after Roswell", p127, 1998

"Initially I was skeptical about this reality but I believe today that the force of evidence commands an honest, scientific look at the facts. The evidence points to the fact that Roswell was a real incident and that indeed an alien craft did crash, and that material was recovered from the crash site."
Apollo Astronaut **Edgar Mitchell**, 1999

"If we extrapolate, based on the best information we have available to us, we have to come to the conclusion that ... other life probably exists out there and perhaps in many places."
Apollo Astronaut Neil Armstrong, Oct 21, 1999.

"Whatever did or did not happen at Roswell in 1947 will ultimately prove to be a rounding error when the implications of

this phenomenon become widely known."
Joseph Firmage, International Space Sciences Organization, 1999

"I'm fairly convinced that we have discovered life on Mars," Clarke told Buzz Aldrin. "There are some incredible photographs from [the Jet Propulsion Laboratory], which to me are pretty convincing proof of the existence of large forms of life on Mars! Have a look at them. I don't see any other interpretation."
Arthur Clarke ~Feb 27 2001

On March 6, former astronaut and Senator John Glenn appeared on the sitcom Frasier and gave a remarkable soliloquy: "Back in those glory days, I was very uncomfortable when they asked us to say things that I didn't want to say, and deny other things. Some people asked, you know, 'Were you alone out there?' We never gave the real answer. We've seen things out there, strange things. But we know what we saw out there. And we couldn't really say anything; the bosses were scared of this. They were afraid of 'War of the Worlds' type stuff, about panic in the streets. And so we had to keep quiet. And now we only see these things in our nightmares or maybe in the movies. And some of them are pretty close to being the truth." Aldrin did not comment.
Senator John Glenn - former NASA astronaut March 6, 2001

In another statement Wednesday, Donna Hare, said that Apollo astronauts saw an alien craft when they landed on the moon, but were told not to reveal it. Hare's source was a man who had been quarantined with the astronauts. **Donna Hare**, former NASA contract employee (reported by ABC News, May 10, 2001)

Former Air Force **Maj. George Filer III** told reporters that when he was at McGuire Air Force Base in New Jersey, an alien craft came down, and an alien got out and was shot by a military policeman.

"Our security police went out there and found him at the end of the runway dead," Filer said.

"They asked me to brief the general staff," he said, but was later told not to. He said he would tell the story in front of Congress. Filer says he also chased an alien ship over England when flying for the U.S. Air Force. "I personally have observed a UFO both visually and on radar." **George Flier III**, Major, USAF (reported by ABC News, May 10, 2001)

Diane Reme interviewed VP Dick Cheney on the first part of her show. A caller asked about UFOs. His reply was something to the effect that '...if I ever was briefed on UFOs it would be classified and I wouldn't be able to talk about it.' Diane Reme followed by asking, "Is there an investigation going on in this administration regarding UFOs?" And he said 'Ummm.... I have not come across the subject since I've been back in gov't since Jan 20th. I've been in a lot of meetings, but none of them about UFO's as I recall." Dick Cheney, VP USA. April 11, 2001. (25 min into the show at: http://www.wamu.org/dr/) As my friend commented, "Once again, Cheney is either suavely regurgitating another lie - or - he's telling the truth, which means he's clueless. Either position is unacceptable for a man in his position, given the critical 'energy /environmental /extraterrestrial situation' now facing all humanity."

"The astronauts are very controlled by military secrecy oaths." **Clark McClelland** - NASA June 6, 2001

Insights, Overview and Context:

"Gradually, I began to accumulate cases that I really couldn't explain, cases reported by reliable, sincere people whom I often interviewed in person. I found that the persons making these reports were often not acquainted with UFO's before their experience, which baffled and thoroughly frightened them. Fearing ridicule, they were often reluctant to report the sighting and did so only out of a sense of duty and a tremendous desire to get a rational explanation for their irrational experience."

"The UFO phenomenon exists, and this fact alone should represent a challenge to science and not a roadblock. We have a responsibility as scientists to support those who accept this challenge even though we may not ourselves be inclined to pursue the matter. In any event, ridicule of those who do consider this subject should not enter, for ridicule is certainly not a part of the scientific method." **Dr. J. Allen Hynek** "Are Flying Saucers Real?"

"UFOs are conceived and directed by intelligent beings of a very high order, and they are propelled by distorting the gravitational field, converting gravity into useable energy. There is no doubt in my mind that these objects are interplanetary craft of some sort. I and my colleagues are confident that they do not originate in our solar system...perhaps not even in our galaxy." It is my thesis that flying saucers are real and that they are space ships from another solar system."
Dr. Herman Oberth, the father of modern rocketry

"One of the principal results of my own recent intensive study of the UFO enigma is this: I have become convinced that the scientific community, not only in this country but throughout the world, has been casually ignoring as nonsense a matter of extraordinary scientific importance..."
James E. McDonald, Senior Physicist, Institute of Atmospheric Physics; Professor - Dept. of Meteorology; University of Arizona, Tucson, Arizona

"No agency in this country or Russia is able to duplicate at this time the speeds and accelerations which radars and observers indicate these flying objects are able to achieve... there are objects coming into our atmosphere at very high speeds."
Admiral Delmer S. Fahrney, former head of the Navy's guided-missile program (New York Times)

"50,000 virtually reliable people have reported sighting unidentified flying objects… From available information, the UFO phenomenon appears to have been global in nature for almost 50,000 years. This leaves us with the unpleasant possibility of alien visitors to our planet, or at least of alien controlled UFO's. The best thing to do is to keep an open and skeptical mind, and not take an extreme position on any side of the question"
USAF "Introductory Space Science", Volume II - **Department of Physics, USAF**

"I've talked with people of stature-of military and government credentials and position-and heard their stories, and their desire to tell their stories openly to the public. And that got my attention very, very rapidly.... The first hand experiences of these credible witnesses that, now in advanced years are anxious to tell their story, we can't deny that, and the evidence points to the fact that

Roswell was a real incident, and that indeed an alien craft did crash, and that material was recovered from that crash site."
Dr. Edgar Mitchell, Apollo 14 astronaut from a taped interview.

"The time will have to come when we realize that we're not the center of the universe. The galaxy may be teeming with life. There may be millions of civilizations."
Richard Terrile, Astronomer, Jet Propulsion Laboratory

"We're way, way past time for bringing this information to the public, acknowledging it and entering into the sort of discussions at the highest levels of congress and the government - to make this information available to the public. It's far, far past time for this. If we don't do it here, I don't know when we'll ever be able to do it."

"I think our representative democracy is in danger.... I think events are moving so fast, so very rapidly, that no one is really on top of it, and if we don't get the people mobilized here to demand that we get to the bottom of these issues we're talking about today...we're not going to have an opportunity forever. This is a key issue that we are talking about." **Dr. Edgar Mitchell**, Apollo 14 Astronaut Jan 5, 1998 on the Art Bell Show

As the Federal Government continues to deny the existence of other worldly life forms, the American people only lose trust in the Federal government. The truth is, the knowledge that we are not alone is buried deep within our cellular memory. We already know the truth. This alone accounts for the deep fascination with all things which deal with this topic. **Dr. Heather Anne Harder James Harder**

UFO 'research by proclamation':

"Characterized by fantastic tales and an utter lack of research into possible explanations. 'I have no doubts' is the most common figure of speech...and they are doubtlessly sincere, if arguably deluded." **James Oberg**, NASA

"It is difficult for those to see, whose paycheck depends on them not seeing." (Upton Sinclair)

"All truth passes through three stages: first, it is ridiculed; next it is violently attacked; finally, it is held to be self-evident." **Schopenhauer**

"Scientists and skeptics; they spend more time and energy explaining the uninvestigated...rather than investigating the unexplained." **George Knapp**

UFO quotes by Steve Myers (2002)

This is a list of UFO crashes up to 1992 with recovery information:

DATE--- LOCATION---BODIES

Unknown - Beaver Oklahoma (ancient crash site still believed by some to be buried under Sand Hills of Beaver State Park) Bodies Unknown

Unknown - Steppes Mountains (ancient crash site, some wreckage reported recovered in Arch Dig 1956, No Bodies)

October 1865 – Cadotte Pass, Montana, no bodies

June 1884 – Dundy, Nebraska, no bodies

August 1897 Aurora, Texas 1 Body (buried in Local cemetery)

July 4, 1947 Roswell, New Mexico 4 Bodies

Oct 1947, Paradise Valley Arizona 4 bodies

Feb 13, 1948 Aztec, New Mexico 12 Bodies

July 7, 1948 Mexico, south of Laredo 1 Body

1949 Roswell, New Mexico 1 ET Living

1952 Spitsbergen, Norway 2 Bodies

Aug 14, 1952 Ely, Nevada 16 Bodies

Sept 10, 1950 Albuquerque, New Mexico 3 Bodies

April 18, 1953 S.W. Arizona No Bodies

May 20, 1953 Kingman, Arizona 1 Body

June 19, 1953 Laredo, Texas 4 Bodies

July 10, 1953 Johannesburg, S. Africa 5 Bodies

Oct 13, 1953 Dutton, Montana 4 Bodies

May 5, 1955 Brighton, England 4 Bodies

July 18, 1957 Carlsbad, New Mexico 4 Bodies

1961 Timmensdorfer, Germany 12 Bodies

June 12, 1962 Holloman, AFB, New Mexico 2 Bodies

Nov 10, 1964 Ft. Riley, Kansas 9 Bodies

Dec 9, 1965, Kecksburg Pa

Oct 27, 1966 N.W. Arizona 1 Body

1966-1968 5 Crashes IN/KY/OH/ areas 3 Bodies and Disc Intact

July 18, 1972 Morocco Sahara Desert 3 Bodies

July 10, 1973 NW Arizona 5 Bodies

Aug 25, 1974 Chihuahua, Mexico Bodies and Disc intact

May 12, 1976 Australian Desert 4 Bodies

June 22, 1977 NW Arizona 5 Bodies

April 5, 1977 SW Ohio 11 Bodies

Aug 17, 1977 Tabasco, Mexico 2 Bodies

May 1978 Bolivia No Bodies

Nov 1988 Afghanistan 7 Bodies

May 1989 South Africa 2 ET Living

June 1989 South Africa 2 ET Living Disc Intact

July 1989 Siberia 9 ET Living

Sept 2, 1990 Megas Platonos Greece

Nov 1992 Long Island, New York

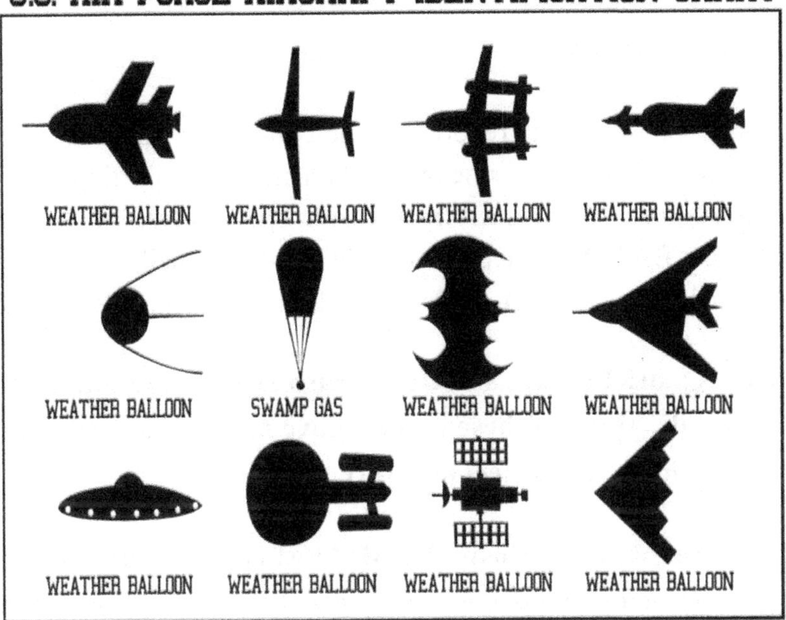

The Mystery Man:

Robert Bigelow was born in Nevada in 1945 and made his wealth in real estate and *Budget Suites* hotels. He founded the *National institute for Discovery Science* in 1995, 1994 funded the *UFO Research Coalition* made up of *MUFON, CUFOS* and the *FUFOR*, purchased the Utah *Skinwalker* ranch in 1996, founded *Bigelow Aerospace* in 1999, received government funding from 2007-12 to investigate UFOs, funded *MUFON* investigations for $672K in

2008, got the FAA to send UFO reports to him in 2010 and went on *60 Minutes* in 2016 and said there is an alien presence here. I believe Bigelow and not Tom Delonge is in charge of the *To the Stars Academy of Arts and Science*. You can view my *String Theory of the Unexplained* lecture on my reasoning.

9-8-1. GENERAL

a. Persons wanting to report UFO/unexplained phenomena activity should contact a UFO/ unexplained phenomena reporting data collection center, such as Bigelow Aerospace Advanced Space Studies (BAASS) (voice: 1-877-979-7444 or e-mail: Reporting@baass.org), the National UFO Reporting Center, etc.

This is a brief synopsis of UFO Crash reports and military retrievals. Many of these reports have not been investigated and could be the subject of future research.

1. July 4, 1947 (Roswell, NM) Most famous of the UFO Crash cases and most thoroughly investigated. William (Mac) Brazel, a local rancher, reported hearing a loud explosion during the night of a thunderstorm. The next day Brazel found a debris field on his ranch. Word reached Major Jesse Marcel at the Roswell Army Air Field and he investigated. Marcel reported finding a debris field scattered over a mile. The material recovered from the debris included small beams with hieroglyphics on them; metal that was as light as balsa wood, but couldn't be dented with a sledgehammer, although flexible. The material would not burn. The scrap material was flown to Carswell AFB in Fort Worth. Witnesses have described a second site where the main body of the craft was found along with the bodies of its crew.

2. Oct, 1947 (Cave Creek, AZ) Not much is known about this crash. There is still one living witness in Prescott, AZ.

3. Mar 25, 1948 (Aztec, NM) though still considered a hoax by most researchers; others have left the door open on this one. A new first-hand witness has been found in Las Vegas. Story is that a large disc said to be 99 feet in diameter came down in Hart Canyon and that a military recovery team was dispatched from Durango, CO.

4. Mar 1948 (Socorro, NM) a second craft came down in this vicinity that was much like the Aztec craft according to an ex-army private.

5. Aug 14, 1952 a disc crashed near Ely, NV, and 16 bodies were recovered.

6. May 20, 1953 (Kingman, AZ) An engineer who reported this event said 1 or 2 bodies were recovered. He rode a bus with darkened windows from the Nevada Test Site to the crash location. The disc was found embedded in the sand and canted at an angle. His job was to determine the disc's trajectory and velocity.

There have been rumors of additional crashes including a controversial report of a South African Mirage jet fighter shooting down a disc over the Kalahari Desert in Botswana on May 7, 1989. There are also reports of a disc crash in Chihuahua, Mexico on August 25, 1974 and one in Megas Platanos on September 2, 1990 in central Greece. Few of these reports have been investigated as thoroughly as Roswell, but that does not mean they should be dismissed.

An FBI MEMO from March 22, 1950 alludes to 3 saucers recovered in New Mexico. This memo also states that it was believed that a radar station interfered with the saucers' control mechanisms causing them to crash. If that were true, then such a discovery would suggest the idea of a weapon that could be used to bring saucers down.

7. In Beaver Oklahoma crash site (alleged) believed to be the cause or effect of phenomena known as the "Beaver Sands Portal." A supposed dimensional doorway to other worlds first experienced by Native Americans of the area, and then white men starting with Coronado's Expedition who camped near the sand dunes. Green light and eerie sensations on the skin mark this experience, along with a small number of disappearances in to the Portal spread out over the last 4 centuries.

Here is another file of alleged crashed disks researched by The Phoenix Foundation:

Alleged UFO Crashes

The following list of UFO crashes was compiled by the Phoenix Foundation from numerous sources within the Gemstone Intelligence Network (GIN), an international intelligence organization founded and operated by the Phoenix Foundation. For further information on Phoenix Foundation membership or to receive the organization's newsletter, please contact:

The Phoenix Foundation, Research Division, P.O. Box 92008, Nashville, Tennessee 37209.

April 17, 1897 - Aurora, Texas

A mysterious airship is said to have crashed in this town, exploding into many small fragments. Reportedly, the occupant was child-size and greenish, and the craft contained papers covered with hieroglyphics. The pilot's body is supposed to be buried in the local cemetery. Although the case was widely regarded as a hoax, new investigation brought to light a peculiar alloy that was eventually analyzed by the McDonnell Aircraft Company.

Dec. 22, 1909 - Chicago

Six years after Kitty Hawk, newspapers from New York to Chicago were astounded by national reports of a huge airship flying across the nation and seen by thousands. It crashed west of Chicago, but was never found. The story was front-page news in the nation's major newspapers.

1933 or 1934 - Ubatuba, Brazil Witnesses on a beach are said to have seen a disc dive and explode, showering the area with silvery fragments of highly pure magnesium.

May, 1947 - Spitsbergen, Norway

A report by journalist Dorothy Kilgallen stated that British scientists and airmen were excavating the wreckage of a mysterious flying ship. The Swedish military acknowledged its extraterrestrial origin and reported 17 bodies were found. The story appeared as a tiny blip for only one day in the U.S. news media before it was silenced by the military. I personally saw this news story years ago.

July 2, 1947 - Roswell, New Mexico

The most famous and thoroughly investigated by journalists, this is the crash that launched Majestic-12. It was the first and only time the U.S. government publicly admitted it had recovered a crashed flying saucer. Within hours, the craft was whisked off to Wright-Patterson AFB and a new cover story emerged, claiming it had been only a weather balloon. In recent years, the officer responsible for that cover story has recanted. Three or four humanoid bodies were recovered; one was alive for a short time.

February 13, 1948 - Aztec, New Mexico

Three radar units tracked a falling UFO. Secretary of State George C. Marshall requested a search party be dispatched from Camp Hale in Colorado. A helicopter team found a crashed 30-foot disc 12 miles northeast of Aztec and recovered 2-12 badly burned humanoids. The disc is stored in Hangar 18 at Wright-Patterson AFB near Dayton, Ohio.

August 1948 - Laredo, Texas

Four officers witnessed the crash of an object and the recovery of bodies 38 miles south of Laredo, Texas, in Mexico. The information came from an NBC affiliate in Chicago, who received it from a source in Army security.

August 19, 1949 - Death Valley, California,

Two prospectors named Mace Garney and Buck Fitzgerald claimed to have watched an object crash in the desert. It was a 24-

foot disc. The story appeared on page 13 of the local Bakersfield newspaper the next day.

Before 1950 - Mexico

Roy L. Dimmick, sales manager for the Apache Powder Company of Los Angeles, spoke with a man from Mexico and another from Ecuador who had seen a disc crash near Mexico City.

April 1950 - Argentina

Mr. E.C. Bossa found a strange disc and four small dead pilots in a remote region of Argentina. He returned with a friend the next day and found only a pile of warm ashes. A cigar-shaped object was seen briefly as it flew overhead at a high altitude.

1953 - Brady, Montana

Mr. C.M. Tenney, returning from Great Falls to Conrad, saw an oval object that followed his car while balls of fire fell all over the road. Later that day a colonel phoned him from Malmstrom AFB who asked him to come to the base at 10 a.m. the next day. He was escorted to a windowless room inside a fenced-off compound and asked to sign a statement. While doing so, he says he saw two men carrying large laundry bags containing humanoid bodies.

May 21, 1953 - Kingman, Arizona

A USAF veteran claims to have participated in the recovery of a crashed aluminum-like disc impacted 20 inches into the earth. It was oval, 32 feet wide. Inside were two swivel chairs, an oval cabin and numerous instruments. One 4-foot-tall occupant was recovered, dead. It had a dark brown complexion and wore a silvery metal suit with no helmet. Respected UFO researcher Ray Fowler in UFO Magazine, April 1976, released the witness' affidavit.

Mid-1950s - Birmingham, Alabama

When a disc crashed near Birmingham, the area was cordoned off and humanoid bodies were flown to Maxwell AFB, according to a man who claims to have flown the helicopter with the bodies to a waiting aircraft.

Spring 1954 - Mattydale, NY

In this suburb of Syracuse, at 3 a.m. on a Sunday, an information specialist and his wife saw a 20-foot-wide object being examined on the ground by several men who were taking pictures. The next day an officer told them the event was a military secret. Later, police denied the whole incident ever took place.

1959 - Frdynia, Poland

An object was reported to have fallen into the harbor. Divers recovered pieces of shiny metal, which were examined by the Polytechnic Institute and Polish Navy. Some material was reportedly lost. Several days later a small humanoid was found on a nearby beach; its remains were sent to the Soviet Union.

March 1960 - New Paltz, NY

Local law enforcement authorities captured a small humanoid outside his craft while two copilots escaped. The alien was turned over to the CIA and died 28 days later.

January 1967 - Southwest Missouri

A Mr. Loftin found a 40-inch disc and gave it to the U.S. Testing Company for analysis.

November 9, 1974 - Carbondale, Pa

A glowing object fell into a small lake outside town. Three teenagers saw it fall at 7:30 p.m. on a Saturday. They observed a yellow-white glow under the water that shifted to a point 25 feet offshore. The boys were kept in a police car for three hours while a number of vehicles with floodlights and cranes removed a disc-shaped object and put it into a van. The following Monday, a railroad lantern and battery were recovered from the lake and officials called the whole thing a hoax. Hoax or cover story?

May 17, 1974 - Chili, NM

An Air Force team allegedly removed a 60-foot-wide metallic object from an impact area and moved it to Kirtland AFB.

May 6, 1978 - Padcaya, Bolivia

A large luminous object crashed on a 13,000-foot mountain. An expedition of soldiers and scientists was dispatched to the site, but was delayed by bad weather. They found nothing.

1978 - Soviet Union

After a collision with a Soviet fighter plane, a disc-shaped object fell into the ocean off Finland, where it was recovered with humanoid bodies - by a Soviet salvage team.

-Researched by the Phoenix Foundation and expanded by the author.

Fact: In a 1977 interview with J Allen Hynek, he said, “The ETH runs up against a big difficulty. We are seeing too many UFOs. I am very much afraid that UFOs are related to psychic phenomenon. We only try to study it with physical sciences but it is absurd to exclude others. UFOs may come from a parallel reality. I don’t talk about the occult because the general audience will think it’s crazy”.

(Courtesy Craig Fackrell)

Music to the Cosmos; encoded radio waves:

SETI searches for signals- 1977 Big Wow signal.
1960- Language for a cosmic call created.
1974- Carl Sagan sends by radio from Arecibo.
1977- Voyager 1 gold plated record.
2001- Ukraine blasts Beethoven to stars.
2004- NASA blasts Beetles.
2016- EU message, S Hawking warns against.
2018- METI Inst sends music to Luyten star.
Classical music has been used most.

5 Arguments against ET contact by Jacques Vallee:

1. Unexplained close encounters are far more numerous than required for any physical survey of the earth;

2. The humanoid body structure of the alleged aliens is not likely to have originated on another planet and is not biologically adapted to space travel;

3. The reported behavior in thousands of abduction reports contradicts the hypothesis of genetic or scientific experimentation on humans by an advanced race;

4. The extension of the phenomenon throughout recorded human history demonstrates that UFOs are not a contemporary phenome-non; and

5. The apparent ability of UFOs to manipulate space and time suggests radically different and richer alternatives

The John Ventre Collection

After four chapters, I've proven UFOs are real because they are unidentified but there is no physical proof that Flying Saucers are from space that science will accept. The following are articles and book reviews that I wrote that have appeared in seven publications that I occasionally write for (U.S.-MUFON Journal, FATE mag., Intrepid and Conspiracy Journal. U.K.- UFO Truth Mag., Phenomena Mag. and UFO Today. India- UFO India) but listed here in no particular order except for the last six. It is much easier for you to read a recap of everything I have researched which has led me to my conclusions:

"The suppression of uncomfortable ideas may be common in religion and politics, but it is not the path to knowledge, it has no place in science." -- Carl Sagan 1980

Chapter 5

MUFON on the ANDERSON COOPER SHOW

In March of 2012, MUFON Exec Dir. Dave MacDonald contacted me regarding representing MUFON on the Anderson Cooper show in NYC. Having grown up in NY, I immediately said yes. When the show's Producer Ty Peterson contacted me, he told me that he is a huge believer in UFOs and had his own sighting as a youth. He did add that Anderson believes in life in space but not in the UFO phenomena. Ty said that we would have 3 witnesses, a skeptic, a psychic and me. The skeptic turned out to be Joe Nickell.

The show would be taped on Friday April 13 and air in the next two weeks. They flew me in on JetBlue and put me up at the Hudson hotel across from their studio. The hotel room was smaller than my kitchen and the hotel was very dimly lit. Even the shuttle driver told me that the Hudson is a very dark place. In case you are wondering if there is money to be made in Ufology, they gave me $40 for expenses, which didn't cover my gas, airport parking, tips and meals. Fran Drescher was the guest on right before us. She looks even better in person and was very friendly and hugged and spoke with us all back stage. We were both in the same class in third grade in Queens NY.

Our witnesses included Denise Murter from our 2008 UFO wave in Bucks County Pa, two 22-year-old witnesses from Kentucky, Jennifer and Brittany, who both had a very interesting sighting and a CE4 in April 2011. An ET-Spiritual communicator named Cassandra. There were five witnesses to the Brittany and Jennifer case where they saw over a dozen UFOs of different shapes. Under hypnosis, the two ladies recalled two ET's and a room with a counter around its perimeter. Brittany had a positive experience; Jennifer did not as she was roughly handled and had a migraine headache afterward. When our two witnesses said they got out of their car and stood right under the UFO, I immediately thought of chapter 13 of the Fire Officers Guide to Disaster Control which has a chapter on UFOs (The UFO Threat-A Fact pg. 471) and a warning to not get out of your vehicle or approach or make contact with a UFO. There were seven witnesses to the Denise case along with trace evidence. Linda Moulton Howe gave permission to the show to use Prof Levengood's lab report. I explained that Boron, magnesium and anthocyanin were found on the leaves where Denise claims probes were dropped into and that boron is used in stealth aircraft because it doesn't reflect radar. It is also used in the enamel that coats the inside of nuclear reactors.

Our portion of the show lasted approximately 40 minutes and went well. Joe Nickell used the typical debunking tactics that our witnesses saw Jupiter, were still dreaming at 4am during their sightings, are prone to fantasy and misidentified lights in the sky. He also said the O'Hare airport incident in 2006 was a natural hole-punch cloud formation even though pilots, crew and the

Tower saw it and there are voice transcripts. Hole punch clouds form at temperatures below 32 but the O'Hare temperature was 53. The only reason this case of a violation of Class B restricted air space came to the public was that a United Airlines Supervisor called the Tower and it was recorded. The FAA and United denied the incident until the tape surfaced. Nickell also accused MUFON for using hypnosis on the girls and said that it doesn't work. I countered that hypnosis is a tool just like a polygraph or interviews or video analysis. The live audience applauded when I stated that these three witnesses have the courage and integrity to say what they saw even though it is not politically correct and not believed. I went on to say that the two cases had 12 witnesses, which are enough to make up a jury. If they were a jury and had just decided on a court case and saw a UFO while exiting the courthouse, they would be not believed outside but would be believed inside the courthouse.

Anderson was fair with his questions. He asked how UFOs could be kept a secret. I said that we kept the Manhattan Project a secret. A woman in the audience asked our witnesses why there were no pictures taken. Our witnesses countered that their camera's shut down. Anderson polled the audience as to whether they believed in UFOs and unfortunately only around 25% raised their hands. The audience also laughed when Anderson interviewed the psychic. She told Anderson that he was from Lemuria. When polled, only one person in the audience believed Cassandra. Denise and I spoke afterwards that we had a pretty good discussion going with Anderson, the skeptic and ourselves until they introduced the psychic. I have nothing against psychics since the police use them and we only use 3% of our DNA and 8% of our brain capacity; I'm sure some people use more of their abilities than others.

Overall I thought the show was fair. Afterward, I used my Hilton hotel points and spent Friday night at the Waldorf Astoria. They upgraded me to a $700 a night suite on the 32nd floor of the Towers for free. What a great hotel, what a great show experience. It turned out to be one of those perfect days. . . . .

The show actually aired on Tuesday April 24th after I had submitted the above article to the MUFON Journal and of cause they edited out my best responses to the skeptic. They did not edit out anything the skeptic said. They did edit out the audience's laughter when Joe said the witnesses saw Jupiter. Edited out was my response that regressive hypnosis is a tool we use no different than a polygraph and that Joe Nickell has no medical background. Edited out was my statement that the witnesses showed courage and integrity, which received applause from the entire audience. Edited out was my analogy that the 12 witnesses to these 2 cases could make up a jury yet they would be believed inside the courtroom but not outside the courtroom if they witnessed a UFO. Edited out was my statement that we kept the stealth fighter a secret for 12 years when asked how the government can keep this a secret. It's not like I said they kept Anderson's orientation secret for years, now that's something that should be edited out. Anderson coincidentally came out of the closet shortly after this show. . . . . .

The skeptic received twice as much air time and the last word on the show. The shows website had nine pages of comments; more than any other show that they have done. All the comments were against the skeptic and psychic. I should've known the Producer was playing me when he said he was a UFO fan but never heard of Project Blue Book or the 1952 UFO wave over DC. They introduced a psychic medium to minimize the seriousness of the show. I had asked Cliff if he wanted to be on the show but he declined when he found out it is not a live show. To date, only Larry King has shown he could do an unbiased interview regarding UFOs. They also indicated on the show that the most recent AOL poll shows 34% of people believe in UFOs when in fact the poll shows that 60% believe in UFOs and 80% believe in life in space and 75% believe the government knows and is lying. Is it any surprise that NBC edited the interview? They edited the police phone call from George Zimmerman regarding Trayvon Martin to make it appear racist when it wasn't. This is what NBC does. Just like Project Blue Book and following the Brookings Institute's recommendations to not tell the truth regarding UFOs, the outcome was predetermined. I read this quote on PAKALERT News last week, "Do you ever get the feeling that the mainstream media is feeding you a very watered-down and twisted version of the news? Do you ever get the feeling that the government does not believe that the American people can actually be trusted with the truth? It is exasperating to realize that the news that the public is being fed every single day is very heavily filtered and very heavily censored. In a world where "spin" is everything, simply telling the truth is a revolutionary act. Fortunately, the Internet has helped fuel the rise of the alternative media, and millions of Americans that are starting to wake up are turning to the alternative media for answers to their unanswered questions". It is situations like this that convince me that there is a conspiracy to discredit Ufology and only make my belief stronger in it.

On April 30th, Ty Petersen did call me and explained that after the filming it goes to the editing department and there was no malicious intent to cut out our responses. He said it ran a little longer than planned and needed to be edited back. He did say the psychic medium was a little eccentric but thought that it was a good show. I said the UFO community would like to see a show done where just the facts are presented. You don't have a skeptic with a rape victim or a woman who claims she was abused so why is there always a skeptic with UFO witnesses? You'll have to decide based on the facts I just presented as to whether there was a bias against Ufology.

Interestingly, when the Anderson show returned for its second season in September 2012 it was no longer taped but a live show. I don't know if the UFO communities' numerous complaints regarding the shows editing led to the change. I would welcome an invite to do another show but this time LIVE.

Chapter 6

70 Years ago- The Battle of L.A.

Up until the release of last summer's movie *Battle L.A.*, this was a much unknown and highly overlooked case. On February 25 1942, just three months after Pearl Harbor, 15 objects were picked up on radar approaching from the Pacific with eyewitness confirmation. The city was blacked out from 2:25am to 7:21am as the Army's 37th Coast Artillery Brigade shined eight spotlights on a 100-foot domed shaped object and fired 1433 rounds of anti-aircraft shells at it. Six civilians died that night; three from shell fragments and three from heart attacks as air raid sirens and canon fire awoke nearly two million residents who believed they were under attack by the Japanese. Even though direct hits were reported, it had no effect on the object. This was the first time we fired on a UFO and the first time UFOs were officially denied. The front page of the February 26 L.A. Times headline read "Army Says Alarm Real" and showed a picture of the object. This was also the first time the weather balloon excuse was used. Although six weather balloons were released 12 hours earlier, wind patterns would've put them well up the coast. The incident was denied by U.S. Navy Secretary Frank Knox. The press responded with the classic line, "If you can't shoot down a weather balloon at 9000 feet with nearly 1500 rounds, then how are you going to protect us from a Japanese invasion?"

General George Marshall issued a memorandum on March 5 1942 that a saucer was recovered off the coast and that it was not earthly. The memo was released in 1974. He also ordered the creation of a special Interplanetary Phenomenon Unit.

A side note to this case is that a 10 year old witness to The Battle of L.A. was Charles W Bahme J.D. who grew up to become a Naval Reserve Captain, Attorney and Assistant Fire Chief of L.A. and co-authored the *Fire Officers Guide to Disaster Control.* This FEMA approved hazmat manual sits in every Fire Dept. in the U.S. and interestingly has a chapter on UFOs. If you go to Chapter 13 on "Enemy Attack and UFO Potential", it starts out with a description of the Battle of L.A... If you go to page 458; "*The UFO Threat-A Fact*" you'll find 13 pages of some of the best UFO advice ever presented.

Los Angeles Times

ARMY SAYS ALARM REAL

U.S. Flyers Reap Indies Victories

Storm Grows Over Delay in Alien Ouster

INFORMATION, PLEASE

Five Deaths Laid to Raid Blackout

Roaring Guns Mark Blackout

Chapter 7

1952-THE RESPONSE

Many believe that the modern UFO era started on June 24 1947 with the Kenneth Arnold sighting and we honor that day by referring to it as National UFO Day. Others say that it started with the Roswell crash two weeks later. Those events may have inaugurated the UFO era but the response came in 1952.

On two weekends in July 1952 UFOs buzzed our Nation's Capital. Up to a dozen UFOs flew over our Nation's Capital on July 19 and 26. The objects were picked up on radar and spotted by pilots and civilians. They were seen cruising at 130 MPH and then take off at incredible speeds of 1000 MPH.

With the runway closed for repairs at Andrews AFB, F-94 interceptor jets were scrambled from New Castle AFB in Delaware. As our jets approached the objects, they turned and disappeared from radar. As our jets returned to New Castle AFB, the objects then returned. When our jets soared back to DC, our pilots saw the objects but couldn't catch them.

General Samford called the largest press conference since WWII. He mentioned that "UFOs have been around since biblical times but these were probably temperature inversions. He went on to say that we have analyzed up to 2000 sightings and most are explainable. It is this small percentage made by credible witnesses that they are attempting to resolve. These objects represent no pattern or purpose or threat to the US. The UFOs are not a secret US craft." Samford would go on to direct the NSA.

Project Blue Book had just replaced Project Grudge a few months prior to these July sightings and was headed by Captain Ruppelt. The CIA sponsored Robertson Panel started in 1953 with the goal of debunking UFOs. Project Blue Book concluded in late 1969 with the Condon report and concluded that UFOs were not a threat to our National Security and that the Air Force would no longer investigate them. It is interesting to note that the original 19 scientists on the Condon panel all resigned once they realized that the conclusion had already been reached before they even started. This effectively ended the era of UFO media and military "cooperation" with civilians in this country. Even though General Bolander went on to say that UFOs that were a threat to national security were not part of Project Blue Book and that the Air Force would continue to investigate those under JANAP 146 and Air Force manual 55-11, this ended the UFO era for all intent and purpose with the media. It did give rise to the Mutual UFO Network to do the job that the Air Force claims they no longer do. The Air Force also pulled their Physics 370 course that they taught to Cadets at the Air Force Academy in Colorado Springs. Chapter 33 of the Physics course was on UFOs.

A chain of events was also set in place after the DC sightings. On Nov 18 1952, the Eisenhower Briefing Document was presented on MJ-12 and the world of UFO secrecy began. See Stanton Friedman for more on MJ-12.

Winston Churchill did make a request in 1952 asking "What all this flying saucer stuff amounted to. What did it mean? What is the truth?"

In September of 1952, an air battle with UFOs took place off the East coast of the US and resulted in the infamous Flatwoods WV case where a disabled UFO crashed in Braxton County WV and a group of teens saw an ET in a hover pod. A second UFO came to rescue or repairs the first craft and so was born the Flatwoods Monster case. See Frank Feschino's book *Shoot them Down* for more on that case.

The Weather

The Washington Post FINAL

Seventy-fifth Year in the Nation's Capital

NO. 27,801 — MONDAY, JULY 28, 1952 — FIVE CENTS

'Saucer' Outran Jet, Pilot Reveals

U.S. Protests Soviet 'Hate' In Aviation Day Posters

Air Chase Pictures Held Admission of 3 Attacks; Envoys Shun Big Red Show

Conquest by Terror — Russians Rule Satellites By Torture and Murder

By Leland Stowe

Stevenson And Truman Head 'Big 4'

Barkley, Sparkman Also Will Enter Stumping Campaign For Party Victory

Eisenhower, Nixon Plan Campaign

Will Invade South; Spirit of Unity Growing in GOP, Senator Declares

Investigation On in Secret After Chase Over Capital

Radar Spots Blips Like Aircraft for Nearly Six Hours; Only 1700 Feet Up

Dwight D. Eisenhower, Republican presidential nominee, shows his running mate, Sen. Richard M. Nixon of California, correct angling technique at the two conferred on campaign strategy yesterday at Ike's mountain retreat in Fraser, Colo.

Subject File

PRIME MINISTER'S PERSONAL MINUTE

SERIAL No. M. 412 /52

5

~~SECRETARY OF STATE FOR AIR~~

~~LORD CHERWELL~~

What does all this stuff about flying saucers amount to? What can it mean? What is the truth. Let me have a report at your convenience.

W.S.C.

THE MUFON FILES (PT. 1)
?
AN INTERVIEW WITH JOHN VENTRE
Photo: Los Angeles Times, February 25, 1942 - "The Battle of Los Angeles"

Chapter 8

Life, Liberty and the Pursuit of UFOs

I've read a number of articles recently regarding Gary McKinnon, the Scottish chap that hacked into NASA's computers 10 years ago looking for UFOs and free energy for the benefit of humanity. What he claims he found was a secret Air Force space program and references to 300 non-terrestrial officers. In fact, the Air Force has had its own space program since 1982 and it has always been funded slightly higher than NASA at $8.8B a year. One could say that NASA and SETI are the public view while the Air Force runs the private view. Gary has been fighting extradition to the US to stand trial as a terrorist. His hacking into NASA's computers is a zero tolerance crime and shouldn't be downplayed but it brings to mind a similar situation from a generation earlier.

In July 1969, the Extraterrestrial Exposure Law was added to US law under Title 14, Section 1211 of the Code of Federal Regulations. The law prohibited anyone from coming into contact with any object that has been in outer space. The purpose of the law was to prevent a virus or contagion from spreading. If a person broke the law, he or she could be fined up to $5000 and be jailed for up to a year along with being quarantined by NASA without a hearing. The law was so vaguely written that anyone coming into contact with a meteor fragment, extraterrestrial or its vehicle, or reporting being abducted or a CE3 or 4 would be a criminal. Based on this law, Travis Walton and every hybrid or abductee that Dr David Jacobs has interviewed would be a criminal. One effect of the law would be to silence witnesses. The law was on the books until April of 1991 when it was removed and placed into reserved status, which means it could be reinstated. No one was ever prosecuted under the law because it was unenforceable and in the case of UFOs, it would first require the admission by NASA or the Air Force that UFOs are real. Here in lies the lesson for the Gary McKinnon case. Should someone be prosecuted for "googling" for fantasy topics like Bigfoot, UFOs, ghosts, fairies or elves? We all know that they are not real. Right?

So is the real issue hacking, containing contagions or controlling the truth? You decide.

Note: President Ronald Reagan's diary also speaks of an out space fleet with 300 officers yet the 8 space shuttles could only carry 40 total officers. The charges and extradition of McKinnon to the U.S. were dropped in December of 2012.

Chapter 9

AMERICA SHRUGGED

I decide to retire this week (May, 18 2012) at 55 after a 35-year career at UPS. I could've easily kept working for 5 more years and earn $1M at my current compensation but I refuse to continue to pay a 35% Federal AMT rate while 47% of Americans pay nothing. You see, I have no debt, no write offs, and no second or third home to declare. I understand that even my credit rating is just average because I pay all my bills on time. I started work at 12 as a paperboy and paid my own way through college and rose to a "Director" level based on my own effort. There is nothing that this government does for me that is worth 35% or $350K over the next 5 years. I don't believe the top 5% of earners were given what they have; actually 90% of the rich were born into middle class or poor families. They are hard driven workaholics with degrees and skill to match their pay.

In one lifetime, the country I was born into has completely changed into a socialist nightmare where we drive the wrong behavior. Here in lies the lesson for our President who doesn't believe in individualism and people who achieve. I'm tired of sharing my wealth. I do contribute over $10k per year to charities and am a Tocqueville Society member. Handouts don't work. They breed laziness but they do buy votes. Capitalism is the only social system that allows people to live in peace based on individual effort. I am hereby on strike from mediocrity, big government, EEOC quotas, welfare, Affirmative Action and political correctness. The inconvenient truth is that most people end up exactly where they belong in life.

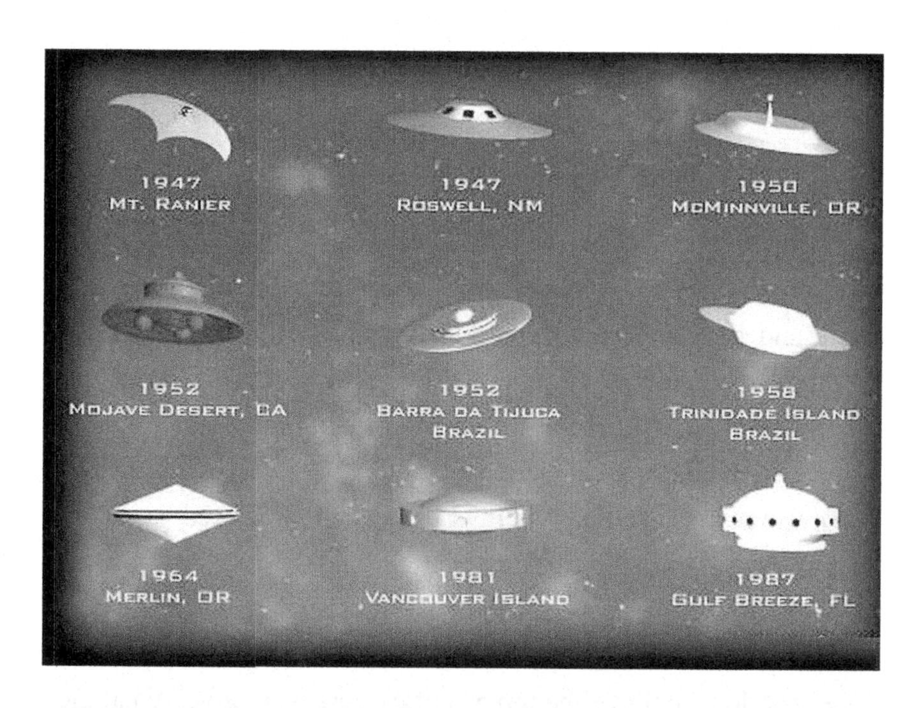
1947
MT. RANIER
1947
ROSWELL, NM
1950
MCMINNVILLE, OR
1952
MOJAVE DESERT, CA
1952
BARRA DA TIJUCA
BRAZIL
1958
TRINIDADE ISLAND
BRAZIL
1964
MERLIN, OR
1981
VANCOUVER ISLAND
1987
GULF BREEZE, FL

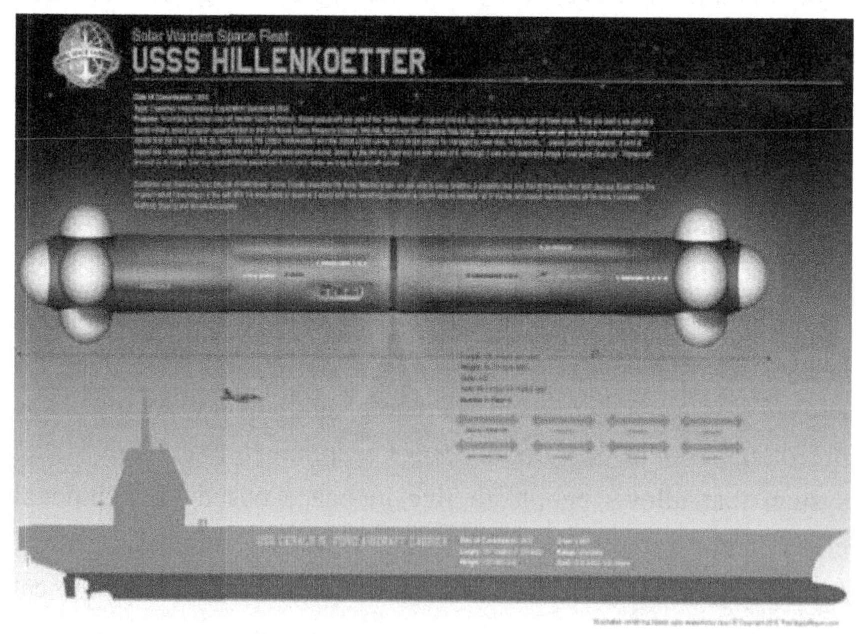
Solar Warden Space Fleet
USSS HILLENKOETTER

Chapter 10

THE OTHER SPACE PROGRAM

We've all read recently that NASA has shut down the shuttle program and SETI, the search for extraterrestrial life, has also shut down due to funding. The truth is that NASA and SETI were always the public view while the Air Force has had its own space program since 1982 with a budget that exceeds NASA. The Air Force Space program receives nearly $9B a year in funding and currently flies the X-37 which is a smaller unmanned version of the space shuttle. They also secretly fly the delta shaped TR-3B which has been seen extensively over Pa the past 3 years. As for SETI, why were they searching for radio waves from a distant galaxy when the Mutual UFO Network has already proven that "They" are already here? When the President asked NASA for a bolder plan for the future, he already knew we have the next generation technology already in use and that is what we will see in the near future.

A July 12, 2012 Huffington Post article by Darren Perks said that the "Other Space Program" was actually called "Solar Warden" and Darren confirmed it with a FOIA. He was told by NASA that the program was cancelled but did exist. Gary McKinnon hacked into information that described its present existence with a fleet of eight 600 foot craft and 43 scout craft and at least 300 personnel assigned. Cancelled or hidden? President Reagan's 1985 diary said we have a space capacity of 300 crew members. You decide.

The scary part is that the government does not have our best interests at heart and if necessary, will leave us behind and start humanity all over again elsewhere. . . . .

TR-3B Pattern filings:

Cited Patent	Filing date	Publication date	Applicant	Title
US3675879 *	Sep 2, 1969	Jul 11, 1972	Fuchs Harry B	Method and means for creating artificial gravity in spacecraft
US5269482 *	Sep 30, 1991	Dec 14, 1993	Shearing Ernest J	Protective enclosure apparatus for magnetic propulsion space vehicle
US6974110 *	Dec 27, 2002	Dec 13, 2005	Peter Grandics	Method and apparatus for converting electrostatic potential energy
US20030209635 *	May 9, 2002	Nov 13, 2003	St. Clair John Quincy	Electric dipole moment propulsion system
US20030209637 *	May 9, 2002	Nov 13, 2003	St. Clair John Quincy	Rotating electrostatic propulsion system
US20060038081 *	Aug 4, 2004	Feb 23, 2006	St Clair John Q	Electric dipole spacecraft

Chapter 11
Nazi UFO

The subject of Nazi involvement and preoccupation with UFOs is something I've learned about recently and I find intriguing. As the legend goes, a UFO crashed in the Black Forest in 1937 near Freiberg Germany and it was taken to Himmler in Westphalia and attempts to reverse engineer it took place. These attempts lead to the Vril project, which created the Haunebu series of three different prototype antigravity craft. They were small disc's that were hard to maneuver.

In 1938, Hitler sent his SS agents to Antarctica, Argentina and Chile to search for the Vril-ya and purchase a swatch of land as a fallback plan for WWII. Hitler was heavily involved in the occult, astrology and ancient relics and interacted with the Vril and Thule societies. The Thule Society was founded in 1918 and focused on the origins of the Aryan race. The Vril Society was founded in 1921 by a group of female psychic mediums and was led by Maria Orsic. Maria claimed to have met with Aryan aliens from the Aldebaran space system who claim to have settled ancient Samaria. Maria also claimed to be able to channel information on constructing an anti-gravity craft and was in communication with Hitler. The Thule and Vril Societies received official state backing from Hitler in 1933 and in 1942 fell under the authority of the SS. In 1938 Hitler also started his research into the "Bell" project in Czechoslovakia. Testing at this site killed five scientists and all depleted chlorophyll in plant life. In 1945 Hitler ordered the killing of 62 scientists, engineers and prisoners that worked at the site.

In 1929, Admiral Byrd was the first person to fly over Antarctica and map it. In 1938 retired Admiral Byrd was invited to Hamburg Germany to tell of his Antarctica exploits. Hitler then laid his plans for "Neu-Schwabenland" or New Germany in Antarctica. The Germans proceeded to map the continent from the air and discovered areas free of ice, warm water lakes and numerous cave openings. One ice cave extended 30 miles into a geothermal lake. Hitler believed this would lead to contact with the Vril-ya race and started construction of underground bases. A second base was built in the Argentinean Andes. The Germans built eight large cargo submarines that were used to transport construction materials to Antarctica. These eight subs were never located after WWII. Also gone were 100 German U-boats. Two U-boats, 530 and 977, were captured carrying 96 barrels of red mercury, which is used for antigravity experiments, and members of their antigravity-disk research and development team. Juan Peron of Argentina also issued 1000 patterns to Nazi scientists.

The Germans were on the verge of fantastic discoveries with the Vril Series V-7 in 1945 and needed a few more months to extend the war but obviously lost. The Russians and Americans were then in a race to acquire the German technology. The Americans formed Operation Paperclip where 2000 German scientists, engineers and Officers were interviewed in Alexandria Va. at a location called POB 1142 and then given immunity and homes and salaries to work for the U.S. Military and NASA. Wernher von Braun was the most famous of these scientists.

Hans Kammler was in charge of these special projects and he loaded his JU390 large transport plane with many special project plans and took off at the end of WWII. This plane was capable of flying 6000 miles without refueling. Many believe he turned over his findings to the U.S. in exchange for immunity since he was never tried or mentioned in the Nuremburg trials.

In August 1946, Navy Secretary James Forrestal initiated Operation High Jump, which in December sent Admiral Byrd, 13 vessels including the aircraft carrier USS Philippine and 4700 troops to Antarctica for a 6-8 month mission that lasted just two months. In March of 1947, Admiral Byrd was quoted in the Chile *El Murcurio* newspaper as saying to Lee van Atta that in case of a new war, the continental U.S. would be attacked by flying objects which could fly from pole to pole at incredible speeds. Many believe that Admiral Byrd's mission was turned back prematurely by these same craft. Interestingly this Antarctic location falls directly on the South Magnetic Pole.

In 1957, Australians discovered a 16mm film of the German V-7 project. It showed an operational disc craft. The Antarctic Treaty is signed where no military operations in the Antarctic would be allowed until the year 2000. In 2003, seismic activity at Lake Vostok indicated military activity.

Some people believe the modern UFO phenomena are actually Nazi craft from this time period or have been upgraded by the Americans and there are no ETs. Were the Nordic's just a spin on the Aryan race and who created the legend; man or alien?

War Department
Bureau of Public Relations
Press Branch
Tel. RE 6500
Brs. 3425 and 4860

October 1, 1945

IMMEDIATE RELEASE

OUTSTANDING GERMAN SCIENTISTS BEING BROUGHT TO U.S.

The Secretary of War has approved a project whereby certain understanding German scientists and technicians are being brought to this country to ensure that we take full advantage of those significant developments which are deemed vital to our national security.

Interrogation and examination of documents, equipments and facilities in the aggregate are but one means of exploiting German progress in science and technology. In order that this country may benefit fully from this resource a number of carefully selected scientists and technologists are being brought to the United States on a voluntary basis. These individuals have been chosen from those fields where German progress is of significant importance to us and in which these specialists have played a dominant role.

Throughout their temporary stay in the United States these German scientists and technical experts will be under the supervision of the War Department but will be utilized for appropriate military projects of the Army and Navy.

END

DISTRIBUTION: Ao, Af, B, Da, Dd, Do, N,
4:30 P.M.

Chapter 12

MILITARY UFO OFFICERS

A few months ago I put a request in the Journal for anyone who was or knew someone that served as a UFO Officer in the military in the 1940's or 50's. I received two replies.

Jerry Severs, a former MUFON Indiana State Dir., called me and confirmed that the Air Force had a UFO Officer at every base. He said that he had a retired friend in Air Force Intelligence with a high clearance as a Russian translator (no, it's not James Carrion) who told him 20 years ago that there were personnel assigned to UFOs. They both had a mutual interest in UFOs and would often discuss them. This individual joined during Korea and also served in Europe, Antarctica and Alaska and has since passed away.

Jack Clicks, a New York MUFON subscriber, also called me and said he had a friend that confirmed there were UFO Officers.

We also discussed the USS FDR in 1956-58 that had an X Division UFO Officer assigned. We also discussed a 1952 ship that encountered UFOs and a 1958 60 ton carrier off of Spring Florida that struck a possible USO that rocked the large vessel and snapped a 27 foot propeller. Jack tried to contact his military friend at my request but this individual got angry and did not want to discuss UFOs anymore.

Audio tapes from the October 7 1965 UFO over Edwards AFB say that the "UFO Officer was notified".

Chapter 13

The Robertson Panel

After the UFO wave of 1952, the government decided to create a policy and react to the situation. In the 1940's, our intelligence didn't know what they were dealing with regarding UFOs and that is why many sightings made front page news such as the Battle of LA, Roswell and the UFOs over DC. It was time for a coordinated response to calm the public.

"In 1953 the CIA formed the Robertson Panel. The Panel recommended a systematic debunking of flying saucers and Air Force Regulation 200-2 restricted the military from making public reports of UFOs. They went so far as to strongly recommend that teachers refrain from giving students credit for school work based on UFO books." (1)

The Robertson Panel was President Truman's last official act and it was held in secret and not revealed to the public until 1958. H.P. Robertson said, "That their job was to reduce public concern of UFOs." The CIA ordered a national debunking campaign, planting articles in magazines and arranging broadcasts to make UFO reports look like poppycock. They were ordered to hide sightings where possible. Make up something to kill the UFO report. Ridicule the witness and discredit their own pilots. (3)

The official title of the 24 page report was: "REPORT OF MEETINGS OF SCIENTIFIC ADVISORY PANEL ON UNIDENTIFIED FLYING OBJECTS CONVENED BY OFFICE OF SCIENTIFIC INTELLIGENCE, CIA". . . . . January 14-18, 1953.

They looked at 75 cases from 1951 and 1952. The Panel's concept of a broad educational program integrating efforts of all concerned agencies was that it should have two major aims: training and "debunking." (2)

The Panel recommends that the national security agencies take immediate steps to strip the Unidentified Flying Objects of the special status they have been given and the aura of mystery they have unfortunately acquired.

The "debunking" aim would result in reduction in public interest in "flying saucers" which today evokes a strong psychological reaction. This education could be accomplished by mass media such as television, motion pictures, and popular articles. Basis of such education would be actual case histories which had been puzzling at first but later explained.

The Panel concluded unanimously that there was no evidence of a direct threat to national security in the objects sighted. (2)

In 1966, trusted CBS news reporter Walter Cronkite hosted a CBS TV special organized by the CIA to debunk UFOs. The CIA proudly bragged about their efforts. Unfortunately, that's what the public remembered since they seem to believe everything they see on TV especially if said by a figure of authority. Project Blue Book concluded in late 1969 with the Condon report and concluded that UFOs were not a threat to our National Security and that the Air Force would no longer investigate them. It is interesting to note that the original 19 scientists on the Condon panel all resigned once they realized that the conclusion had already been reached before they even started. This effectively ended the era of UFO media and military "cooperation" with civilians in this country. Even though General Bolander went on to say that UFOs that were a threat to national security were not part of Project Blue Book and that the Air Force would continue to investigate those under

JANAP 146 and Air Force manual 55-11, this ended the UFO era for all intent and purpose with the media. It did give rise to the Mutual UFO Network to do the job that the Air Force claims they no longer do. (4)

The CIA sponsored Robertson Panel set policy for the next 60 years and beyond. They made the witness the enemy. I applaud those of you who have the fortitude to come forward because you know what you saw. The CIA policy has been so effective that the largest UFO conference with TV stars as speakers can only draw 400 attendees a day compared with 250,000 attendees at the San Diego Comicon. I can only imagine if the CIA had targeted comic books as the threat in 1953 there would be no Superman or Spiderman or X-Men movies. . . . . .

Sources:

1. Human Devolution by M Cremo- pg. 387
2. CUFON website
3. UFOs and the Nat'l Security State by R Dolan- pg. 122-130
4. UFOs over Pennsylvania by J Ventre

Chapter 14

JOE ROGAN FAILS TO INVESTIGATE

On August 21st, SyFy aired *Joe Rogan Investigates Everything.* This is a fun show similar to Chasing UFOs and is brought to us by Joe Rogan who is a comedian and by SyFy who specializes in Sharknado and Sharktopus shows. Rogan said he believes there is life in space but needs to see physical proof. He opened his show with the same line Anderson Cooper used last April when three witnesses and I appeared on his show. Rogan, like Cooper, would not accept any evidence as proof unless he could feel and touch a UFO or Alien.

I "Googled" Rogan and listened to three of his pod casts where he constantly related UFO witnesses to drug users and said all UFO cases occur at night so they must be dreams. Rogan also said that people live boring lives and UFO contact gives their lives importance. Rogan had his mind made up before he investigated. Rogan interviewed Bill Birnes, Stephen Bassett, Senator Gravel, Jason McClellan and a few experiencers. He failed to interview anyone from MUFON. If you were going to do an investigation, shouldn't you speak to the people who actually do the investigations? For many people, the UFO experience happens only one time. For others, it is a lifelong and generational experience.

Here is some evidence for Joe.

1. 1942- General George Marshall issued a memorandum that a saucer was recovered off the coast of California and that it was not earthly.

2. A July 18 1947 memo from Major General George MacDonald to J Edgar Hoover asks the FBI to get involved in UFO investigations.

3. The Sept 1947 Air Technical Intelligence Center report on flying saucers concluded that they are real.

4. Gordon Cooper saw multiple UFOs over his airbase in West Germany in 1951. He again saw photos of a landed UFO on May 3 1957 at Edwards AFB

5. On July 29 1952, President Truman issued an order to shoot down any UFO that couldn't be talked down. That same afternoon, the Air Force held a press conference and stated that UFOs were not a threat to national security.

6. A memo by Gen. Twining on July 14 1954 stated that UFOs are real. Capt. Ruppelt released the *Twining Memo*.

7. On June 16 1966, a UFO hovered over Whiteman AFB for two hours and shut down all 150 nuclear missiles.

8. On March 16 and 24 1967, a UFO shut down eight nuclear missiles at Malmstrom AFB.

9. In July 1967, a UFO started a launch sequence at Minot AFB.

10. Congressional hearings on UFOs were held on April 5 1966 and July 29 1968.

11. The Air Force taught a UFO class to its cadets from 1968-70 in a Physics 370 class (chapter 33).

12. November 1986- Japan Airlines flight 1628 over Alaska confirms a UFO by ground and air radar and is seen by pilots and confirmed by the FAA.

13. The FEMA approved Fire Officers Guide to Disaster control has a chapter (13) on UFOs.

These are just a few examples. I like Joe Rogan. He is intelligent and quick witted but he didn't do his due diligence and should stick to the UFC, not UFOs!

References

1. UFOs over Pa by John Ventre

(Courtesy L. Woodruff)

Chapter 15

LIFE BEYOND EARTH

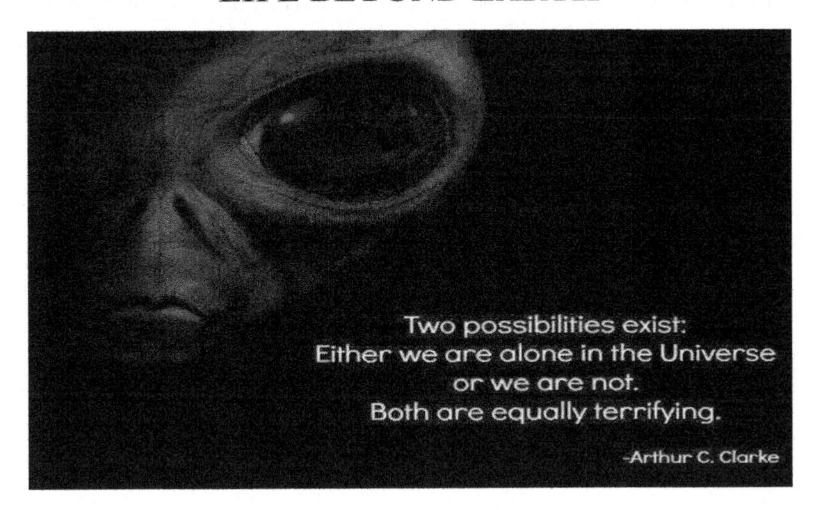

Two possibilities exist:
Either we are alone in the Universe
or we are not.
Both are equally terrifying.
-Arthur C. Clarke

In the Nov 5 article by the Associated Press entitled *Life beyond Earth just got more likely*, I was taken aback by the studies co-authors comment that "If we aren't alone then there is a deafening silence in our Galaxy". The article went on to say that the Milky Way Galaxy has 8.8 billion earth-like planets and has more habitable planets than humans living on earth. I find it amazing that main stream media and science ignores the over 10,000 UFO reports filed each year with organizations like the Mutual UFO Network. NASA, SETI and our Defense Department will concede that there has to be life in space but won't admit it is already here. Every Roper or AOL poll that I have seen reports that 14% of Americans have seen a UFO and 3% believe they have been abducted. That amounts to millions of witnesses or victims if they have experienced abduction. In the Tribune Reviews daily poll last week, six of seven respondents said they believe in UFOs.

MUFON has 75,000 UFO reports on file with pictures, video, radar, and sonar and witness testimony. This is the same type of evidence that would hold up in a court of law. I believe the more pertinent question is why won't our Government disclose the truth regarding UFOs? Is it about acquiring the technology or is there a more sinister explanation to "Their" motives on earth?

Chapter 16

WHY DO PRESIDENTS LIE?

He said he would stand with the Muslims against us.
That is the only promise he has ever kept.

Isn't honesty the best policy? Weren't you always told that you can't get in trouble if you tell the truth? In my lifetime there has been LBJ's Gulf of Tonkin lie that resulted in the death of 55,000 Americans and 4 million south east Asians, Nixon's Watergate, Carter's oil shortage, Reagan's Iran Contra, Clinton's Monica, Bush's WMD and now Obama's Mexican gun running, Benghazi, voter fraud, NSA monitoring, use of drones in our own country, giving 123 Technologies $300M right after it declared bankruptcy and was sold to the Chinese, arming the Muslim Brotherhood, IRS targeting conservatives, DOJ spying on the press, shaking down health insurance executives, giving Solyndra $500M 3 months before they declared bankruptcy and was sold to the Chinese, ordering the release of nearly 10,000 illegal immigrants from jails and prisons and falsely blaming the sequester, threatening to impose gun controls by Executive Order in order to bypass Congress while DHS purchases 1.6B hollow tip shells, the death of Seal Team 6, making a bad nuclear deal with Iran and lastly telling the public you can keep your doctor with the Affordable Care Act.

I truly believe this man and his bulldog faced bowl legged wife hate America. In 2008, I thought Obama was a left wing liberal Manchurian candidate who fit Jean Dixon's description of the anti-Christ. I was wrong. He has turned out to be a good American President (in reality, the worst President since Carter). Actually he has exceeded all past Presidents; in lies…unless Hillary gets elected in 2016. I hope the next President loves America and is nationalistic!

30 ROCKEFELLER PLAZA
NEW YORK, N.Y. 10112

ROOM 5600

(212) 649-5600

November 1, 1995

11-1-95
JHG.
Staff
Gohr

Dear Jack,

Attached are: (1) A draft letter to the President which Laurance has been discussing with Mrs. Clinton and her staff; and, (2) A draft report on the "best evidence" about UFOs.

Laurance thinks that it is perhaps timely to send a letter to the President. We think the "best evidence" report, although we haven't reviewed it in detail or analyzed it, is a good piece of work.

Laurance would like to discuss these items by telephone, perhaps on Thursday, November 2 between 11:30 and 12:30, if this is convenient for you.

Sincerely,

Henry (signed in absence)
Henry L. Diamond

Doctor John H. Gibbons
Assistant to the President for
Science and Technology
Old Executive Office Building
Room 424
Washington, D.C. 20500

Enclosures
Via Federal Express

(1995 memo that proves the Clintons met with Rockefeller)

Chapter 17

HOW IT IS DONE

I have a few anonymous benefactors who occasionally mail me UFO related documents. In September, this "friend" mailed me a five page article with a hand written note on it entitled "This is how it is done". I incorporated this information into the end of my "Do you Know, Should you Know" presentation at the Philly MUFON Conference in October. What I am about to relate to you is a true life scenario of how the government covers up the truth. It is very verifiable so please trust but verify what I tell you here.

I will paraphrase an article written by Richard Lardner of the Associated Press on July 8 2013 entitled "Pentagon secretly moved Bin Laden raid files to keep them from public".

"The top U.S. special operations commander, Adm. McRaven, ordered military files about the Navy Seal raid on Osama bin Laden's hideout to be purged from Defense Department computers and sent to the C.I.A. where they could be more easily shielded from the public. The secret move set off no alarms in the Obama administration even though it side stepped federal rules and the Freedom of Information Act. An acknowledgement by Adm. McRaven was also removed from the inspector general's report.

Secretly moving the records allowed the Pentagon to tell the Associated Press that it couldn't find any documents inside the Defense Department that AP had requested more than two years earlier and would represent a NEW strategy for the U.S. government to shield even its most sensitive activities from public scrutiny. "Welcome to the new shell game in place of open government". The C.I.A. has special authority to prevent the release of "operational files" in ways that can't be challenged in federal court.

The Defense Department told the AP in March 2012 that it could not locate any photographs or video taken during the raid or showing bin Laden's body. It also said it could not find any images of bin Laden's body on the U.S.S. Carl Vinson, the aircraft carrier from which he was buried at sea. The Pentagon also said it could not find any death certificate, autopsy report or results of DNA tests for bin Laden. It said it searched files at the Pentagon, Special Operations HQ and Navy command.

The Pentagon also refused to confirm or deny the existence of helicopter maintenance logs even though one of the stealth helicopters that carried the SEALs in Pakistan crashed during the mission and its wreck was left behind."

I think it would be safe to say that every human being on earth with a TV saw the CNN reports and read the news regarding the raid that killed bin Laden. There have also been Hollywood movies released yet the Defense Department and C.I.A have managed to expunge the evidence from the public. It no longer exists just like the Roswell and Kecksburg crash files. As a matter of fact, all are most likely filed in the same warehouse. If the C.I.A. and Defense Department can make the evidence for the most widely known assassination since President Kennedy disappear, it can make any UFO case evidence or investigator disappear also!

It wasn't until I spoke at an October conference that I also noticed a similar pattern by "G-Men" when they speak at conferences. Col Thomas McCabe, John Alexander, Antonio Paris and Storey Musgrave all said the same thing regarding UFOs. Their line is that there is life in space, which gets the UFO audience listening and less hostile, but that there is no way to travel the great distances. They also say that the government can't keep a secret and is grossly incompetent and we have no advanced technology beyond the 37 year old stealth fighter. Anderson Cooper used that same line on me last year when I appeared on his show. It caught my attention when McCabe, Paris and Alexander said the exact same thing at a conference in Maryland. It seems like they've been coached with this new strategy. I for one believe the C.I.A. and Defense Department are highly competent and the best in the world at what they do and this is how it is done.

Chapter 18

45 Years Ago-Casting a Symposium

I was asked by Jan Harzan to host our 45th Annual MUFON Symposium which will take place in Cherry Hill, NJ just outside of Philadelphia. Our first Symposium took place in Peoria Illinois on June 13, 1970 with the theme of "UFOs- an Unexplored Scientific Horizon". Our 2014 theme is "UFOs and the Media". I think this could be a Pandora's Box of interesting perspectives.

I'm a big fan of movies and have 600 DVD's at home. I've always found it interesting as to who was selected for a movie and why and I would enjoy watching the BIO channel for the inside scoop. For example, Anthony Quinn was originally cast as the

Godfather but Marlon Brando stole the role from him. So it is with casting our 45th annual Symposium. No one steals a spot but the selection process is interesting. So far we have:

George Knapp	Dinner Keynote:
	"Area 51- 25 years after Bob Lazar"
John Ventre	MC
Ben Hansen	"Media, Technology and Belief"
Bill Birnes	"UFO Hunters: Season One"
Dr Lynn Kitei	"After the Phoenix Lights"
James Fox	"UFO Film Making"
John Ventre	"UFOs and the Media"
Lee Spiegel	"UFOs- From Cave Walls to Modern Linda
	Reports to the United Nations and
	Internet"
Linda Moulton Howe	"Gobekli Tepe's 12,000-Year-Old Stone
	Circles Enigma"
Stanton Friedman	"Press Coverage of Flying Saucers a Study
	in Laziness"
Roger Marsh	"Covering UFOs"
Stephen Bassett	"Congressional UFO Disclosure"

I asked one speaker at a time to fill the openings. I had asked radio host Kevin Smith to speak. He agreed but unfortunately died of a heart attack at age 60 the week after we spoke. I issued Stanton Friedman's debate challenge to Dr Neil deGrasse Tyson but was told through his aide that Dr Tyson doesn't work on weekends and requires a $75,000 fee. I can see why he doesn't work on weekends. Jacques Vallee, Dan Ackroyd and Paul

Stonehill all declined due to other commitments. Art Bell said he is still trying to correct the Sirius mess on internet radio but doesn't really do conferences. Other speakers who didn't reply were: Michio Kaku, Daniel Sheehan, Derrick Pitts, M Night Shyamalan and James Callahan.

As you can see, it has been an interesting process. The last time the Symposium was on the east coast was in 1999. That was also my first Symposium due to the fact that I joined MUFON in 1998. Please plan on attending the Symposium July 17-20 2014 and sight-seeing in Philadelphia, the home of the Constitution, Liberty Bell, Boathouse Row, Franklin Institute, Mutter and Mummer Museums and Phillies baseball.

MUFON
EVOLVED
Mutual UFO Network
PRESENTS
HANGAR 1
THE UFO FILES
SERIES PREMIERE
FRIDAY FEB 28
10E 11P

UFO Network

Chapter 19

HOW WE SPENT OUR SUMMER INSIDE *HANGAR 1*

I kept a diary:

Nov 10, 2012:

While lecturing at a Metaphysical Conference in Pensacola Florida regarding End Time Prophecy, I receive an email from Frank Prather of Go-Go-Luckey Entertainment in Los Angeles California. He said I was one of a handful of people that they were considering for a MUFON based UFO TV show on the History Channel. He asked that I do a Skype call with him on Monday November 26 that will be taped and presented to the Producers. I had never applied to be on the show but Frank told me they saw me on the Anderson Cooper show a few months earlier in April and they wanted my "fire" on the show.

Dec 17, 2012:

I fly to Los Angeles and meet Jeremy Ray from Colorado MUFON. I know Jeremy from past Symposiums. We discuss the show and realize we know very few details. We are given a script to familiarize ourselves with regarding the Feb 1954 Eisenhower encounter with UFOs at Muroc (Edwards AFB).

Dec 18, 2012:

We meet our shuttle ride at 7:15 am and go to their sound stage in LA called "One Big Stage". The LA traffic is so congested that we arrive 40 minutes late for makeup. We meet the Executive Producer Paul Villadolid and the Producer/Director Bill Castonzo. Both are very professional and focused on their vision for the show. Makeup goes fairly quickly and Jeremy and I start our shoots. We average five takes on each line covering a three hour period. The teaser reel is scripted so there is not much ad-libbing. The three hours of shooting will probably boil down to three minutes of edited dialogue each. It appears the theme of the show is the Eisenhower opportunity to sign an agreement with the Nordic Aliens to exchange technology for our giving up our nuclear weapons. Eisenhower refuses to make the U.S. vulnerable to the Aliens or the Soviets. This theme of "what if" will run through season one. Alien influence on humanity will also be a theme regarding their interference at nuclear bases and power plants. Is it a test, toying with us, or a recharging of their energy needs?

The set is a warehouse with maps and files and monitors. There are three actors who portray MUFON investigators in this office situation. They are thumbing through records and looking at maps. I'm glad they selected three young attractive actors who will hopefully attract a younger crowd to the show. Elijah Howard is a black male, Jonathan Krebs is a Hispanic male and Taylor Murphy-Sinclair is a white female. The other person in the show is Jason McClellan from Open Minds magazine. Jason used to be a MUFON investigator. He portrays a radio personality. We did not meet him today since he completed his scenes over the first two days of filming. Both Jason and Jeremy are in their early thirties and I appear to be the only grizzled authoritative veteran in the show. I believe it is a good idea to target a younger audience.

We have time in between shoots to talk and Paul tells me the name of the show will be either *Alien Agenda* or *Hangar One* since MUFON HQ keeps its evidence and documents in Hangar One at Lunken Airport in Cincinnati. I suggest the *M-Files* as the title as a takeoff of the *X-Files* since the show is based around the MUFON Case files. I also suggest that the Nordic Aliens have solid blue eyes with no whites, no eye brows and an elongated skull. The Mayan, Dogan and other tribes that claim to have encountered Nordics say they had elongated skulls. These tribes also started the practice of strapping boards to their infant's heads to emulate the Nordics.

Jeremy and I leave the sound stage around 4 pm and are told that this demo episode will be sent to History Channel at the end of January and we should get the OK to film six episodes starting in April and then fourteen more if the ratings are good.

April 25, 2013:

I received the following email from Paul Villadolid:

Hey guys,

Congratulations on H2's series pick-up of our MUFON show! And thank you for your contributions to the tape! I'm finally able to share this with you.

Besides the two of you, I've only shared this with Dave and Clifford Clift, so please follow Dave's lead and don't share this link with anyone else. Also, when you watch this, please keep in mind that for this pilot we didn't have the resources or manpower to conduct comprehensive research on your archives, so some of the case files cited is made up, as are some of the references to MUFON research. Also, the way that some of the storylines unfold reflect specific instructions and notes that we received from History. For instance, they asked us to add the character of the electrician, who represents a homegrown conspiracy theorist. Finally, this tape was just a sales tool and is not intended for air.

Thanks again for your help and excellent interviews! I'm looking forward to a long, successful series with MUFON!

September 11 2013:

I receive my itinerary to fly to Los Angeles and film eight episodes. I'm told Dave MacDonald has been replaced by Jan Harzan who is now the MUFON Executive Director; Conrad Holden and John Greenewald will not be in the show either. John Schuessler will replace them.

September 13, 2013:

I receive the scripts for the first eight episodes and they total 200 pages. Wow, I hope there is a teleprompter for my lines. I notice that John Schuessler is not in the show but many big names in the field are; Michio Kaku, Richard Dolan, Leslie Kean, John Callahan and Grant Cameron. It looks like Michael Schratt has taken John's place in the show. I send Paul a list of documents that should be included in the show including the 1963 Kennedy UFO memo. The first eight episodes are entitled:

1. Space Weapons
2. Secret Underground Bases
3. American Hotspots
4. Crashes, Landings and Cover-ups
5. Unfriendly Skies
6. Shadow Government
7. Presidential Encounters
8. Alien Technology

September 18, 2013:

I leave the Holiday Inn Express at 7:45 am and I arrive at the studio at 8:30 am and we start filming after make-up at 9:15 am. I meet the new Co-Producer, Doug Segal who produced City of Angels, Three Kings and Bullet Proof Monk. It seems like nearly everyone who filmed the pilot in December has been replaced except for Paul, Jeremy, Jason and I. The new extras who portray MUFON investigators are actors Katie Eichler, Mark Kingsley and Nik Petkov.

This is the most grueling day of my life as we film my lines for seven episodes over the next thirteen hours. I was absolutely exhausted after filming the first three episodes but the dinner break seemed to revive me. There were times when my brain didn't want to cooperate as I was asked to recite whole paragraphs back for the camera. There are no Teleprompters and everything is done by repetition and memory. It doesn't appear that they received the budget that they had expected and corners are being cut and too much filming was being done in order to save cost.

September 19, 2013:

I return to film the last episode and do still shots and file footage in the warehouse reviewing old case files. Paul tells me I got the role on this show due to my appearance on the Anderson Cooper show and he wants me to show that same fire and anger that I did with Anderson and the skeptic. I ask Paul why we are not being paid per episode like he originally said. He replies that History didn't give them the budget they wanted.

For all the MUFON haters, nay-sayers and conspiracy theorists, this show clearly pits MUFON against the U.S. government cover-up of UFOs.

Feb 8, 2014:

On a MUFON Board Meeting call, Producer Paul Villadolid announced that the *Hangar 1* show will air Friday Feb 28 at 10 pm. It will air between *Ancient Aliens* and *America Unearthed* which are History's top two rated shows. TV ads should start this weekend. Paul said that the format of the show changed three times over the last year at History's request. Originally, Paul flew around the country and filmed with MUFON Investigators but that format was scrapped. History is already planning season two and a possible spinoff. Paul said it was important that MUFONs brand and reputation were protected. History chose the people that will appear on a regular basis and the demographics of the audience were males between 18-54 years old. Paul said the first season was done on a budget approximately half of what he was expecting.

Feb 2014 MUFON Journal article:

"As you know, MUFON Board member Debbie Ziegelmeyer and I research and write the historic anniversary cases that you have been reading entitled "Looking Back". In a season where every network has a UFO show, History Channels new show on H2 is set apart. What makes it different than the others is it is based on the actual files of the Mutual UFO Network. MUFON has been around since 1969 when the Air Force closed Project Blue Book and concluded that UFOs were not a threat or worthy of investigation. MUFON conducts the investigations that the Air Force claims it doesn't.

In the area of cinema, 60 years ago was the release of the movie *War of the Worlds*. This is actually a significant movie since the Brookings Institute and our Government based its policy regarding UFOs on the panic that followed the original Orson Wells Panic Broadcast on radio in 1938. The policies regarding the implications of extraterrestrial contact are that we cannot tell the public the truth regarding ETs out of fear of riots and a breakdown of the religious and scientific communities. My guess is that it has more to do with the control of technology.

Twenty years ago, we had another cinematic anniversary with the pilot of the TV show, the *X-Files*. This show featured two FBI agents investigating bizarre events with an underlying conspiracy as one agent was a believer and the other a semi skeptic. The *X-Files* also influenced a generation of baby boomers as did *Star Trek* almost 30 years prior to the *X-Files*. In the UFO genre, it appears that a classic show comes around every 20-30 years. We now have the MUFON based TV series on History channel's H2 station entitled *Hangar 1* premiering on February 28 2014. *Hangar 1* may eventually replace *Ancient Aliens* which has run from 2009-2015 which replaced UFO Hunters which ran from 2007-2009 which replaced UFO Files which ran from 2005-2007.

The cast includes Jan Harzan, John Ventre and Jeremy Ray of MUFON and Jason McClellan of Open Minds radio along with other cameo cast members including Richard Dolan, Grant Cameron, Leslie Kean and Michael Schratt.

The premise of each show is to piece together three MUFON cases that tie in to historic UFO events and try to show what the alien agenda may be. Actual footage, recreations and narratives will be used along with expert testimony. The *Hangar 1* title comes from the actual Hangar 1 where the vast archive of 75,000 MUFON cases and evidence are stored including the Leonard Stringfield files. The show clearly pits MUFON against the U.S. government cover-up of UFOs.

Ventre drives a black SUV with a "MUFON 1" license plate. If you see it in your neighborhood, you'll know the MUFON hunters are in your area. Most summers are spent vacationing and tending to the lawn or backyard barbeques. Our summer was spent researching the archives and filming the first eight episodes in Los Angeles. Stay tuned because the "truth is out there" or shall I say, it's actually in *Hangar 1*.

March 4, 2014:

The ratings are in and *Hangar1* did well:

TV Recaps reports *Hangar 1* as 25th ranked; 0.634 is in millions of viewers. Rating .18 is for ages 18-49.

August 9, 2014

I decide to fly to California two days early and spend the w/e in San Diego. What a beautiful city with so much to do. It's one of the best kept secrets for a travel destination.

August 11, 2014

We have a new warehouse set to film in. MUFON has moved its headquarters to L.A. I arrive on set at 2 pm and don't start filming until 6 pm. After 2 hours of filming, they realize there is a camera problem and the 2 episodes I filmed didn't take. They have to be redone. I bring 3 suites, 5 shirts and a vest for filming per instructions but am told that again, I will wear one outfit for all ten episodes that I'm in. This time, wardrobe decides to put me in a light grey suit with a pink shirt.

August 12, 2014

Our Uber driver has the wrong location and Cassidy O'Connor and I arrive 45 minutes late. We can't get the teleprompter to work on Paul V's laptop so we try it on his IPad but it crashes half way through the script. Filming gets delayed almost two hours and we officially start at 11 am and do all 10 episodes in 10 hours. Last year it took 18 hours to film my 8 episodes over two days. I'd say I had about 2/3 less lines this year.

I have a drink with Mike Bara and he tells me what he got paid per shoot with *Ancient Aliens* which is in line with what H1 pays. He was sure that Giorgio and David Childress were paid much higher. I was surprised when Mike said *Hanger 1* had a much larger film crew and staff and that the meals were better. He said Prometheus really skimped on everything with *Ancient Aliens*.

August 13, 2014

Last day of filming for me; no lines, just hallway and warehouse shots looking at files. It doesn't appear any of my script suggestions were used since they sent me the scripts days before shooting started.

Paul tells me that we added seven Hosts and five episodes to this season. It doesn't appear from the scripts that Jason McClellan of Open Minds made the cut. MUFON wanted more of their own members in the show.

I waited all day to film and got into 30 seconds of "B-roll" filming in the warehouse. They had me planned for other shots but decided not to pay the camera crew overtime or reschedule my flight so my scenes will be given to someone else.

After note:

I wrote the article for the MUFON Journal before the show aired. There have been many changes along the way. The characters and the format changed. Producers never really want to tell you anything that might get out. Season two was delayed twice as they moved the show from H2 to History. Season two started with 865,000 viewers for the first two episodes and ended with a high of 1.55 million but with two thirds of the viewer's being males over 50. The advertisers want the 18-49 viewers for ads. The show reflects our membership and conference attendance demographics.

For those of you who think there is money in UFOs, I only got paid $800 for 20 episodes. One could say that the History Channel really took advantage. The show moved from the small H2 channel to the large History Channel and was dubbed and aired all over the world with re-runs. I get friended on Facebook from all over the world. The CEO of the GoGo Luckey Production Company, Henry Capanna, drives a Lamborghini and we get paid chump change. I guess that's better than the zero I was paid by Discovery Science for three episodes of Close Encounters and then they didn't even list it on IMDb so I could update my profile. My biggest disappointment with season two of H1 was having so many non Mufon co-hosts. Dwight Equitz became the face of *Hangar 1* because he is the co-producers sons Boy Scout troop leader and has acting experience. Who knows where they found Brian Mathieson?

Season three rumors are that Go-Go-Luckey got sold and the History Channel is reorganizing and may eliminate the H2 channel or change its name to *Viceland* with different programing. We're waiting on the go ahead for season three and hopefully Paul Villadolid remains as Executive Producer and we change the shows name to the *M-Files.* If not with History Channel, we will sell the concept to a different network. Did History string us along until the contract expired so we couldn't make a quick move to another network and would lose a season? I was so certain that our factual show would replace the made up *Ancient Alien* series with its scripted lines from *Fakespear*. Shame, the truth didn't prevail with the public. . . . Yet!

On the set for season 1

If SETI got their own TV series, every episode would be the same with them sitting around doing nothing and listening to nothing. They might as well be searching space for the best Chinese restaurant . . . . .

In July of 2014, I decided to attend a social gathering at the Fox Chapel Yacht Club in Pittsburgh. The Producer of Pittsburgh Community TV, Carl Cimini, is there and approaches me with his idea to do a UFO talk show. I told him I was thinking the same thing and we decided to move forward. I decide to name the series, *UFOs over Pittsburgh* which is in line with my book, *UFOs over Pennsylvania* and a take-off of the first TV series I appeared in-in 2008, *UFOs over Earth*. We film two episodes a month and our first episode was recorded on October 9, 2014. I asked WV MUFON State Director Fred Saluga to co-host with me. I also write each episode and really enjoy doing this. In 2017 after 54 episodes, I converted the show to my entertainment group called the *String Theory of the Unexplained* and I air these episodes on zoharstargatetv.com.

Here is an outline of the first episode:

EPISODE 1: 10am Oct 9, 2014

Intro- "Welcome to UFOs over Pittsburgh. I'm your host John Ventre. I'm the Pa State Dir of the Mutual UFO Network.

Our guests are Fred Saluga who is the WV State MUFON Dir and W-Pa regional Dir and George Doc Medich who heads up our Abduction Research team for Pa. George is a doctor and former pitcher for the Pirates".

1. Show 4 slides from PPT.
2. Fred reviews a case.
3. Medich discusses abductions.

That's our show for this week. Be sure to look for our next episode and visit www.mufonpa.com for more information.

Although each episode airs on PCTV21 they are also available on YouTube, Carl tells me the network wants to restart it on July 11, 2015 and re-run each episode three times a week. We have 32 episodes completed at this time and here is the press release:

Pittsburgh Community Television
1300 Western Avenue
Tel: (412) 322-7500
www.pctv21.org

News for Immediate Release
July 11, 2015

PCTV21 SERIES PREMIERE UFOS OVER PITTSBURGH

On Saturday, July 11th 2015, *UFOs over Pittsburgh* will take us on a journey exploring the cryptic world of paranormal phenomena. With UFOs and extraterrestrials as the primary subject matter, the show is a medium for professional discourse on topics and case files ranging from paranormal zoology to frontier science. The show is one of the many new shows in PCTV's coming fall lineup.

Each episode, John Ventre mediates discussion between paranormal experts, witnesses, and scholars from the interstate area. Ventre himself is the PA state director of the Mutual UFO Network (MUFON). In addition to authoring several books on the subject of UFOs, he has made previous television appearances on Discovery Network, History Channel, and Anderson Cooper.

Air Date: July 11, 2015.

PCTV has been Pittsburgh's only community access channel for over 30 years. PCTV21 allows all Pittsburgh residents to explore making media at their newly remodeled studio on the North Shore.

On May 13, 2017, I transitioned away from PCTV and started my own YouTube channel entitled ***Make Ufology Great Again*** for obvious reasons.

Chapter 20

Captain Ruppelt

Occasionally, I receive an email exclaiming how wonderful it was to live in the 1950's. It was the height of American success and know-how after WWII and it was the wonder years for America. As I was researching material for my new book, I decided to go back and read some classic UFO books from the 50's and 60's. I had always ignored these books because they were old news but I found myself immersed in the moment when UFOs were new-news. One important book was by Blue Book Director Captain Ruppelt. He wrote *The Report on UFOs* in 1956 and mysteriously added three new chapters in 1959. There is an extraordinary history to UFOs during this time period that pitted Captain Ruppelt, Admiral Hillenkoetter and Major Keyhoe's NICAP organization against the CIA and Air Force cover-up headed by Dr Condon. Eventually, Ruppelt and Hillenkoetter were turned leaving just an aging Major Keyhoe to fight for Congressional hearings similar to Stephen Bassett's current efforts.

Admiral Hillenkoetter was our first CIA Director but was also on the Board of NICAP with Major Keyhoe and asked for Congressional hearings on UFOs. Hillenkoetter dropped out of NICAP on the verge of Congressional hearings after having a meeting with the CIA. Ruppelt was the first Blue Book Director in 1952 but was also pro-UFO. He changed the name from flying saucers to UFOs. He supplied Major Keyhoe the 51 classified UFO documents he needed to write his book. He said the heat inversions from the 1952 UFOs over DC could not have caused the radar returns. He supplied the best UFO footage available for the 1956 United Artists UFO movie. He released the Twining memo and was asked to join the Board of NICAP in 1957. He seemed to be the opposite and equal reaction to J. Allen Hynek who was hired to match up UFO reports to natural phenomena and debunk UFOs. Ruppelt asked for a transfer out of Blue Book once he realized it was a cover-up. His transfer was denied and he resigned from the military. After writing his classic 1956 UFO book, while he was a civilian working for Northrup, he was pressured into adding three additional chapters to his books reprint in 1959 that basically said there was nothing to UFOs. Ruppelt, at age 37, suffered his second heart attack and died six months after debunking his own UFO book. Here are some quotes from *The Report on UFOs*.

"Project Blue Book was given the second highest Air Force security code. Unknowns consistently made up 20% of the sightings. By the end of 1947, the UFO security lid was down tight. Memo's indicated it was considered to be very serious. Every time a reporter went to interview a witness, an intelligence person had already been there. The Air Force report on the Mantell incident was weasel worded and the original evidence was damaged when microfilmed. UFOs are normally peaceful but some pilots got too inquisitive and the UFOs made ramming attacks. General Vandenberg rejected Project Signs "Estimate of the Situation" that concluded UFOs were interplanetary. Although the reports were getting better, there was a drastic change in official attitude which was hard to explain. I wondered if there wasn't a hidden reason and didn't want to be the front man to a big cover-up. The Pentagon decided that it was easier to say UFOs didn't exist and everyone felt better. Project Sign was too pro-UFO and everyone was replaced with Project Grudge whose name did have a significance. Grudge was intellectual Dark Ages. Every case would be solved on the premise that UFOs couldn't exist. I was told to report on the solved cases and not mention the unknowns. Newspapers were skeptical and conducted their own investigations. A 1950 nationwide poll showed 94% of the public believed in UFOs. Defense location UFO sightings were on the increase. The Air Force was taking UFO reports seriously in June of 1952 when many good reports were coming in from Korea and sightings were bunching up on the east coast over Virginia. Unknowns rose to 40%. The Washington DC sightings garnered more press than the Democratic Nat'l Convention. They were seen by civilians, airline and fighter pilots and radar. General Samford didn't have the answers but told us to enlist top ranking scientists. A good source told me that tower operators and pilots were convinced to change their stories. Temperature inversions were not strong enough to cause the radar sightings. The final proof came six days later over Michigan where a UFO on radar lock made a

180 degree turn and changed speeds from 200 to 1400 MPH and stayed just out of range of the F-94 jet yet the report wasn't believed and the frustration was pitiful to see. A group of intelligence officers were fighting hard to get the UFO recognized. Giving a final answer to the UFO question would be the most serious decision since the beginning of man. I was betting 5-3 in favor of the UFO. If UFOs weren't intelligently controlled then why were they always over important locations rather than the general population? An analysis of the motion of the UFOs proved that they were intelligently controlled. The Tremonton and Montana films were analyzed by the countries best photo labs and were true unknowns. In 1953, a panel of top scientists was convened and the best evidence was reviewed. They concluded that it was impossible for other planets to be inhabited so therefore UFOs can't exist. All evidence presented was circumstantial. The Pentagon decided that there would be no new publicity and another intelligence agency took over all investigations. In August of 1953, I turned my command over and walked out the door into civilian life. I am sure that within a few years there will be a proven answer."

Little did Captain Ruppelt realize that the "other intelligence agency that got involved" was actually the CIA and that his Robertson Panel had been orchestrated by them with the goal of debunking UFOs. Ruppelt did indeed become a pawn in a game of psychology. In 1959, Ruppelt added three chapters to his classic book and it was sad to read in Chapter 20 that he concluded that pilots and scientists did not make good witnesses and it isn't the UFOs that give us trouble, it is the people. There was no truth to the rumor that the Air Force conspired with the media to stamp out the UFO. Again Ruppelt had no idea that hundreds of media outlets had a working arrangement with the CIA. Ruppelt stated that Carl Jung was misquoted when Dr Jung said UFOs were real. The Air Force managed to get the unknowns down to 1% and there was not one shred of material evidence. Radar was unreliable as was the operators and Ruppelt concluded by stating that he was positive that UFOs didn't exist and they were a Space Age myth.

Not only did the Michigan UFO do a 180 turn but so did Captain Ruppelt. He died six months after debunking his own book and it is up to the reader to decide if the CIA or Air Force played a role in changing his mind. In my mind, Ruppelt's death goes in the same file with JFK, MLK and the host of other Ufologists that met an untimely death.

Reference:

1. The Report on UFOs by Edward J. Ruppelt.
2. An Alternative History of Mankind by John Ventre

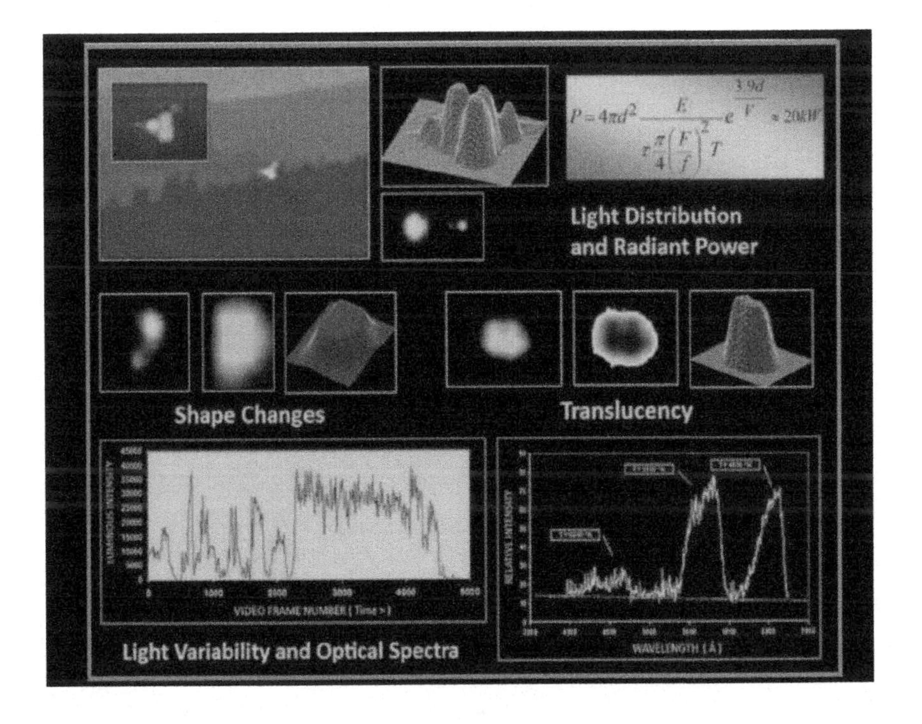

Chapter 21
Morris K. Jessup

After thoroughly enjoying Captain Ruppelt's book, *The Report on UFOs*, I moved on to read a strange book entitled *The Case for the UFO* by astronomer Morris K. Jessup who wrote four books from 1955-57 including *The UFO and the Bible.* I got my hands on the *Varo Edition* which adds to the strangeness of this book. Frank Edwards described this book as "The most unusual and comprehensive volume on the subject of flying saucers". Gray Barker wrote, "On the evening of April 20 1959, an astronomer committed suicide. His book, *The Case for the UFO* alienated him from his colleagues and had relatively few sales. The 1956 *Varo*

Annotated Edition represents a contribution to the literature of Ufology which began in 1947 with Kenneth Arnold".

In 1956, two naval officers informed Jessup that a man had annotated his book. The Navy decided to reprint this version for Naval Research in 1956 and copies were reprinted by the Varo Company of Texas which had a Navy contract. The annotated version contained notes by three "persons" in different color ink with unfamiliar terminology and alluded to the Philadelphia experiment of October 1943 involving the USS Eldridge, time travel, teleportation, and two species of "others" living here on earth and in space. Carlos Allende also wrote a series of three letters to Jessup from New Kensington, Pa discussing Einstein's Unified Field theory and the experiment on a navy destroyer that he witnessed. He went on to say that man is not ready for space flight and is too petty and jealous and materialistic. Although he thoroughly described the Philadelphia experiment, he told Jessup that if he was hypnotized and given truth serum, he could remember every detail including sailors names involved with the experiment. The return address on the letters led to an abandoned farm house in Pa. Allende disappeared but resurfaced in 1969 in Tucson Arizona where he gave affidavits to APRO stating that he witnessed the Philadelphia experiment.

In reading Jessup's book, he made the following statements:

"The world is full of unexplained oddities from ghosts to flying saucer reports that go back as far as 1500 BC. We have named these events paranormal but we have never explained them. We segregate these into two groups of physical and psychic. There are three major areas; things that fall from the sky, people and ships that disappear and observational data. There are megalithic works of stone that have been standing for ages prior to any written record where lifting engines of space ships were used. Indian and

Tibetan records indicate wingless flight took place 70,000 years ago. Moon lights have been seen and shadows cast on the moon and earth by something flying has also been observed. Gold chains and steel constructed objects have been found that date back 300,000 years. Archeological studies break down at approximately 7000 years ago and will topple the house of cards built by science. If the effort and money poured into rocket technology were instead spent on gravity propulsion, we would have space flight within a decade. Abundant observations by astronomers indicate UFOs between the earth and moon in the gravity neutral zone of 170,000 miles from earth. We see their small craft on exploratory missions and they have developed a source of power far superior to ours. It is not necessary to explain where they come from since they are part of our immediate family. They chose to stay in space after a cataclysm occurred here on earth. Something sudden terminated the work on Easter Island and Baalbek. All strange lights in the sky are from UFOs or their reflection and fireballs are their weapons. Could they be tending to us as sheep? Can we be owned? The comet of 1881 that erratically moved is verifiable proof of UFOs. Science and religion should have at least one thing in common; the truth. This book is a serious attempt to bring order out of chaos".

The annotated notes from the three "others" went on to say that, "One arrogant scientist's opinion can nullify what many had seen. There are remnants of cultures of unspeakable age. All science breaks down when confronted with the origin of man's intellectual development. Humans die due to gravities wear and tear. Rocket propulsion will never solve space travel. They have been here before the dawn of civilization. Man's ego is at stake. They will not allow humans to blow this planet up when it is the only one in a great distance which offers supplies and a haven for space travelers. The moon is a recent acquisition of earth. There are two distinct species that have come here and live in the ocean and in space. Water is a gravity neutralizer. They are small in stature with four fingers; one is good, one evil. The open seas are a natural home and provide an easy catching place of men and fish. Deep space is not for every man. Sailors can take the long voyage so they are kidnapped. A diseased person, once taken, may not be desirable and is dropped. Both species regard humans as valueless and destructive. Humans love to impose their will and make war. We learned not to war. The great temple building has not been equaled in twenty centuries. They went home after a war involving small asteroids as weapons. The remnants are under the sea. Humans must overcome their racial ego and free themselves of the idea that the space life here came from a planet. Round discs have always crossed the sun in great arks".

Many of the notes were hard to understand, misspelled or made no sense. Jessup went on to give numerous examples citing the missing crew of the Roanoke colony, Marie Celeste and Ourang Medan to a 1500 mile wide shadow that held its position on the moon for hours. Falling ice, rain deluges and frogs and fish from the sky indicates intelligence in space as mother-ship holding tanks are dumped and cleaned. Many of his sources of information came from Charles Fort and Ray Palmer's FATE magazine such as the Devils Footprint in Devon England. It would be easy to understand why the scientific community shunned Jessup's work. The Naval Research Office was obviously interested in the information leak of the Philadelphia experiment since this was the first time that it was exposed. Jessup may have been the first Ancient Alien theorist since he visited many of the ancient sites in Cuzco and Baalbek and around the world. As far as the question whether Morris K. Jessup was killed for what he knew or committed suicide, I have to side with suicide in this case. Jessup's realization that we may be “their cattle” surely preyed upon his mind. This entire field of research can cause someone to question our very existence and purpose. Yet no autopsy was performed even though it was Florida state law and the water soaked rags he stuffed around the carbon monoxide hose in his window from his car exhaust never revealed a bucket or bottles that contained the water that was used. His book was strange and he was taken in by everything Fortean.

References:

1. The Case for the UFO by Morris K. Jessup
2. An Alternative History of Mankind by John Ventre

Chapter 22

Frank Scully

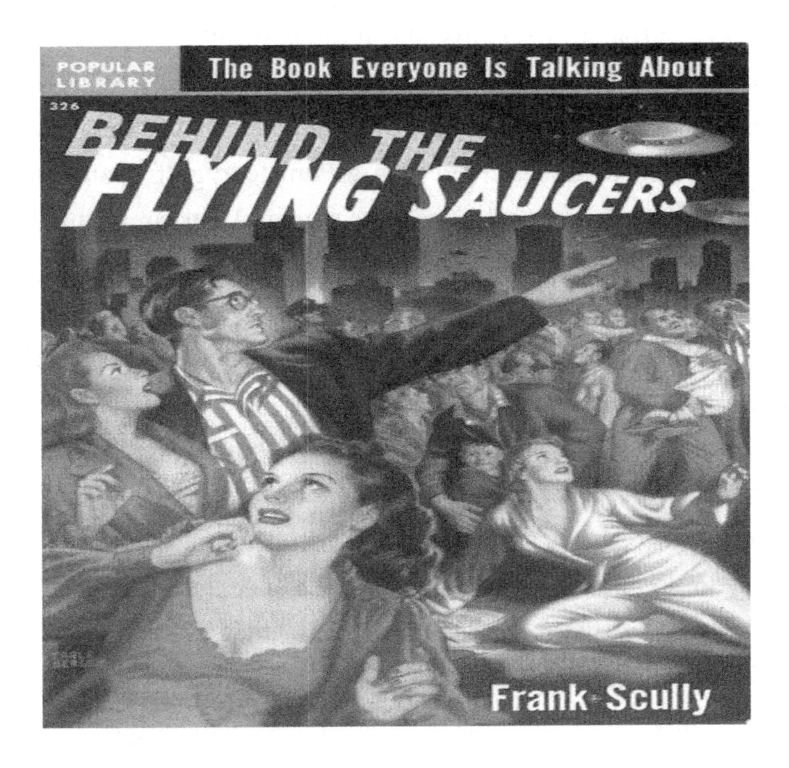

I picked up a copy of Frank Scully's *Behind the Flying Saucers* to add to my UFO book collection. I've always wondered if the Aztec New Mexico crash of 1948 was the real smoking gun since we supposedly recovered an intact craft and sixteen bodies as opposed to just fragments and debris eight months earlier in Roswell. I was unaware of the bazaar story written by Frank Scully who was a writer for *Variety*. Scully was a Hollywood writer with no interest in flying saucers. He received a tip from actress Linda Darnell that Silas Newton and Leo GeBauer had the facts on a saucer crash. Scully knew Newton and proceeded to write the first book on the subject which spoke about small men, only there were no witnesses or physical evidence.

Nick Redfern recently filed FOIA's on this case and unlike Roswell, received hundreds of pages. Redfern received 200 pages on Leo GeBauer, a scientist but the rest of his 400 page FBI file was marked classified for national security reasons. Silas Newton was a successful oil man who was involved with the Republican Party, donated to charities, was an amateur golf champion and Yale graduate and was described as a great American. Why did the FBI have a thick file on a wealthy oil man and a scientist? Newton was discovered by the FBI to be the source for Scully's book. Newton and GeBauer were later charged with being "Confidence Men" and Newton was ordered to pay $18,000 back to an oil investor. One has to ask why 31 investors were completely satisfied with working with Newton but only one complained even though all 32 were making money. Sounds like the FBI found one patsy to go after Newton's reputation. Hence the FBI files on both men and they were discredited because they were the source of information on the Aztec crash.

Scully wrote that there is a double standard whereby the military claims everything scientific is secret for security purposes but this secrecy breed's fear instead of security. Any man that has worked in "Intelligence" is a man that can no longer speak the truth. Scully planned to expose their tactics and had very little good to say about the Air Force and Pentagon in 1950.

Scully's book starts with a mysterious man giving a lecture at Denver University on March 8, 1950. This man gives a scientific lecture on a crashed saucer and fully describes the craft and its inhabitants. He said there were three recovered saucers of different sizes made of unknown metals that flew faster than the speed of light by using magnetic forces. The craft was so light that two men could lift it. A total of 34 human looking men standing three feet tall with peach fuzz hair and perfect teeth in uniforms with no insignia were recovered from the three craft. The thread on the uniforms took 450 pounds of weight to break. The craft carried no weapons, had no seams or rivets but did have porthole windows. The only way the military was able to enter the craft was through the porthole. Concentrated food wafers and heavy water were found. When mixed, the food overflowed from its container. The lecture created such a stir with the media that the FBI launched a manhunt to find this mystery speaker. Ten days later the skies over Farmington New Mexico were full of flying objects making right turns with no noise or vapor trails and witnessed by over 50 residents. It was later revealed that the mystery speaker was millionaire Silas M. Newton who was President of Newton Oil.

Scully had known Newton among Hollywood circles but was introduced to his partner, scientist Leo GeBauer. Dr Gee had worked for the government for seven years and was called in to examine the Aztec crash. Dr Gee specialized in magnetism and created the system by which we were able to identify Japanese subs by their magnetic signature during WWII. Dr Gee claimed that the craft were disassembled and many souvenirs were taken by Army and Air Force personnel. He had in his possession a small cigarette sized radio that had no tubes or wires or antennae. He also had some gears and film he shot but the film was damaged. Scully examined the radio and gears. Dr Gee said there was a time piece on the craft that used a 29 day magnetic calendar. He said the military had no knowledge of magnetic propulsion. Every object has a magnetic field which can be demagnetized and destroyed. The various colored lights in the sky from the saucers used the same principle as the Aurora Borealis which was a magnetic disturbance. At this same time, Project Saucer was shut down due to the conclusion that saucers were “hallucinations seen by psychos”. It was discovered that the Project ran four months longer than admitted to and that 34 of the 270 cases investigated were unknowns.

Scully believed that we were invested in jet technology and didn’t want to change to magnetic or gravity technology because a lot of careers and money were already tied up. He believed that many times these craft are beyond our range of vision similar to a planes propeller when spinning.

All of Scully’s evidence was just summarized for you in the above paragraphs. The rest of his book spoke about hoaxers, astronomers, magnetism, famous cases like the Thomas Mantell crash and George Gorman dogfight with a saucer. Mantell’s plane was demagnetized which disintegrated him and destroyed his craft. Gorman had a 27 minute dogfight with a craft over Fargo where the craft made right turns and were seen by witnesses in the Tower. Scully identifies Hynek as Joseph A. Hynek. Who knew the J. stood for Joseph? Scully spoke of many newspaper and magazine articles on saucers like the True magazine Major Keyhoe article where Keyhoe said we have been under observation by “Them” for 175 years, there were three types of craft and that “They” were 225 years ahead of our technology. It is interesting to note that Keyhoe’s 175 years in 1950 takes us back to 1775 or the birth of our nation. His 225 years takes us to 2175 when we would most certainly have this or better technology.

Scully went on to conclude that the visitors showed no belligerence unless attacked first. Why is our policy to shoot first? Why does our military say they don’t exist when everyone sees them? Someone is lying or ignorant or both! How did the opposing saucer races learn not to blow each other up? Why does the military get first crack at them when they are least equipped to handle delicate matters?

This was a well written book by a real writer who had very little evidence to go on. It's a little hard to believe that three craft with 34 human looking short ETs were recovered though. There were a few notes in his appendix worth looking into:

1. Jan 23 1950 Kansas City Times by Dick Williams. In 1941 in Appleton Wis., a 15 year old boy using his short wave radio came upon a magnetic frequency that shorted every motor vehicle in a three mile radius.
2. April 10 1950, LA Times. In Amarillo Texas, a 12 year old boy named David Lightfood touched a blue gray round object the size of a truck tire. It was warm and slick but then released a gas and took off burning David's arms and face causing welts.

Canadian scientist Wilbert Smith confirmed that in a meeting with Dr Robert Sarbacher in 1950, Sarbacher said that the Frank Scully book was correct and that UFOs are the top U.S. classified subject.

Scully was discredited when oilman Newton was charged with fraud but in June of 2017, *Ultra Top Secret* documents were leaked to *Midnight in the Desert* radio show host Heather Wade. The documents were authenticated by Stanton Friedman.

Chapter 23

1973

In 1973, I was 16 years old and busy playing sports, delivering my paper route and making super 8 Horror movies similar to the Steven Spielberg movie, *Super 8*. I had no idea there was a large UFO wave spreading across the country.

1973 ended with a UFO wave that started down south in Pascagoula, Mississippi and made its way north through Tennessee, West Virginia, and Ohio and across Pennsylvania ending in New Hampshire. NICAPs website describes the 1973 wave as, "Concentrated in the last half of the year and featured the largest number of humanoid occupant sightings in years. Several abductions were reported. The sightings peaked in mid-October with October 17 as perhaps the most extraordinary single day in UFO history." Many of the creatures were described as stocky strong mummy wrapped beings. Many of these cases were investigated by the Air Force who three years earlier stated that they would no longer investigate UFOs unless they were a threat to National Security. Even future President Jimmy Carter decided to file a UFO report with NICAP 4 years after his October 1969 Leary GA sighting with multiple witnesses.

On the evening of October 11, 1973, 42-year-old Charles Hickson and 19-year-old Calvin Parker were fishing off a pier on the west bank of the Pascagoula River in Mississippi. They heard a whizzing sound, saw two flashing blue lights, and reported that a domed, cigar-shaped aircraft, some 30 to 40 feet across and 8 to 10 feet high, suddenly appeared near them. The ship seemed to levitate about 2 feet above the ground.

On the ship, Hickson claimed that he was somehow levitated or hovered a few feet above the floor of the craft, and was examined by what looked like a large football-shaped mechanical eye, about 6 to 8 inches in diameter, that seemed to scan his body. Parker claimed that he could not recall what had happened to him inside the craft, although later, during sessions of hypnotic regression he offered some hazy details. The men were released after about 20 minutes and the creatures levitated them, with Hickson's feet dragging along the ground, back to their original positions on the river bank. Hickson did pass a polygraph while Parker declined to take one. (1)

On October 17, Falkville Alabama police Chief Jeff Greenshaw saw and photographed an alien in a reflective suit. The town's folk burned down his home and he was forced to resign. Greenshaw took the only photo of the 1973 wave. He has always contended that he told the truth and that government agents told him they tracked a UFO on radar.

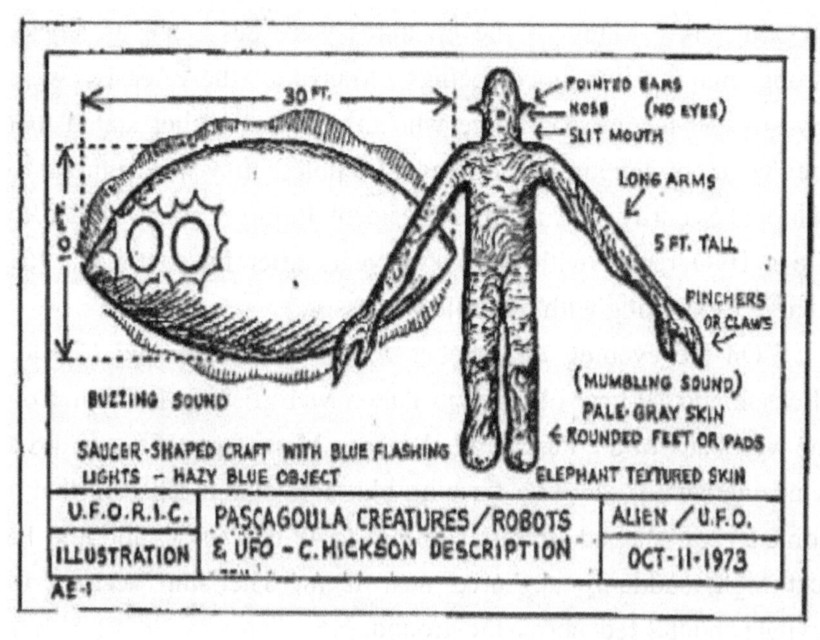

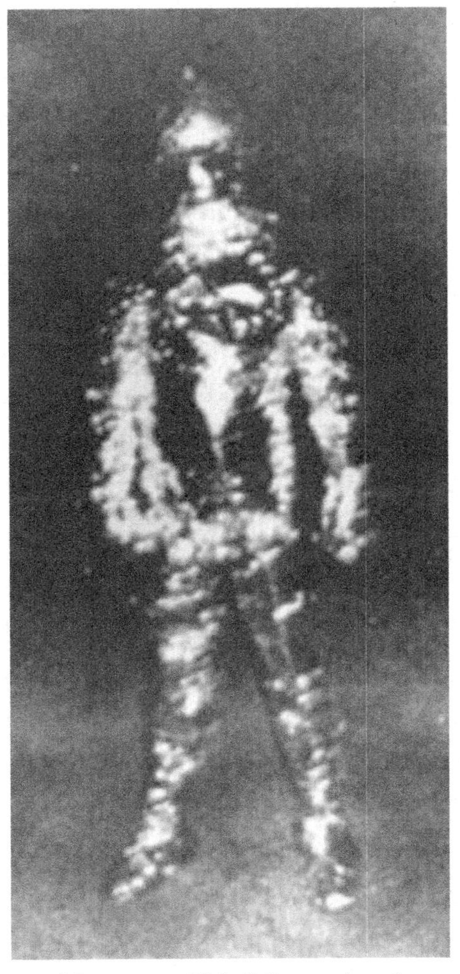

(Courtesy Chief Greenshaw)

"There was actually hundreds of UFO observations reported in Pennsylvania during the wave of 1973. It was a major outbreak for strange observations in the sky. Many of these sightings were not just of lights in the sky, but involved very close observations of what appeared to be solid constructed craft. There were sightings of various shaped and sized objects, including glowing spheres, as well as domed and cigar shaped objects. Additionally, there were reports of UFO landings, strange aerial objects hovering low off the ground, car chases, and detailed close encounters with strange craft". (2)

On the night of Oct 25th, a craft is seen landing near Uniontown Pa and hunters observe 2 eight foot tall creatures near it. They fire their rifles and hit one creature. The creatures disappear into the woods and the craft literally disappears. An arriving State Trooper at the scene reports that the ground is flowing in a 150 foot diameter. Investigators on the scene report animals won't enter the circle and they themselves feel nauseous and can't breathe due to a sulfur smell. One witness becomes delirious and starts howling. His dog tries to attack him but runs off when it enters the circle. The witness collapses and has visions of an apocalypse.

Philadelphia reporter Jerry Jonas writes, "Two of them were daughters of one of my close friends, who had what they described as a terrifying experience while attending a movie at the Roosevelt Drive-In Theater on Rt. 1 in Langhorne (where the Target shopping center now stands). According to their panicked descriptions to their father, and later to me, the girls insisted that they saw a large circular object with bright pulsating lights descend from the sky and hover in front of them. Other witnesses claimed to have seen a large V-shaped object hovering over, Morrisville Borough just a couple of miles north of the drive-in and across the Delaware River from Trenton, New Jersey. Some said they witnessed the same object over the U.S. Steel plant just a couple of miles to the east. Later that year, I learned that there seemed to be a great many individuals who had reported seeing that same V-shaped object in the skies over Lower Bucks County". (3)

This UFO wave seemed to coincide with the Nixon administration's response to the Middle East war and Soviet intervention by putting our nuclear forces on DEFCON 3. The

1973 wave seemed to signal the return of the UFO phenomena after a few sparse years. (4)

October 1973 events:

1. Oct 1, Tennessee- Three teens see an egg shaped UFO and hairy robotic creature. Landing imprints are found.
2. Oct 4, Simi Valley Cal- Triangular craft lands and humanoid creature spotted.
3. Oct 6, Quebec Can- Domed object lands with 5 creatures in yellow outfits.
4. Oct 11, Mississippi- Pascagoula abduction.
5. Oct 16, Burbank Cal- Being tries to coax a teenager aboard craft.
6. Oct 17, Lehi Utah- Pat Roach and 4 children are abducted. Report seeing neighbors on craft.
7. Oct 17, Berea Tenn. - UFO in woods; landing traces found.
8. Oct 17, Falkville Ala. - Jeff Greenhaw takes the only known photo of a being during this wave.
9. Oct 17, Danielsville GA- Paul Brown fires his pistol at 2 beings near cone shaped craft.
10. Oct 17, Loxley GA- Clarence Patterson and his truck are levitated into a large UFO.
11. Oct 18, Savannah GA- Small being spotted by side of highway. Susan Ramstead abducted as her car stalls and small beings take her aboard craft.
12. Oct 18, Mansfield Ohio- An army helicopter nearly hits a stationary UFO and is pulled and suspended by a green tractor beam.
13. Oct 19, Ashburn GA- Woman's car stalls and small creature approaches car.

14. Oct 19, Copeland NC- Blue oval craft spotted and small humanoid in gold colored clothing seen.
15. Oct 20- College student Leigh Proctor abducted for 4 days.
16. Oct 21, Coverdale OH- Grey humanoid and craft seen and ground traces found.
17. Oct 22, Indiana- Small creatures in silver outfits are seen by 4 witnesses in 3 separate incidents.
18. Oct 25- FBI Director Clarence Kelley denies the Agencies involvement in UFO investigations.
19. Oct 25, Uniontown Pa- Shots fired at aliens and trace evidence found.
20. Oct 31- U.S. and European forces are removed from DEFCON 3.

The 1973 wave seemed to end with 3 reports in Goffstown NH on Nov 1-4 where small beings were seen gathering soil samples. One woman was chased from her car and managed to run to a neighbor's house for safety. (5)

The 1973 wave was a departure from the norm. There were dozens of landing reports and occupant sightings. Abductions may have been the intent. There seemed to be a plan of harvesting samples and people who were abducted from their vehicles in remote locations. Female crew members were also reported. It appears that a single species of aliens were operating on earth with a limited time frame agenda to gather data and samples to be analyzed at a later time. What separates 1973 from other UFO waves was that there was a pattern and scientific purpose. The aliens had a short window to do their work and get out. (5)

Sources:

1. Wikipedia
2. UFOs over Pennsylvania; Chapter 1 by Stan Gordon
3. UFOs over Pennsylvania; Chapter 15 by Jerry Jonas
4. UFOs and the National Security State by Richard Dolan
5. Faces of the Visitors by Kevin Randle and Russ Estes

(Courtesy Getty Images)

Chapter 24

CITIZENS HEARING

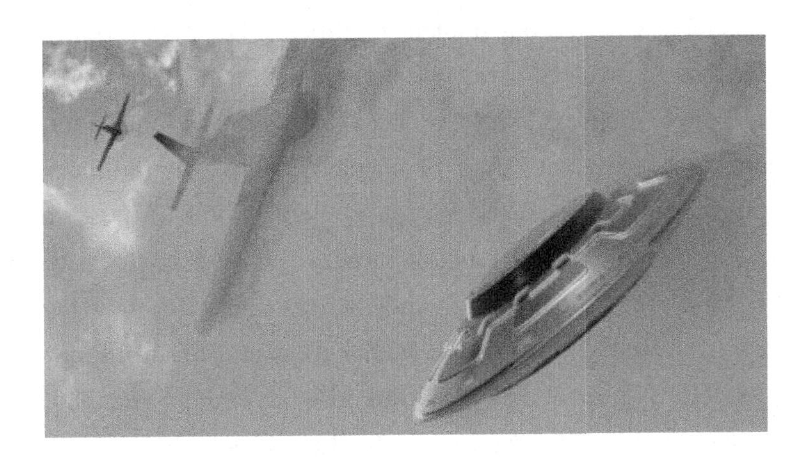

I was able to attend the first three days of Steven Bassett's Citizens Hearing on Disclosure at the National Press Club in Washington DC prior to having to leave for the Erie Pa MUFON Conference. This was the fourth such hearing held at the Press Club in the past 12 years. Let me first give you some history on the first three.

In the past decade, a group of distinguished witnesses gathered three times at the National Press Club in Washington DC and signed affidavits that they were willing to testify before Congress. In 2001 Dr Steven Greer organized 21 military, government and scientific witnesses that told their story. He also identified 350 additional witnesses that were willing to come forward. Their affidavit requested a Congressional inquiry and to utilize this new energy source for good and to stop the weaponization of space.

In 2007 Investigative Journalist Leslie Kean and Producer James Fox organized 19 witnesses; 13 pilots, 5 foreign Generals and former Arizona Governor Fife Symington who testified to what they saw regarding UFOs.

In 2010 Robert Hastings organized seven US Military officers and one enlisted man to testify at the National Press club that UFOs have violated our nuclear facilities. They also produced 120 additional signatures from witnesses on an affidavit that is being ignored by Congress. The Air Force response was that "There have been NO significant cases to warrant an investigation since the conclusion of Project Blue Book in 1969". Somehow they missed our Minuteman missiles being turned off at Malmstrom AFB in 1967 and 2007 even though they do not have a turn off switch. They also missed the same at Nellis AFB in 2003 in the presence of a UFO. Since Project Blue Book ended we have had Bentwaters, the Phoenix Lights, O'Hare airport, Stephenville, the Pennsylvania UFO wave in 2008 and a host of other sightings. CNN and the Tribune Review covered the National Press club story in a positive light. The Washington Post debunked and mocked the officers. (1)

The Citizen's Hearing in 2013 was facilitated by five former Congress-people; Carolyn Kilpatrick, Merrill Cook, Darlene Hooley, Roscoe Bartlett, Lynn Woolsey along with Senator Mike Gravel and Attorney Daniel Sheehan. Steven Bassett organized the hearings. The setting was a Congressional Hearing where all 38 speakers were sworn in and testimony was given and witnesses were questioned by the panel. Topics covered included UFO history, the Rockefeller Initiative, RAF Bentwaters, Nuclear bases, documents, Roswell, International cases, pilots and technology. What follows are quotes from the Hearing:

Congr. Bartlett- "The First Amendment gives the people the right to petition the government."

Dr Edgar Mitchell- "We are not alone. They have been here for a very long time. We need to be able to leave this planet because we are using up the natural resources. Astronaut Gordon Cooper saw a UFO at Edwards AFB."

Paul Hellyer- "We must regain the peoples trust. We are not alone."

Richard Dolan- "There have been hundreds of military and UFO encounters including recovery, injuries, radar and F-16's. President Truman was briefed quarterly on UFOs. MUFON and NUFORC get over 10,000 UFO reports per year."

Grant Cameron- "President Truman stated that UFOs were discussed at every conference. Gen Curtis LeMay refused Sen Barry Goldwater access to the UFO room at Wright Paterson AFB. In 1981, President Reagan stood up at the showing of Steven Spielberg's ET movie and announced that the movie was real."

Stanton Friedman- "We are being visited, it is covered up, there are no good arguments against UFOs, 5 independent studies show that UFOs are real. Project Blue Book did not include UFO cases that affected National Security."

Linda Moulton Howe- "Cattle mutilations are real and she was shown a document in 1983 at Kirkland AFB that was a briefing document on UAV's, the history of retrievals and that a 1949 captured EBE was reptile like."

The Congressional Committee acknowledged Rev Louis Farrakhan in the audience.

Sen Gravel- "It is the height of arrogance to think that we are alone. Why is this kept secret?"

Stanton Friedman- "There are military applications to the technology and some say there would be social chaos or that they are demonic and where would people's allegiance be if disclosed."

Linda Moulton Howe- "I believe some ETs are androids who have been here since the dinosaurs and they take DNA and we are their research project. Our detonating an atomic bomb got their attention and we became aware of them."

Congr. Cook- "Couldn't the sightings have been Nazi or Soviet technology?"

Dolan- "Only low level documents are available through FOIA, not top secret documents. UFOs are part of our history. We must have access to the documents"

Congr. Bartlett- "UFOs are not anti-biblical. Read the book of Job. There are plenty of pre 1940 cases. UFOs won't reveal themselves due to our violent behavior. How many cases of radar are there?"

Antonio Huneeus- "There were UN hearings on UFOs in 1978 and astronaut Gordon Cooper testified and asked for a policy on how we should or would interact with them. ET contact would unify the planet."

Daniel Sheehan- "Pres. Carter asked CIA Dir. Bush to brief him on UFOs. Bush refused to brief Carter since Carter was replacing Bush as CIA Dir. Sheehan was asked to get access to the Vatican library which was denied by the Vatican. Sheehan was given access to the classified documents of Project Blue Book and saw UFO pictures with strange symbols on them. The Vatican has since said that UFOs are not in conflict with religion. Congress is not in control of the information on UFOs. Disclosure must come from the religious community."

USAF Col French- "I worked on Project Blue Book and my job was to make up stories and debunk UFOs. We have shot UFOs down. I saw the Truman Majestic report in person."

Sen Gravel asked the speakers to draft a resolution that can be presented to the UN.

Steven Greer- "UFOs have been kept secret because the lie goes too deep and it has gone on too long. We have free antigravity propulsion and the oil industry keeps it silent."
Sheehan- "I was involved with the Iran-Contra and Karen Silkwood cases. There are levels of secrecy beyond Congress and classifications beyond what we know. There is a cosmic classification for UFOs and Pres. Gorbechev told him that UFOs are real. I believe ET's and our government is complicit in not wanting to be revealed."
Cameron- "The Roswell and Lawrence Rockefeller documents have gone missing from the General Accounting office. Hillary played a key role in UFO discussions with Rockefeller."
Congr. Bartlett- "Welfare, Education and Healthcare are not in the Constitution. We ignore the Constitution to do some good things. This can go wrong."
Greer- "We have zero point energy. This is about oil and military spending. Secrecy undermines our Democracy. The practical applications of this technology should be released; not the bomb making capabilities. Billions of dollars disappear into the Defense budget with no oversight. I have a memo where 5135 patents were confiscated for national security. The media won't cover UFOs since the CIA got involved with Disney and debunking in 1953. The internet is the new media. Congress and the courts have the power to get access."
Cameron- "All media of any consequence is controlled."
Steven Bassett- "The six year Rockefeller Initiative was ignored by the media. Hillary Clinton, Leon Panetta, Bill Richardson, and John Podesta were all ready to disclose UFOs."
Sen Gravel- "When good people do nothing, they endorse evil."
UK Det. Gary Heseltine reviewed 42 cases of police witnesses; most with multiple witnesses.

We viewed Steven Geer's Sirius film. The corpse involved is a male and six inches tall and lived up to eight years old. Testing shows that it is 91% human (chimps are 96% similar to us) and its mother is from Chile. It only has 10 ribs and an oversized skull. Since it is male, there is no mitochondrial DNA regarding its father. Only females carry our genetic history. A comment in the film also said that since gravity bends light it must move faster than the speed of light and so would antigravity propulsion.

Nick Pope- "Many of the files on Bentwaters have gone missing by the military. Sgts. Penniston and Burroughs are unable to obtain their medical records from the military."

The real question will be if these six retired politicians can convince Congress to again have hearings on UFOs. Although I found the proceedings to be very interesting and well done and the Hearing testimony would be an eye opener for the media and lay people, there were only 100 attendees in attendance to a free conference that was open to the public. There was also a live simulcast taking place on the internet. My point is who is winning the media battle for truth? If Kim Kardashian held a press conference there would be thousands in attendance. Until the people demand that the media asks the right questions, the CIA policy to debunk and ridicule as spelled out in 1953 at the Robertson Panel continues to win out.

References:

1. UFOs over Pennsylvania pg. 34.

Chapter 25

1983 Hudson Valley, NY UFO Wave

The Hudson Valley NY UFO wave actually started on Dec 31, 1982 with a sighting of a large triangular craft by a retired police officer. It culminated with 7046 reported sightings and 256 creature reports over a 13 year period. On March 26, 1983, the "wave" made the front page of the Westchester-Rockland Daily newspaper as hundreds of witnesses reported seeing a silent "V" shaped object with numerous lights on March 23, 1983. A hot-line was opened by Bob Pratt, Philip Imbrogno and J Allen Hynek which resulted in 300 more reports. The object was described as 300 feet in size, silent and had the ability to turn or rotate on a dime. It would cruise at 30 MPH and then take off at tremendous speeds. Witnesses said the object would block out the stars in the sky. This description is similar to the Phoenix Lights case in 1997.

In June of 1984, the craft was twice spotted over the Indian Point Nuclear reactor. There were a total of 18 security guards that saw the craft hover 30 feet from the reactor # 3 dome resulting in the security system shutting down. The guards were told to forget about the incident as false reports of Cessna pilots faking the UFO were circulated. A spokesperson for the Reactor did confirm that an object hovered over the reactor making it the first time a UFO was confirmed over a nuclear reactor.

Video from Bob Pozznoli was analyzed by ABC TV and the Jet Propulsion Labs in Pasadena and both confirmed that it was a solid object and not a group of Cessna's flying in formation. The Air Force received numerous reports and confirmed through Major

Andrews that they were aware of the sightings. Local police said that the FAA said to downplay the incidents.

J Allen Hynek wrote about the utter disregard by the media of a case where there are thousands of witnesses and the safety of a nuclear reactor may have been breached. This case is similar to the 1989 Belgium wave and falls in line with supposed reports of Project Solar Warden.

Chapter 26

Aliens from Space

In my continuing quest to understand our UFO history, I purchased a copy of Major Donald Keyhoe's 1974 book entitled, *Aliens from Space*. The first page of this book reads, "This book was written in defiance of the U.S. Air Force and CIA". I used that for the opening of this book. Keyhoe was a Marine Corp aviator and co-founder of NICAP. In 1958, during a CBS interview, Keyhoe stated that UFOs were under intelligent control and CBS stopped the show and pulled the live feed. Keyhoe was truly the most determined and influential Ufologist of his time period. Here is a compilation of quotes from Keyhoe's last book, *Aliens from Space*:

"The Air Force has full proof of the reality of UFOs but believes it is best for the country to deny their existence. The first fatal UFO chase involved Captain Thomas Mantell in 1948. On August 5 1948, the Air Force "Estimate of the Situation" was delivered to General Vandenberg who rejected it because it would cause a stampede. How could we convince the public they weren't hostile? Project Sign, which concluded that UFOs were real, was renamed Project Grudge and every UFO report was debunked by the Air Force. In 1954, commercial pilots were subject to the same espionage laws as military pilots that reported UFOs. In 1958, we launched bombers against Russia more than once due to misidentified UFOs. The AF (Air Force) then paid $523,000 to Colorado University in 1966 to conduct an unbiased probe of UFOs. The project leader, Dr Condon, immediately stated that there was nothing to UFOs and that the AF was wasting its time. He said teachers should not accept book reports from students on UFOs and if they do, they should be let go from their profession. His project Administrator, Robert Low, then issued a memo describing how to trick the public into believing that they were really investigating UFOs. The hope was that if President Nixon were elected, he would challenge the Condon conclusions since Nixon was a member of the House Committee on Un-American Activities that challenged Condon's security clearance."

Keyhoe goes on to name names and dates of the best UFO reports from his time period including the classified AF Project 10 report, the AF Academy analysis for cadets, and numerous NICAP and AF cases. "If an unfriendly country were to acquire this knowledge then they would be master of the world and could determine the survival of the U.S. If the U.S. were first to build an armed UFO force, then it would mean freedom from war for an indefinite period. At least five other nations were engaged in this battle for UFO technology. It appears the aliens are peaceful but can defend themselves. There are not enough UFOs here to launch a full scale attack on us and they repeatedly avoid harming humans. UFOs are not invulnerable and have crashed or been crippled. In 1963, a naval surface to air missile scored a direct hit on a UFO. In 1964, seven aerospace companies had top secret anti-gravity projects in place; Bell, Boeing, Convair, Douglas, Hughes, Lockheed and Martin".

Keyhoe wondered if our broadcasts were being monitored by "Them" and in 1963 the Department of Justice was asked if killing an alien would be considered murder. The reply was that it would be classified as cruelty to animals or disorderly conduct. Other scientists speculated that we would establish large colonies on other planets even if they were already inhabited. What if they heard that? What do they think of our news casts describing murders and hijackings and TV shows like Bewitched and I Dream of Jeannie? What of our constant wars? Would they fully understand and recognize humor and satire?

Keyhoe described the first ET transmissions that were picked up by Nicola Tesla in 1899 and again in 1959 by NASA monitoring a craft circling earth. "In 1960, Project Ozma was headed up by Dr Frank Drake. Strong intelligent signals were immediately picked up from the Tau Ceti region of space. Project Ozma was immediately shut down and moved to Arecibo Puerto Rico under AF control. The CIA takeover of the AF UFO investigations took place in 1953. The five day Robertson Panel was completely run by the CIA. Newsmen were not allowed to ask questions and there would be no disparaging remarks allowed about the AF. Chief of Press Al Chop and later Captain Ruppelt resigned. Ruppelt died of a heart attack due to the pressure put upon him to edit his tell all UFO book. The AF started smearing its own pilots that reported UFOs. In 1962, the CIA went after NICAP. Two CIA agents convinced Admiral Hillenkoetter not to testify in Congressional hearings and he resigned his NICAP Board position".

Keyhoe went on to describe UFO sightings by astronauts James McDevitt, Frank Borman and Michael Collins. "The CIA got us into this mess and the AF caught the heat. Frank Edwards agreed to blast the AF on the air with Keyhoe prior to the release of the Condon report but Edwards suddenly died of a heart attack. In 1967, the Soviets announced they had proof of UFOs made by their astronomers. There was speculation that the Mars moon Phobos was a hollow craft since it defied the laws of physics and circled Mars faster than the planet rotated. Every 26 years when Mars was closest to Earth, there was an increase in UFO reports. The first stealth UFO report occurred on May 13 1967 when a craft flew 200 feet over NORAD in Colorado Springs and was strongly picked up on radar but was invisible to sight. In 1968, the Soviets abruptly reversed their position regarding UFOs but Henry Ford II went public with his UFO sighting. Keyhoe was told by Dr Robert Low that, "the AF doesn't know how to prepare the public and the CIA doesn't think the public can ever be prepared for this disclosure". UFOs received a higher classification than Top Secret and it concerned plans for emergency defense measures if they proved hostile. The Project Saint program was put in place to shoot them down.

Keyhoe goes on to name names and details of case after case in the most detailed description of UFO encounters that I have ever read. In his appendix, he names 122 scientists, military and pilots who dispute the Air Force conclusions. He obviously had the proof in his NICAP files and the 51 classified reports given to him by Captain Ruppelt. Keyhoe goes on to describe the great 1965 blackout as being caused by UFOs. The first report came from Syracuse Deputy Aviation Commissioner Robert Walsh who saw a UFO at Hanford airport followed by reports from flight instructor Weldon Ross and tech James Brooking. A Time magazine reporter even took a photo. President Johnson, fearing a panic, decided not to announce a national emergency even though power companies could not explain the loss of electricity. A broken circuit breaker was blamed but an industry Power publication disputed that claim. Later that year, more blackouts occurred in Minnesota, Texas and New Mexico after UFOs were spotted.

In the end, even the National Academy of Scientists praised the Condon Report and Project Blue Book was closed even though only 59 cases out of over 13,000 were actually investigated by Blue Book; 701 cases were classified as unknown. In 1970, the Air Force Academy analysis was made public and it was quickly replaced by the Air Force censors. The AF retaliated against Dr Hynek's criticism of the Condon report and dropped him as a consultant. The AF wrote a blistering letter to the RAND Corporation for their support of the UFO reality. Lt. Col. Corbin told Keyhoe that the AF was still investigating UFOs under Project's Blue Paper and Old New Moon but they will deny it.

Operation Lure was put in place to attract the UFOs to a designated location and obtain undisputed photographic proof of their existence. It would cost less than one Apollo launch. It should also be considered that Earth is located on the outer edge of the Milky Way galaxy and is a perfect way station and launch location for alien missions beyond our galaxy!

Upon Keyhoe's ouster from NICAP in 1973, he commented that there was a complete reversal of NICAP's policies. Most investigators and advisors resigned after it was disclosed that NICAP would no longer criticize the AF.

Little did Major Keyhoe know that the Agency that he had fought so hard against for so long had infiltrated NICAP and were now running it. The CIA was now in charge of NICAP and eventually bankrupted it with overblown expense accounts and salaries and NICAP closed its doors in 1980. From all I've read, it seems as though the ETs that were here in the 1950's were not hostile. That seemed to change in the 1970's as a new species may have arrived. I also find it interesting that Dr Frank Drake who was in charge of Operation Ozma went on to Direct SETI. George Santayana once said that "one must understand history in order to avoid repeating its mistakes". It seems obvious to me that SETI and NASA are the public view while the real space program is operated by the Air Force or Navy.

References:

1. *Aliens from Space* by Major Donald Keyhoe
2. *An Alternative History of Mankind* by John Ventre

Chapter 27

So Where Is It?

(Courtesy Natural News)

In March of 2014, I went out on a limb and posted my personal belief that the 239 passengers of Malaysia Flight 370 were still alive but abducted by ETs. I received a lot of push back for saying that; mostly from the scientists in the UFO communities after I said in writing what many of them were only thinking. Time and again the so called UFO experts are oblivious of our UFO history and turn out to be the biggest skeptics. I'm still scratching my head as to why it is ok to say the plane crashed or exploded or is in a terrorist camp but not that it was abducted. What prompted me to write my opinion piece to my local media contacts was an article I read that stated that there were only six possible explanations. This prompted me to go on record with a seventh possible explanation. Do I know for sure? No, but neither do the experts with their theories!

I feel very confident in knowing our UFO history to state that this type of disappearance has happened before and will happen again.

Here are four examples regarding planes:

1. December of 1945, five bombers from Fort Lauderdale took off and disappeared in clear weather. A large Martin Mariner was sent up to find flight 19. They disappeared also. Six planes and twenty seven crew "vanished".
2. In 1953 General Benjamin Chidlaw said, "We have stacks of flying saucer reports. We take them very seriously when you consider how many men and planes we have lost trying to intercept them".
3. On November 23 1953, an F-89C Scorpion jet was scrambled from Kinross AFB to intercept a UFO. On radar, the 2 merge and the jet and its 4 member crew vanish.
4. Oct 21, 1978, Melbourne Australia pilot Fred Valentich radioed in that he saw a shiny elongated object with four lights and that, "It is not an aircraft". His plane then disappeared and no debris field was found.

(Courtesy Phenomena Magazine)

If a Carnival cruise ship was found abandoned off the coast of Miami with dinner on the tables of the banquet room, would mainstream media say it was pirates, engine fumes or ET abduction? ET wouldn't even be mentioned yet this scenario did take place in 1872 with the 10member crew of the Marie Celeste Merchant vessel. The largest naval vessel to disappear was the USS Cyclops on March 4, 1918 in the Bermuda triangle. None of the ships 306 crew or wreckage was ever found from the 19,360 ton ship. German records show no record of sinking it.

What happened to the Roanoke North Carolina colony in 1585? Even the passive Indians were baffled as to where they all went to? Roanoke was very similar to the 1930 Eskimo village residents that disappeared and left all their clothes, shoes, rifles, dogs and dinner cooking on the fire. Did they wander off never to be found or were they all taken? If you look further back in history, in 1917- 800 British troops disappeared at Gallipoli Turkey and in 125 AD the 6000 man Roman 9th Legion disappeared near Rendlesham Forrest in England.

My other point was that this plane was headed into Chinese air space which is monitored by U.S. and Chinese satellites. The military knows exactly what happened to a plane that suddenly stopped transmitting signals. Transponders, cell phones and emergency signals just ceased as if the craft was hit by an EMP. In a world where every cell phone call, text and email is monitored, how do we lose a plane? We were told the plane turned west; then the search headed south near Australia and then it was reported that files from the pilot's hard drive had been deleted. Why hasn't the Malaysian government been forthcoming with information? How do you get to the truth and when did the cover-up begin?

According to Dr.Wahid Ibrahim, "Over 50 UFO's were seen near Phuket, Thailand after Malaysia Flight 370 went missing – a UFO was seen on radar passing Flight 370 tripling its speed. (Thanks to Dr.Wahid Ibrahim from Cairo/Egypt).

"Malaysia's air force chief, Rodzali Daud, said military radar detected an UFO in an area in the northern Malacca Strait at 2:15 a.m. local time on Saturday about an hour after the plane vanished from air traffic control screens".

So far, no one knows what happened; not the media, not the experts and not me. I still receive a lot of push back from the UFO community for writing this article and I have lost as much respect for them as they have for me. I do know that very strange things occur on this planet which is outside of scientific explanation. How prophetic were the pilot's last words, "All right, good night".

Update: On July 29, 2015 a flaperon from a Boeing 777 was found on a remote island 1000 miles west in the Indian Ocean. Since there are no serial numbers on the flap, experts are pinning there proof on the age of the barnacles attached to the flap. Most consider this to be proof. Mr Raza, the Honorary Consul of Malaysia, transported the pieces back from Madagascar. When he returned in August 2017 to do the same with more alleged pieces, he was gunned down for his involvement. What truth is being hidden and why?

The search was officially suspended in January of 2017 after searching 120,000 square miles of the ocean floor at a cost of $160M with zero results. Where did the plane go? The Australian Transport Safety Bureau's final report said the "Location is an almost inconceivable mystery".

Chapter 28

3 TV-Movie Reviews:

~ Chasing UFOs ~

Last month I decided to help Roger Marsh with the Journal by writing a monthly movie review even though he needs help with book reviews. I read every word in a book and it would take me too long to get a book review done. I love movies and have over 600 in my home theater room. After watching NatGeo's *Chasing UFOs* I felt compelled to do a TV review. I solicited comments from my Pennsylvania MUFON team and added my own.

Roger was kind and classy with his TV show review in his Examiner.com article. I grew up in New York so I'll just call it as I saw it. Let's start with "Safety First" as we have all heard at our places of employment. Do not walk into a known radioactive zone. Do not handle evidence without gloves when you intend to have it tested. Do not trespass on Airport grounds. Do not repel cliffs when you can walk to a clearing. These acts all made for good entertainment but no real UFO investigator would do any of them. MUFONs own Chuck Zukowski could probably repel to a cattle mutilation site but I doubt that he ever has. MUFONs Board member Debbie Zigelmier can dive to a depth of over 100 feet but it won't get her to the artifact on the floor of the Baltic Sea.

The show was filmed with a Blair Witch style of night vision and camera's on the actors so we could see their reaction. I can only imagine what Bigfoot hunters must think of James Fox's scared reactions to something in the woods. I can only imagine what conservatives think of the bleeped out foul language throughout the show. After three years of faked ghost hunting shows I thought we would be done with staged evidence. Did Ryder really capture a UFO on video at the end of episode one or was that CGI to get you hooked for the next show? I found that insulting. The public might have liked it but for real UFO investigators it would be like a surgeon watching the Alien Autopsy video and being told it was real. I expected better from James Fox who has produced three quality UFO documentaries but I would question whether any of these three so called investigators have ever really done an actual investigation. They've conducted interviews, but they are not investigators. I don't blame them because as I learned from the Anderson Cooper show, the power belongs to the editor. The show seemed to bounce around with no real conclusions and I learned nothing.

As for what they did right; I liked the actual UFO video clips shown at commercial breaks. I liked the interviews of authorities like police and retired military. I liked MUFONs logo on the paranormal van window but I'm not sure we would want that association.

The three actors in Chasing UFOs seemed to be having fun and their goal was entertainment. This show could've aired on the Comedy Channel. The public may like this show. I believe the season of more UFO shows will begin in the fall and I bet at least one will stick to the scientific method . . . for the benefit of humanity.

~ Prometheus ~

I went to see Prometheus while visiting my son and his girlfriend in DC. The movie starts off with the Ancient Alien theme that we were visited centuries ago and the Gods of old were them. Rock cave drawings are found in seven locations around the world in countries that had no contact yet each drawing is the same pointing toward a star system. This reminds me of the primitive Dogan tribe of Mali (Africa) that knew of the Sirius star system yet there is no way they could have that knowledge.

The year is 2092 and we launch the Prometheus craft with 17 crew headed to make contact. I would've liked to have seen more on the Ancient Alien theory in the beginning but the movie moves past that quickly. Outside of Charlize Theron, who we are not sure is human, the cast is non-descript and the movie lacks action or a fast pace. Prometheus also left more questions than answers. If this is an *Alien* movie prequel, then why does the alien look different? Why did the ten foot tall human looking Titans in the movie create us? Why did they plan to destroy us? Why did they change their mind? Prometheus clearly left those questions unanswered and there will be a sequel. If done right, the sequel can be one of those rare movies that exceed the original like T2 or Aliens. I'm certain I will buy this DVD and watch it 2 or 3 more times. The one answer we think we got was who created us. But the real question is who created them? My guess is we'll find out that the same creator created us and them and this movie is nothing more than a sibling rivalry. . . .

~ Battleship ~

Since I'm a retiree now, I went to the Tues matinee to watch the sci-fi movie *Battleship*. I was very pleasantly surprised by this movie starring Liam Neeson and directed by Peter Berg who has switched from acting to directing. The premise of the movie is Stephan Hawking's statement that we shouldn't contact other space species because it would probably turn out for us like it did for the Indians when Europeans arrived in North America. Of course we build radio transmitters on the top of mountains in beautiful Hawaii and start transmitting. The response soon arrives in the form of five spacecraft and the battle for our species ensues. The aliens are human looking with four thumbs for fingers and wearing ecto-suits that increase their strength. What I really liked about the movie was how a group of WWII vets help jumpstart the USS Missouri from a tourist attraction to the savior of the battle. Our current military didn't know how to operate the steam engines or work the old technology. I also liked how another hero in the movie was a young vet who lost both his legs. The movie really paid tribute to our vets. When I heard about the movie a few months ago, I laughed and said to my kids that we don't even have a Battleship in our military.

Our last two battleships, the Iowa and Wisconsin, were turned into museums off the coasts of Stockton, California and Newport News, Virginia six years ago. Their replacement, the DDX destroyer, was due out in 2014 at a cost of $4 billion. The DDG-1000 will use electromagnetic rail guns. I didn't know the theme of the movie was to put a Battleship back in use.

As a side note, there are no remaining military persons who served in WWI still alive. The last two passed away last year; Harry Landis of Sun City Florida and Frank Buckles of Charles Town West Virginia. They were the last of the generation to fight in the "War to end all Wars".

This was a great movie to watch and I would recommend it to all seniors and vets and not only sci-fi fans. Brooklyn Decker is also easy on the eyes in her role as the Admirals daughter.

On May 2, 2014, I received a letter marked from the CIA. The person said they were one of the CIA's "Anomalous Sighting" Investigators. The person said the CIA is still involved and has 41 agents investigating UFOs.

The person said the CIA "Anomalous Sighting" Investigators are happy MUFON exists and want the truth told that we are not alone and owe our technology to five friendly alien species. "Please keep doing what you folks are doing. And for the record, I saw the original Roswell files. They are in the CIA archives and can't be copied. Two saucers crashed, one hovered intact and bodies were found. The aliens had no immunity to our airborne pathogens".

Cordially – A friend in the agency

Doug

Chapter 29

UFOs and the Media

I was awarded the 2014 MUFON Symposium to manage in July of 2014 and we held it outside of Philadelphia in Cherry Hill, NJ. I gave a lot of thought to the theme of the event and selected "UFOs and the Media". I thought it was a very pertinent topic and also knowing the mentality of people on the east coast, I knew they needed a topic and speakers with showmanship as opposed to boring scientific reviews. I researched the topic for my lecture and here is what I presented on why the media has failed in its responsibility to cover UFOs properly.

When you listen to President John F. Kennedy's 1961 speech on secret societies, you have to wonder what the young President had discovered. His speech sends chills through my spine every time I listen to it. Kennedy said, "We decided long ago that the dangers of concealment of pertinent facts far out way the dangers cited to justify it. There is a grave danger that an announcement for increased security will be ceased upon for censorship and concealment. No one should censor the news, stifle dissenters or withhold from the press and public the facts they deserve to know. There is a conspiracy which relies on covert means. Preparations are concealed not published. Mistakes are buried not headlined. Its dissenters are silenced, not praised. No expenditure is questioned, no secret is revealed." Those are powerful words which we can view in a different light 57 years later.

I next moved on to review my appearance on the highly edited Anderson Cooper show in April of 2012. The show actually aired on Tuesday April 24th ten days after it was taped and of cause they edited out my best responses to skeptic Joe Nickell. They did not edit out anything that Joe said. They did edit out the audience's laughter when Joe said the witnesses saw Jupiter. Edited out was my response that regressive hypnosis is a tool we use no different than a polygraph and that Joe Nickell has no medical background. Edited out was my statement that the witnesses showed courage and integrity, which received applause from the entire audience. Edited out was my analogy that the 12 witnesses to these 2 cases could make up a jury yet they would be believed inside the courtroom but not outside the courtroom if they witnessed a UFO. Edited out was my statement that we kept the stealth fighter a secret for 12 years when asked how the government can keep this a secret. Edited out was my response that whole punch clouds only occur during freezing temperatures and it was 53 at O'Hare airport for that sighting.

The skeptic received twice as much airtime and the last word on the show. The shows website had nine pages of comments; more than any other show that they have done. All the comments were against the skeptic and psychic. I should've known the Producer was playing me when he said he was a UFO fan but yet never heard of Project Blue Book or the 1952 UFO wave over DC. They introduced a psychic medium to minimize the seriousness of the show. Just like Project Blue Book and following the Brookings Institute's recommendations to not tell the truth regarding UFOs, the outcome was predetermined. I read this quote on PAKALERT News last week, "Do you ever get the feeling that the mainstream media "press-titutes" is feeding you a very watered-down and twisted version of the news? Do you ever get the feeling that the government does not believe that the American people can actually be trusted with the truth? It is exasperating to realize that the news that the public is being fed every single day is very heavily filtered and very heavily censored. In a world where "spin" is everything, simply telling the truth is a revolutionary act. Fortunately, the Internet has helped fuel the rise of the alternative media, and millions of Americans that are starting to wake up are turning to the alternative media for answers to their unanswered questions". Internet news is a problem also but it is situations like this that convince me that there is a conspiracy to discredit Ufology and only make my belief stronger in it.

One comment I made of significance was that the government monitors every cell phone call, text, email and website. Anderson disagreed. I had just read an article in March 2012 in *Wired Magazine* regarding the NSA monitoring center in Utah. I also referenced this in my book *Apophis 2029* on page 131. When the story broke in the spring of 2013, every media outlet and Congress-person denied knowledge of what the NSA was doing. How is that possible when the story was in Wired and my book the previous year? Are they all lying, incompetent or just in bed with the intelligence community? (Did you know that lead paint was banned because it blocks the NSA monitoring?)

I next reviewed the state of the media in America. During WWII, our media and the Pentagon were working together to protect the Manhattan Project and that working arrangement stayed in place through Operation Mockingbird when UFOs started to menace Washington DC in 1952. I mentioned a study which cited that 45% of people believe 100% of what is said by an authority figure; 30% believe 90% which means 75% believe everything they are told and only 25% question what they are told. According to recent Pew and Gallop research, ratings at CNN, MSNBC and Fox were down 11% while more importantly, it was down in the key 25-54 age bracket by 59% at CNN and 52% at MSNBC. Newspaper ad revenue was down 33%. The public had lost faith in the media which is heavily controlled by political parties and corporations. Mainstream media should start by telling the truth. News agencies should not have ratings which promote commentaries and sensationalism. If you want to know what's going on in America, watch the BBC.

I next reviewed the SyFy Channels *Joe Rogan Investigates Everything* show which aired in August 2013. Rogan said he believes there is life in space but he needs to see proof they have visited earth. That's the same line Anderson Cooper used. He constantly related UFO witnesses to drug users and said all UFO cases occur at night so they must be dreams. Rogan also said that people live boring lives and UFO contact gives their lives importance. Rogan had his mind made up before he investigated but one has to wonder who did the research for him. Rogan should stick with the UFC and not UFOs.

The media jumped on the Ray Santilli Alien Autopsy charade in 1995 and Hollywood came to the aid of SETI who needed $5M in donations to keep operating. Hollywood makes millions on sci-fi movies which resulted in 8 of their top 30 grossing movies but donate nothing to MUFON. Jodi Foster led the donors with a $250K donation to SETI who searches for radio waves which break up into white noise while MUFON can prove "They" are already here.

You also have to wonder if you can believe the media or are some news items written before they occur. The more important question is what do you believe and why do you believe it? The OJ Simpson trial made CNN. Political campaigns are vastly exaggerated. Some video is re-enacted for the news. Seventy years ago, the rescuing of passengers from the Lusitania was staged for the news. It was filmed in a lake with actors and life preservers. Take a look at the faces in a crowd the next time CNN shows you live footage from a Middle East incident. Everyone is angry in the front two rows but everyone is smiling behind them because it is reenacted. Who killed Kennedy? One shooter and two bullets created seven wounds. Was Flight 93 shot down? Did the World Trade Center Bldg. 7 collapse on its own or was it a controlled detonation? Climatologists believe Climate Change is caused by humans yet Meteorologists say it is caused by the sun. I say it is caused by the earth's core. Where were the WMDs in Iraq? What happened in Benghazi? What really happened to Malaysian Flight 370? It turned west then south with no distress signals or debris found yet U.S. and Chinese military satellites were monitoring the area. Is the stock market being price fixed the past year way beyond the effects of "Tapering" and why did 7 Bankers under 50 commit suicides in January of this year? Did you really believe that Barry Bonds, Mark McGuire and Sammy Sosa were hitting all those home runs legitimately? Has some of our $18T debt been used to build an off world space program? Are we just "sheepel" living in "miceland" since 75% of you believe everything they are told? Did you know that corporations and the government hire web trolls to sway public opinion on social media and in chat rooms?

They reply to you with propaganda! If you repeat a lie often enough, 3 out of 4 people will believe it. The Nazi's proved that.

"What you see depends on what you thought before you looked. Change the way you look at things and the things you look at change." Should we blame the media who is driven by ratings and have given us shows like Honey Booboo and Wife Swap or has the media also been duped? It's no longer, "All the news that's fit to print" but has become a commentary. I do believe that the *Hangar 1* UFO show will change opinions even though every station now has a UFO show. Only *Hangar 1* is based on real UFO files; the MUFON files. All other shows are based on the internet or third party info.

I next asked the audience, "What was the most significant event in UFO history? Of cause they replied with "Roswell". Wrong, the most significant event was the 1938 panic broadcast. It set the tone for non-disclosure for the next 75 years and was referenced in the Brookings Institutes "*Implications of Extraterrestrial Contact*" study as one reason why you can't tell the public the truth. The CIA also cites the public's reaction to ETs in this event as a reason why they can never tell us the truth. Did you know in a November 1980 interview with Cardinal Ratzinger (Pope Benedict 2005-13) regarding the third secret of Fatima, he said, "When one reads that the oceans will flood entire portions of land; that human beings will die in minutes, and in millions, then one should not desire publication of the "Secret"? Knowledge means responsibility. It is dangerous when one only wishes to satisfy his curiosity, if he is not prepared to do something about his discovery, or if he is convinced we can do nothing to prevent prophesized disasters from happening." That is a policy statement that all governments implement regarding events they can't control.

Now it's time to discuss the C.I.A. who is the gatekeeper of the UFO cover-up. The release of 1000's of C.I.A. UFO documents in 1978 exposed the fact that Major Keyhoe and Admiral Hillenkoetter and others were replaced on NICAP's Board by C.I.A. agents in the late 60's. The CIA agents paid themselves salaries and expenses that bankrupted the UFO organization in 1980 that did so much in the 60's to offset the lies of Project Blue Book. "The most effective way of changing the structure of society is to do it silently. Manage the media and you can change everything; as long as you do it covertly. No announcement is made, just a simple policy change".

The C.I.A. got involved in 1953 with the Robertson Panel and their conclusion was to discredit, debunk and infiltrate UFO groups. They also recommended that school children should not receive a grade on book reports involving UFOs. Walter Cronkite hosted a CBS TV special organized by the C.I.A. to debunk UFOs. The Project Blue Book years were marked by the most fascinating spy drama that pitted the C.I.A. sponsored Blue Book and Dr Condon along with J. Allen Hynek against the public and NICAP led by Major Donald Keyhoe, Admiral Hillenkoetter, Captain Ruppelt and later Dr James MacDonald and Leonard Stringfield.

NICAP's efforts to get Congressional hearings were constantly thwarted by the secretive C.I.A. and eventually led to the resignation of Ruppelt and Hillenkoetter from NICAP on the eve of possible Congressional hearings and the eventual infiltration of NICAP by C.I.A. agents and NICAP's demise. Even APRO, a Midwest UFO organization, was under surveillance and infiltration by the C.I.A. and also closed up shop.

On February 17 1954, the C.I.A. and the Military Air Transport Service met with airlines officials and imposed military restrictions on commercial pilot UFO reporting wherein they were subject to espionage laws and a $10,000 fine and 10 years in prison for discussing UFOs with the media or public. On January 22 1958, CBS pulled the live feed on Major Keyhoe when he said UFOs are under intelligent control.

A newspaper article was mailed to me with a note saying that, "This is how it is done" but it is also an example of the media trying to do its job. "The top U.S. special operations commander, Admiral McRaven, ordered military files about the Navy Seal raid on Osama bin Laden's hideout to be purged from Defense Department computers and sent to the C.I.A. where they could be more easily shielded from the public. The secret move set off no alarms in the Obama administration even though it side stepped federal rules and the Freedom of Information Act.

Secretly moving the records allowed the Pentagon to tell the Associated Press that it couldn't find any documents inside the Defense Department that the Associated Press had requested more than two years earlier and would represent a NEW strategy for the U.S. government to shield even its most sensitive activities from public scrutiny. "Welcome to the new shell game in place of open government". The C.I.A. has special authority to prevent the release of "operational files" in ways that can't be challenged in federal court.

The Defense Department told the AP in March 2012 that it could not locate any photographs or video taken during the raid or showing bin Laden's body. It also said it could not find any images of bin Laden's body on the U.S.S. Carl Vinson, the aircraft carrier from which he was buried at sea. The Pentagon also said it could not find any death certificate, autopsy report or results of DNA tests for bin Laden. It said it searched files at the Pentagon, Special Operations HQ and Navy command. The Pentagon also refused to confirm or deny the existence of helicopter maintenance logs even though one of the stealth helicopters that carried the SEALs in Pakistan crashed during the mission and its wreck was left behind."

To top it off, Seal Team 6 dies a year later in an old clunker Chinook helicopter and is not allowed to return fire with the enemy. All the witnesses are gone and that is a crime!

Everyone in the world knows that this event took place but now we have created a conspiracy as to why there are no records of the event. When I hear that the Roswell and Kecksburg files were lost or the two missing minutes from Apollo 11 were lost, I have to think they are in the same room with the bin Laden killing.

The C.I.A. operates as a separate entity from the U.S. government just as the Jesuits operate separately from the Vatican in their attempts to protect the church from itself. They imported cocaine into the U.S. in the 1980's, set up and ruin lives or kill people who are deemed a threat and create disinformation and propaganda that topple governments or cause rebellions. Kennedy was preparing to take the C.I.A. on right before his assassination. But in a perverted sort of way, the C.I.A. does all of this to protect you and I because we don't know and have never been told the truth about the real world we live in. The Air Force wanted to tell the public the truth about UFOs but didn't know how to and the C.I.A. concluded that the public can never be told!

These events take place because the average person believes everything they are told; is more interested in playing with their smart phone, eating at MacDonald's and wondering about who is appearing on Dancing with the Stars.

Now let's take a look at the scientific community. Scientists are funded to find a predetermined outcome. When they solve it, their funding stops. What are the chances of curing diseases if it makes you unemployed? We have only cured two diseases or plagues; polio and smallpox. That's it! Why would SETI ever admit that "They" are here when it would put an end to their donations? The funny thing about scientists is every 20 years they change what they told you. I'd like my tonsils back. But they are completely stubborn with paradigms with their own field of study. Take evolution or out of places archeology finds. Evolution is a theory or philosophy. All the evidence for it can fit on your dining room table. All modern finds are back dated to fit the evolution model. I believe I came from a more superior creature, not a baboon! When archeologists find something that doesn't fit like a gold chain or vase in a 250,000 year old coal deposit, they say it was planted there or they disregard it. I don't believe that we have the kind of science that can solve the UFO enigma. We have consensus science filled with confirmation bias and cognitive dissonance!

How about the oil lie? Every generation there is an oil crisis or shortage which runs the price up drastically. We're told there is just not enough oil; it will run out by 2050. The truth is that there is a 300 year supply of oil that we know of and it may actually be a renewing commodity pushed up from the core of the earth.

How about the "Out of Africa" lies? This was made up in the late 1980's and promulgated in the 90's to support affirmative action. It is a political lie used to support a program that reverse discriminates against white males and violates the 14th amendment. Humans did not originate in Africa because Australian Aboriginal DNA is the oldest ever found followed by DNA from Spain. There is no African DNA found in Russians.

How about the Globalization lie? This was sold to us in the 1990's as good for America yet all it did was move good paying union jobs overseas so that multinational corporations could cut their costs. These former union employees are no longer able to retire, own a home, take vacations or put their kids through college. It is a vicious cycle for those without a college degree. These same people now work in the service industry and cheer $10 per hour and hope for the same in minimum wage yet CEO's earn $20 million dollar salaries on the backs of these dumb loyal Americans.

Did you know the CDC owns 20 vaccine patents and earns $4.6B a year? It regulates itself and is "for profit". Those patents include HIV, SARS, Zika, Ebola, pet booster shots, Hepatitis A, Anthrax and others. Do they cure or spread new strains?

So has the media done its due diligence? No. Has the C.I.A? Yes. Has the scientific community? No. I think the media has been duped by the C.I.A. into believing UFOs are a joke. There are no phone calls made anymore to kill a UFO story; it's just par for the course to laugh at UFOs unless you can produce a body or craft. Only the media has the power to change this soft cover up even though the C.I.A. thinks it has this one 99% licked.

Remember; pay no attention to the man behind the curtain. And it is dangerous to be right on matters in which the established authorities are wrong. . . . .

Here's an email I received when Gary Heseltine printed this article in his British *UFO Truth* magazine:

From: Peter ******
Sent: Saturday, August 30, 2014 11:54 AM
To: jventre1@comcast.net
Subject: re article in Gary's UFO TRUTH magazine
Friend,
For what it's worth – I write almost identical rants concerning the way we are pre-programmed, lied to and generally kept in the dark; particularly with politics, false flags, roman games and UFO's.
Without getting into the details – keep writing and talking – there are some of us out there that are on your side.
Just a comment...Peter

Note:
I tried to book our 2016 UFO Conference at Saint Vincent's College in Latrobe Pa. Stanton Friedman had given a UFO lecture there in 1969 and he was our headline speaker. The college said they could not allow a UFO Conference. The Bishop Connare Ctr did allow our conference in 2017 only to cancel it for 2018 due to violating church principles. Some say UFOs have become more acceptable. I say things have gotten worse, much worse.

Chapter 30

A CASE OF UFO DEBRIS

By John Ventre & Dave Segal

Was Delaware case number 57833 an extraterrestrial craft, black project military craft or a Chinese lantern? That is the question we are asking ourselves as we analyze debris recovered from this sighting. This event occurred on June 29, 2014, having four witnesses that included a man, his wife, as well as two tenants who rent an upstairs room in their house. The tenants were outside just after midnight smoking cigarettes when they observed multiple orange-red unidentified aerial objects descend over their neighborhood.

According to our witnesses, the height of the event presented them with up to twenty four objects. They were silent and floated irregularly. One of the tenants filmed the event using his Samsung Galaxy S5 phone. Toward the end, the objects appeared to slowly and silently move off into the distance, flying in sort of a formation. It was during this time when one of our witnesses observed an orb that seemed to float behind the others, acting irregularly as if it were malfunctioning. With all four witnesses staring intently, the object seemed to jettison something that "burnt wildly" the whole way down to earth. Shortly thereafter, the object instantly "darted" out of sight going in the opposite direction of the other objects. Our witnesses stated, "It went back in the direction it came from."

The 'fireball' dropped straight down, being a fairly windless night, taking about ten seconds. It touched-down fairly close to where our witnesses were standing, roughly four houses up the street. As they approached the debris, one witness claimed that "the yellow flame had reached about two feet in height," which was eventually stomped out to avoid any possibility of causing a fire. The residual fragment was then retrieved and kept in a small Styrofoam container until MUFON field investigators arrived. Only about 10% of the fragment was sent to Frontier Labs, as the witness refused to allow MUFON to take any more, fearing they would never see it again.

The following are photographs of the fragment:

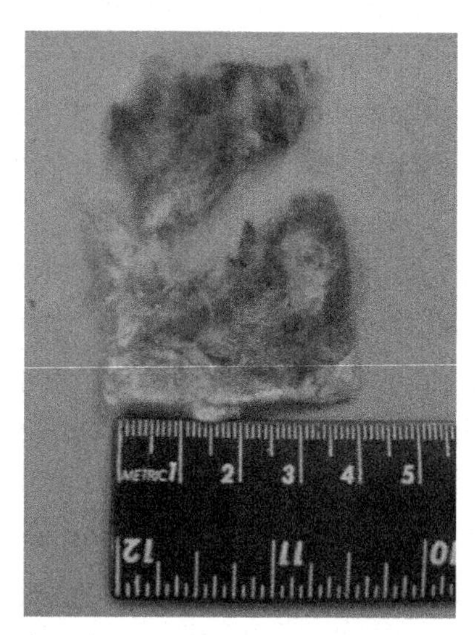

Photo 1: Submitted by Phyllis Budinger, MUFON Analyst

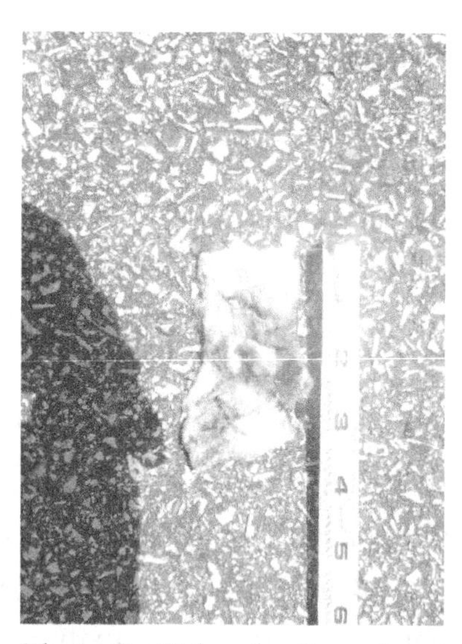

Photo 2: Taken by the witness, at the request of MUFON, prior to the field investigator's arrival

A chemical analysis was performed by Phyllis Budinger, radar analysis by Glenn Schultz, video analyses by Jeff Sainio, Marc D'Antonio and PA MUFON FI Dave Segal.

An excerpt from Phyllis's analysis:

"The fragment is from some sort of energy storage device. The analysis is straight-forward and conclusive. No question on the composition. I find it interesting that the literature article, referenced in the report which discusses palmitic acid/SiO2 composite for energy storage was only published a few years ago. I asked myself if WE could have commercialized that so soon.

The sample is composed of greater than 50 wt. % palmitic acid (a long chain carboxylic acid also known as hexadecanoic acid) which is dispersed in fine glass fibers. Small amounts of other components are present, which are mostly comprised of other long chain carboxylic acids. These are probably impurities that come along with the palmitic acid, i.e. not refined out. There are also trace amounts of quartz which are commonly seen in glass fibers and an unidentified ester-type impurity.

- There are research publications on the use of palmitic acid as a phase change material (PCM)[1] for thermal energy storage.[2] More specifically, one recent publication discusses palmitic acid/SiO_2 (SiO_2 in fibrous glass form) composites for this purpose.[3] There is visual indication that the glass fiber in this fragment may be one that is used in situations where it is exposed to high temperatures.[4]

---

[1] A PCM is a substance with a high heat of fusion which, melting and solidifying at a certain temperature, is capable of storing and releasing large amounts of energy. Heat is absorbed or released when the material changes from solid to liquid and vice versa.

[2] Ahmet Sari, Kamil Kaygusuz, *Energy Conversion and Management,* Volume 43, Issue 6, April 2002, Pages 863-876 (Thermal performance of palmitic acid as a phase change energy storage material); Afif Hasan, *Solar Energy,* Volume 52, Issue 2, February 1994, Pages 143-154 (Phase change material energy storage system employing palmitic acid).

[3] Guiyin Fang, Hui Li, Zhi Chen, Xu Liu, *Solar Energy Materials and Solar Cells*, vol.95, no. 7, pp. 1875-1881, 2011 (Preparation and properties of palmitic acid/SiO_2 composites with flame retardant as thermal energy storage material).

[4] It is estimated that there are in excess of 50,000 chemical compositions for glass (MATERIALS HANDBOOK, by George S Brady and Henry R Clauser).

So a possible speculation is that this fragment is from some sort of energy storage process related to the UAO.

- The most common use of material containing glass fiber is insulation. And, in fact the fragment has the appearance of insulation. However, the presence of palmitic acid appears be unusual. Though one of palmitic acid's properties is waterproofing, no reference was found for it being used in insulating products.
- This fragment does not originate from Chinese Lanterns. Lanterns are made a myriad of recyclable and indigenous materials, none of which are of the composition noted above. In China, they are traditionally made from oiled rice paper on a bamboo frame. The source of hot air may be a small candle or fuel cell composed of a waxy combustible material.[5] Numerous websites describe many construction materials for making homemade lanterns. Indigenous materials like tree bark and fruit shells are used in some locations. Recycled materials are common such as: magazines, newspaper, plastic bottles, ribbon and string. Usually candles are the fuel source."

The video analyses were less conclusive.

Jeff Sainio said, "The video is too poor to tell if the object is moving. Airplanes are easy to recognize in videos due to the strobe lights which must be visible from any angle. None are seen in this video. I have received many Chinese-lantern video cases. They are quite obvious: A red-yellow color, like a candle. Flicker, like a candle. Burn-out, if the video is long enough, in a few minutes like a candle. Sometimes, the paper 'balloon' igniting rather spectacularly and quickly extinguishing, since there is little to burn with random motion of the balloon in the wind. This video

---

contains none of these attributes. Any small hot-air balloon is a very precarious craft with NO margin for excess baggage. Any skeptic must try it; I did. The lift of any balloon increases as to the cube of the size, while the weight increases as to the square of the size, meaning balloons are best BIG. In science or law, the burden of proof lies with the one making the claim. I challenge anybody claiming to talk of Chinese lanterns impregnated with palmitic acid, to find such a device on the market. Especially one that survives fire!! Paper is a better heat-insulator without being soaked in heavy fat."

MUFONs Chief Video Analyst, Marc D'Antonio, stated, "After seeing the image I agree that what Phyllis was given was not a cloth impregnated with paraffin. That looks like the insulating material used to prevent the crossbeam bars from burning during the flight on some lanterns; my opinion of course. This behavior you mention is absolutely consistent with lanterns. And again, judging the object to return to the 'same altitude' is not impossible. It is likely that the flame cake on that lantern was burning out and this is further evidenced by the loss of a piece of it. When it fell, the now buoyant envelop shot up into the air again. The witnesses had NO concept or clues as to the actual 3D separation in the sky of these objects. They didn't know which was closer, which was farther away. None of this could be discerned. Therefore, their observations of altitude, distance, speed, and 'rejoining formation' are all relative to their perceptions of distance and altitude which we know if faulty at best in humans. This is all very consistent with lanterns. So there are many other reasons for the possible arrangement in the sky. I would call this a lantern case plain and simple."

Chief Investigator Bill Weber and Investigator Dave Segal visited the witness. Dave said, "I performed the original video analysis by analyzing almost every frame in this video and importing the frames into Photoshop where they could be zoomed-in and sometimes adjusted in order to pull non-visible color information into the visible spectrum. I did this usually just by adjusting the "LEVELS" of the image to pull what's visible black (but not 0, 0, 0 RGB) into something that can be seen. MOST of the time, I found you didn't really have to do this as the shape of the objects were much defined. I also found there to be no light gradients and no light halos with the illumination, which lead me to believe the illumination was the object itself. All of the objects were canted about 40 to 60 degrees from their X axis while remaining static.

Finally, I think it's worthy to note that the technical aptitude level of the witness, his wife and two tenants were extremely LOW. The video was too large to email and they had no clue how to get the video off his phone. I took his phone and connected it to my Macbook and copied it over myself. The VERY first thing I went to was the meta-data within the file to see when the last time it was saved/edited and the meta-data matched the story completely---- i.e. it was raw, unedited video."

The radar Dave acquired through FOIA proved to be near useless as it was in a different format than usual. One has to wonder if this was deliberate after a lengthy battle for radar on case 47000 the previous year which yielded very good radar returns. Glenn Schultz said, "If there is any useful radar data in this massive data set it is buried under a mass of an un-annotated 79-column excel file. It is one of the poorest responses I have ever encountered. Sorry to be the bearer of bad news. For some reason Dan M. gets a lot more FOIA data with good user friendly formats and file annotations."

The witness never recorded the burning debris as it fell to the ground since he had already put his camera away and it happened so suddenly. That's an important missing link in this case. So we ask ourselves, "What discharged this trace evidence? A military craft, an alien craft or a Chinese lantern?"

Phyllis Budinger will present her analysis on May 16, 2015 at the Erie Pennsylvania UFO Conference, for those interested in attending and seeing the evidence first hand.

A special thanks to Dave, Marc, Jeff, Phyllis and Glenn on their time and effort with this "unidentified" case.

Update: About 80% of the time the science actually prevails. On July 16, 2015 I received this email from Phyllis but it doesn't explain the length of time observed. It only questions the unrecorded trace evidence submitted which breaks the chain of authenticity:

I have analyzed two sky lantern fuel cells from different manufacturers. Thanks go to Bob Spearing for supplying one of them. I found both cells are composed of palmitic acid and a glass fiber. I had hoped that the analysis would turn out differently. To me the identification of the orbs is still in question. There were several orbs. How long was each observed? (Over 10 minutes?) The flaming material was not observed to fall from the orb. At any rate attached is my analysis and comments.
Phyllis

The Philip Klass curse:

"No matter how long you live, you will never know any more about UFOs than you know today. You will never know any more about what UFOs really are, or where they come from. You will never know any more about what the U.S. Government really knows about UFOs than you know today. As you lie on your own death-bed you will be as mystified about UFOs as you are today. And you will remember this curse".

I believe Phil knew the interdimensional nature of UFOs and that they cannot be captured. So far, it has stood the test of time. . . . . . .

Chapter 31

"Phony" FOIA's

If you read *UFOs over Pennsylvania*, I documented the trouble we had with acquiring radar data from the FAA in 2008 even though we visited the Philly Tower and saw the data on the screen. The FAA four times sent me a letter stating that they had no information. The Tower, at the same time, mailed me a CD with the radar screens but the CD was corrupt and copied over with other data. I recently found out that earlier that year (2008) in the Stephensville case, the FAA threatened to fire the radar operator that responded to MUFON with radar data.

More recently in Pennsylvania, we paid $90 for radar data and the file they sent was impossible to read in a format that could not be used. This was done deliberately. The column with paint screens was also deleted. The investigator also sent a certified letter to the FAA which they acknowledged receiving yet never signed for at the USPS. I filed a complaint with the FAA to refund our $90 or provider readable data. I am still waiting a reply. This is no surprise because last year we received radar paints on case #47000 that showed a Cessna like plane nearly colliding with a squadron of UFOs and having to make a hard left to avoid them. Of cause there was zero cooperation from the Allentown airport to ID the pilot for interview. Pa MUFON has received zero FOIA cooperation from the FAA since they "accidentally" gave us good radar on case 47000. Then when we let the FAA know we were getting their ATC antenna data from the military 84RADES Group, they closed down this very responsive military radar source.

I consider myself a Republican Tea Party Patriot but the longer I live, I have no respect for our lying power abusive government agencies. This is akin to the IRS targeting conservative groups. This is not the America I was born into! The F.B.I. showed their dishonest colors during the 2016 Trump election.

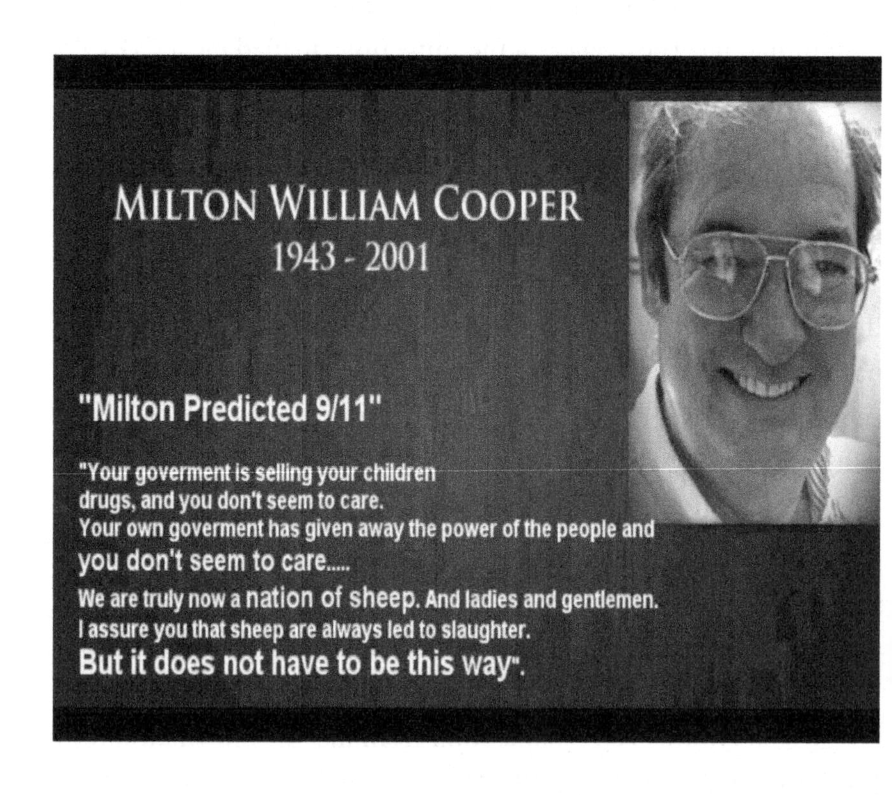

MILTON WILLIAM COOPER
1943 - 2001
"Milton Predicted 9/11"
"Your goverment is selling your children
drugs, and you don't seem to care.
Your own goverment has given away the power of the people and
you don't seem to care.....
We are truly now a nation of sheep. And ladies and gentlemen.
I assure you that sheep are always led to slaughter.
But it does not have to be this way".

Chapter 32

Was Keksburg a GE Mark 2 Reentry Vehicle?

By John Ventre and Owen Eichler

The Mufon Journal appropriately printed this article in December of 2015; Open Minds made no mention of it. All Pittsburgh media outlets covered the story except the Tribune Review but there was inexplicably virtually no national coverage.

On December 9, 1965 at 4:47 pm, something navigated through our airspace and made a semi controlled landing in Kecksburg Pennsylvania. For me, the entire story has been about how it descended over Canada and made a right turn before Cleveland and a left turn before Pittsburgh and slowed down before minimally "crash" landing in rural Kecksburg and avoiding population centers (like Flight 93). The legend has grown to include one witness who saw a scaly, three fingered hand come out of the top of the UFO, similar to the ending of the 1953 movie *War* *of the Worlds*, to seeing an alien body on a gurney at Hangar 18 at Wright Patterson Air Force base alongside a cone shaped craft.

I was contacted in February 2015 by Owen Eichler in regards to his theory that the December 9, 1965 Kecksburg UFO incident was potentially a crash and retrieval of a GE Mark 2 reentry vehicle (RV) with a northern polar launch on December 7, 1965. Owen said he has spent years researching his theory and believes he is correct. The GE Mark 2 RV has never been mentioned as a possible candidate for Kecksburg. This object was a spy capsule that was kept secret until 1991. I posed a few questions that were significant to the case:

1. How did the object turn, slow down and perform a controlled landing? Owen said the GE reentry vehicle had an internal weighting control system for stability and guidance using the coanda effect to glide. Owen also said this was not a NASA project.
2. Why would the military show up in such force for a GE reentry vehicle? Owen said it was used for in-space identification of orbiting space craft and may have contained a Radio Isotope Thermal Generator (RTG) that needed to be recovered in order to control and prevent a radiation leak. The first nuclear power generators were used in 1961. It was also a secret spy satellite of the Soviet Union.
3. What is the explanation for the writing or symbols on the sides of the object? Owen said it was the result of identification welding on the reentry vehicle because there were numerous launches. One symbol, the five pointed star with a circle in the center, is an Army and Air Force symbol. The RV was also attached to the Atlas rocket at the base where the symbols were.

Although I always root for the UFO, Owen got my attention and as the Pa State Director for the Mutual UFO Network, I feel obligated to offer his theory as a possible explanation for the Keckshurg UFO even though I still had questions as to whether GE, NASA or the Air Force can confirm where the loss of the reentry vehicle landed? I contacted experts in the field for a GE phone contact but they didn't have one. I also attempted to contact GE and Lockheed Martin since Lockheed took over the Mark 2 design program and would have the records, but with no luck. I also wondered if the GE Mark 2 didn't collide with Cosmos 96 since the Russians said the Cosmos 96 probe struck something in space. As we approach the 50th anniversary of the event, here's what Owen, who witnessed the in-flight characteristics of the UFO, had to say:

"It was a clear day on December 9, 1965" explains Mr. Eichler, "Myself and several other neighborhood boys and girls were playing baseball in an open area with a wide field of view. As catcher, I saw a bright multi-colored flaming object and called to my playmates to look. I was 13 years old at the time. The predominately green glowing object with wisps of yellow, purple and orange colors was moving from northwest to southeast in my little village of Shafton near Irwin, Pennsylvania. As I had been spending flying time in a small Piper Cub with a neighbor, I was amazed at how low and level the object was moving. I also had spent many hours at a local airport and was familiar with speed and altitude of small airplanes. The object seemed to have a speed somewhat greater than that of small aircraft and a low altitude. In addition, as the object was moving along a path parallel and above the Pennsylvania Turnpike Bridge in the vicinity of the Irwin/North Huntingdon interchange, I can still remember checking the speed against the distance as I was instructed when flying in small

aircraft. As I found out later in life, the object travelled an additional 17 miles to Kecksburg and did not significantly lose altitude. But most of all, I was fixated on the predominantly green color of the object." Mr. Eichler discovered later in high school chemistry that the element copper glows green when incinerated in the open atmosphere. The connection of copper and the object he saw in 1965 put him on an investigative path of the origin of the object for the next 45 years. Moving ahead in time to the present, and after many hours of research, Mr. Eichler has determined the object was an American reentry vehicle designed and manufactured by the General Electric Corporation designated as the MK2 blunt body reentry vehicle.

"During the late 1950s, many reentry vehicles were designed and flown by the United States and the USSR for the original goal of delivery of nuclear bombs. Various American types of designs were tested with the so called "blunt body" design as the design of preference. The blunt body design made use of introducing the reentry vehicle into the atmosphere with a large air-pushing event resulting in a buffering of the atmosphere to dissipate heat from the reentry vehicle. The American design used a section-spherical design while the Soviets used a full spherical design. The American design incorporated controls and jets to "steer" the reentry vehicle while in orbit whereas the Soviet version may not have incorporated such steering controls. Also, the American design used an internal moveable weighted control system for maneuvering in dense atmosphere closer to earth enabling the reentry vehicle to climb, descend and make turns.

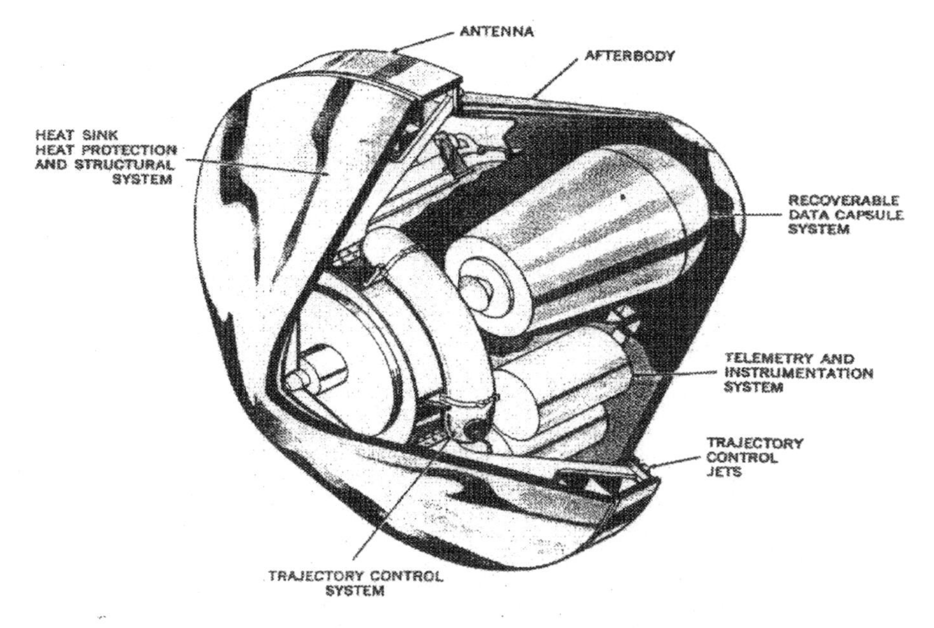

(Figure 1- GE Mark 2 prototype reentry vehicle)

(Figure 2- RV prior to electroplating which covered seams)

THEY DROVE IT, OUT OF THE WOODS.
AND IVE SEEN MANY ARMY TRUCKS
THIS ONE HAD A WHITE STAR ON THE
SIDES. I REMEMBER VERY CLEARLY.

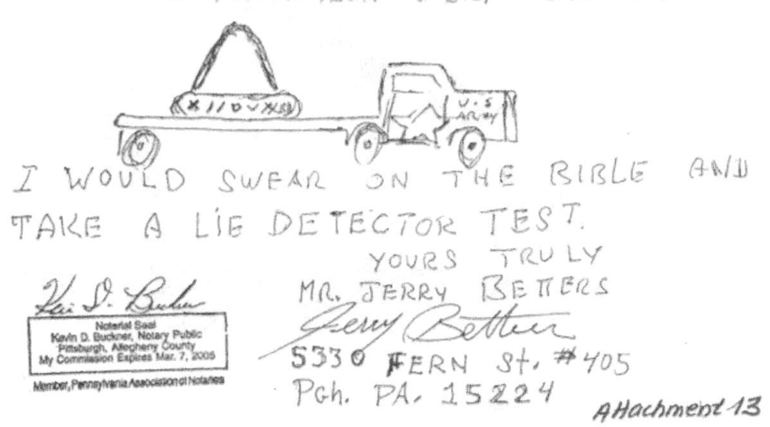

I WOULD SWEAR ON THE BIBLE AND
TAKE A LIE DETECTOR TEST.
YOURS TRULY
MR. JERRY BETTERS
Jerry Betters
5330 FERN St. #405
Pgh. PA. 15224

Notarial Seal
Kevin D. Buckner, Notary Public
Pittsburgh, Allegheny County
My Commission Expires Mar. 7, 2005
Member, Pennsylvania Association of Notaries

Attachment 13

(Figure 3- Notarized deposition of witness Jerry Betters)

"Referring to Figure's 1-3; note the shape of the General Electric MK2 reentry vehicle. Also note the internal components such as a recoverable data capsule system and a trajectory control system. The shape of the vehicle resembles the description given by eyewitnesses as that as an acorn. Also depicted are the control jets used to maneuver while in orbit. When in controlled level flight in the atmosphere, the blunt end of the vehicle encountering the forward oncoming atmosphere can be tilted by the use of the trajectory control system to change the leading edge of the vehicle thereby changing/steering the path of the vehicle. The vehicle then in effect can rise or fall or turn left or right. This in flight capability was demonstrated by the object seen by many observers. And, during the final moments of the event when the reentry vehicle landed in Kecksburg, an eyewitness, Frances Kalp,

remarked about seeing a "four star" object. The "four star" reference most likely was the four control jets used to steer the vehicle while in orbit and possibly used to change the descent speed. Note the similarities between the prototype, the actual MK2 RV and the hand drawn sketch/deposition by musician Jerry Betters who had never seen a MK2 RV or any other space craft up close. As explained below, the MK2 had various capabilities for delivering many payloads such as a nuclear device. Note the funneled end of the MK2 RV. Provisions are made to eject a data capsule, or possibly a camera/film canister for later recovery."

What about the predominantly green color of the object? Mr. Eichler states, "I was able to confirm that the blunt end of the object, the heat sink, was made of copper with minute alloying metals such as beryllium. Reports of green fireballs seen in the southwestern state of New Mexico occurring during the 1950s involving early test flights of reentry vehicles were followed up by "Project Twinkle" ground surveys identifying copper residue over and above normal levels in the low-flying flight path of objects seen flying over the area. Copper heat sinks sound counter-intuitive to protecting a reentry vehicle from heat but the physics of the blunt body design demonstrate that there can be ample heat protection. As a note of record, later RV heat rejection techniques used an ablative material; a design that allows for heat absorption and subsequent stripping of the ablative material from the reentry vehicle to release heat. The ablative design allowed for a completely different physical shape than that of the MK2 reentry vehicle."

For a military perspective, Mr. Eichler added, "This was a cold war project based on the A4 German rocket, commonly known as the V2, designed by Werner Von Braun. The MK2 was the first reentry vehicle to be used to carry an atomic warhead carrying up to 1.5 megatons of TNT equivalent at that time. An historical item of note is WWII Germany and Mr. Von Braun conceptualizing an A10 multi-stage rocket with an atomic warhead to send via air mail to New York City.

"The MK2 reentry vehicle was put atop the United States' Thor and Atlas rocket vehicles. Many of these weapons were deployed in various parts of the world with designations of IRBMs (Intermediate Range Ballistic Missiles). For example, under "Project Emily", up to 60 of the Thor IRBMs were deployed to Great Britain in the early 1960s. The United States sent the missiles and a training team from Vandenberg Air Force Base, here in the United States, to Great Britain. There were other deployments as well. Referring to figures 4 and 5, note the nose of the Thor rocket with provisions to receive the MK2 RV. Also note the general size of the installed MK2 as compared to the Air Force personnel standing below it."

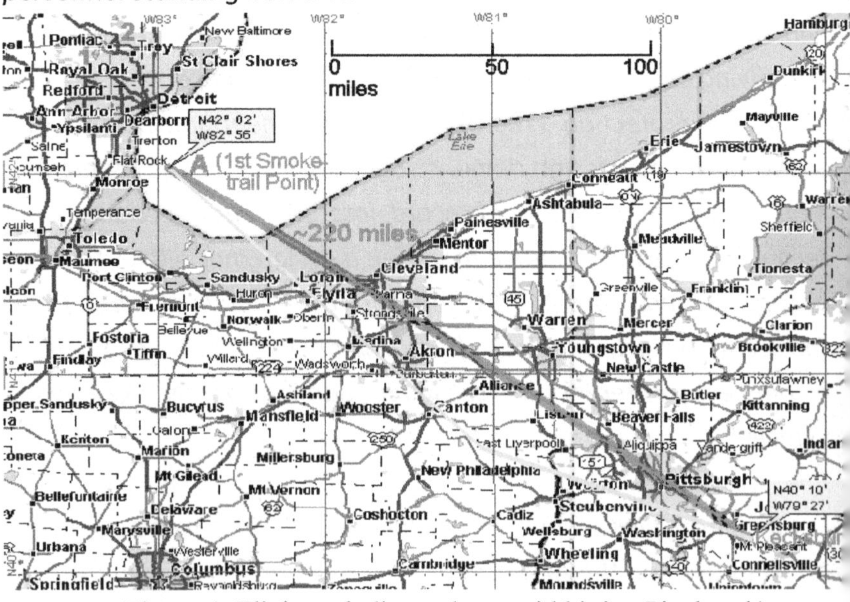

(Figure 4- Flight path diverted to avoid hitting Pittsburgh)

(Figure 5- Mark 2 Reentry vehicle installed at top and ready for lift off. Symbols can be seen on the first black band on the nose which is the RV.)

(Figure 6- Mark 2 Reentry vehicle installed, markings on base)

Mr Eichler further stated, "The deployment of the Thor MK2 armed nuclear missile was eventually recalled from Great Britain as a result of advancing technology and the vulnerability of the MK2 reentry vehicle to intercepting enemy aircraft as the MK2 was slow moving and could be shot down. However, during the 1960s the United States Atlas Rocket was phased in to deliver the MK2 reentry vehicle. The Atlas SM-65 rocket gave some advantages that the Thor rocket was lacking. For example, much longer range and orbiting capabilities. The Thor rocket could only deliver a sub-orbital payload. With the Atlas Rocket, the IRBM became an Inter-Continental Ballistic Missile (ICBM). With the introduction of the Atlas rocket also came smaller and more efficient reentry vehicles. So, then, because there were so many of the MK2's made, possibly over 2000 units, they became useful in other areas of space research and development. Many MK2 vehicles were used to monitor atmospheric parameters in support of the United States moon landing. Another remarkable program employed by the United States was Program 437. The latter program, akin to President Reagan's "Star Wars" initiative, focused on using a nuclear explosion in space to disable an enemy's satellite with Electro-magnetic Pulse waves.

"I also have a suspicion that the strange markings around the base of the Kecksburg UFO may have been caused by the superstructure of a second reentry vehicle being welded to the base of the MK2. After the remnants of the superstructure burned away upon reentry of the MK2 in the atmosphere, all that would be left would be illegible weld spoils in various unintelligible configurations when seen by a common bystander. And, in addition, the base of the MK2 is the only place of attachment of a superstructure as the rest of the MK2 was buried in nose of the

launch vehicle and was made of thick 316 alloy stainless steel sheeting, copper cladded and overall electro-coated with platinum. Also, the strange markings may be identification marks created with a welding stick and a welder to provide positive identification as to the particular model (MK2A, MK2B, and MK2C) of the RV and its payload".

The possibility of the reentry vehicle that landed in Kecksburg of carrying a nuclear warhead is remote. Witnesses stated they saw people dressed in what they describe as full body suits and carrying something resembling what is commonly called a Geiger counter. Examination of Mr. Eichler's research demonstrates many reentry vehicles of the 1960s needed a power source. Mr. Eichler says, "Early power sources utilized batteries, with AC-DC inverters or nuclear thermopiles. The power source of record was a Radio-isotope Thermal Generator (RTG). The generator uses a nuclear material that generates heat. The heat, in turn, heats a thermocouple assembly to generate electricity to power communications and control systems. In the early models, Plutonium-238, Curium 244 and Strontium 90 were used as the heat source. Factually, the authorities would be looking to verify the structural integrity of the reentry vehicle was not breached as a result of the impact potentially releasing radioactive contaminants from the RTG."

All of Owen's proof can be found by searching the internet. I also found this information online:

The Corona program was operated by the CIA with assistance of the Air Force and was used to spy on the Soviet Union and China beginning in June 1959 and ending in May 1972. Program 437 turned the PGM-17 Thor into an operational anti-satellite (ASAT) weapon system; a capability that was kept top secret. The Program 437 mission was approved for development by U.S. Secretary of Defense Robert McNamara on November 20, 1962 and was based at the Johnson Atoll in the Pacific Ocean. Program 437 used Thor missiles and added booster engines to achieve orbital flights. Eighteen more sub-orbital and orbital Thor launches took place from Johnston Island during the 1964–1975 periods in support of Program 437. In 1965–1966 four Program 437 Thors were launched with "Alternate Payloads" for satellite inspection from Johnson Island. Two of the four payloads were designated as APX-1 and APX-2 both of which carried cameras. These launches were evidently an elaboration of a proposed system to allow visual verification of an in-space target before potentially destroying it. These flights may have been related to the late 1960s Program 922, a non-nuclear version of Thor with infrared homing and a high explosive warhead. Care was taken to avoid even the appearance of aiming toward a Soviet satellite. These were U.S. Air Force missions that evaluated reusable, maneuverable, re-entry vehicle designs that might be able to fly to a precise landing point on earth.

There were four launches planned from Johnson Island in 1965; three are listed as successful. The first one on December 7, 1965 does not list an outcome. On December 7, 1965 at 19:29 Military Standard Time (MST), the 10 ADS Air Force crew launched Thor missile Number J8-2299 skyward on an interception azimuth of 153. The target was SPADATS object Number 613; an expended Atlas Agena rocket body. Interception occurred 8:18 minutes after launching following normal lift-off, booster separation, flight path assumption, and payload operation. The camera-bearing capsule registered a miss of .56 nautical miles from the programmed standoff distance of 3.2 nautical miles. All payload functions were performed normally up to separation except for film cutting and sealing operations. The failure was academic; however since the ejected film capsule was stated as never recovered and was visible at 19:45 heading for the ocean. The outcome of this mission is a prime candidate for the Kecksburg UFO although it is listed as a sub-orbital launch!

There would have been a five hour time difference from Johnson Island to Kecksburg Pennsylvania due to daylight savings time in 1965. That would put the reentry vehicle loss at 12:45am eastern standard time on December 8th. Was it actually an orbital launch and could it stay in orbit for over 39 hours? The answer is yes: it could take two hours to three days to come down from low earth orbit. For example, the December 9, 1965 launch from Vandenberg AFB of a Thor Agena-D took two days to recover after an erratic attitude. More complete analysis is required of the RV/rocket separation which altered descent characteristics since the Air Force said they lost track of it at 7:45pm on December 7th. There is no question that the MK2 RV was capable of extended orbital capabilities and controlled landing.

I attended the 50th anniversary UFO festival in Kecksburg in July 2015 where witnesses told their story and did not remember the details very well like the fact that it was glowing green while descending. I also analyzed the testimonials on Stan Gordon's Kecksburg DVD created in 1998 which was more accurate. Although the Air Force said that there were only three Air Force personal on site to recover a meteor, numerous civilian witnesses verified that there were as many as 25 armed military personnel present. Project Moon Dust was in place at that time and the response was consistent with this project's recovery efforts. Witnesses also said, "It glowed green in the sky, it was a burnt orange color on the ground, the site may be radioactive, there was an arcing blue light coming from the woods, it looked like

Egyptian hieroglyphics were welded on a bead in different designs around the base and that four guys in NASA moon suits took a four to five foot box into the area".

There have been a number of theories over the years to explain Kecksburg:

1. A meteor.
2. Extraterrestrial craft.
3. Cosmos 96 Soviet satellite recovery.
4. Nazi Bell project or some other government experiment.

It makes sense that the December 7, 1965 GE Mark 2 launch in the Pacific was tracked on radar. This explains the military response within 30 minutes to the small rural town of Kecksburg. The copper heat shielding would glow green, the stainless steel would turn a burnt orange color, and the technicians on site would wear proper radiation suits and would carry the correct size lead box for a radioactive power source. They may have had to cut the power source out with a blow torch and walked it out of the woods like the arc of the covenant. They could not risk a radiation leak when exiting a residential area. It was equally as important not to divulge we were spying on Russia. (As a side note, the 1968 zombie classic *Night of the Living Dead* was based on radiation from the Kecksburg crash causing zombies).

Since NASA has eliminated the Cosmos 96 probe as the Kecksburg UFO by confirming it came down 13 hours earlier, after our exhaustive research, we are only left with the Nazi Bell Project which Polish author Igor Witkowski made known in 2000, a Mark 2 failure or a real extraterrestrial UFO. Since NASA was ordered by a Federal court to turn over its files on Kecksburg and they responded that the file box was lost, it is doubtful that NASA will confirm or deny our GE Mark 2 theory. Without confirmation from NASA, GE, the Air Force or the Navy, we have the most scientific explanation for Kecksburg but can only add the GE Mark 2 reentry vehicle to the short list of an extraterrestrial craft that maneuvered in the sky and crashed or a government spy reentry vehicle that minimally crash landed. We believe a GE Mark 2 RV landed in Kecksburg. What do you think? After 50 years, we respectfully request that military witnesses involved in the recovery from NASA, the Army and Air Force come forward and provide details and confirmation of the incident.

Although this article graced the cover of the December 2015 MUFON Journal and the Pitt Post-Gazette, the Pitt Tribune Review made no mention of this evidence and the reporter involved kept referencing funding of the Kecksburg fire department through its summer UFO festival. "All the news that's fit to print"?

Additional Pictures:

(Figure 7- Nazi Bell- www.diehanse.tumblr.com)

(Figure 8- Nazi Bell reactor- www.diehanse.tumblr.com)

(Figure 9- GE Mark 2 that was never flown and in a holding rack)

Stan Gordon, who researches unexplained phenomena, wants the government to set the

Production assistant washes mud from a Styrofoam replica of the Kecksburg UFO

Keckburg starring in UFO drama

By Sharon Santus

There it was, just off Kecksburg's main road: a large, unidentified, acorn-shaped object that had fallen from the winter sky into a creek on the Bill Howard [illegible]

9, 1965, witnesses reported seeing a fiery, bright orange object streak across the sky over Michigan, the tip of Ontario and western Lake Erie. The object continued its descent and finally glided to earth in a densely wooded area near Kecksburg.

Shannon McGinn, segment producer, said witnesses were interviewed at the Kecksburg Fire Hall several days ago and additional interviews were conducted earlier this week at Mountain View Inn, east of Greensburg.

Director Michael Mathis said [illegible]

converged at the scene and set up a command post at the fire hall.

Firemen reported seeing a canvas-covered military transport truck head toward the landing area and then leave later that night. The next day, the object was gone. Researchers theorize [illegible]

(Figure 10- replica of crash on its side)

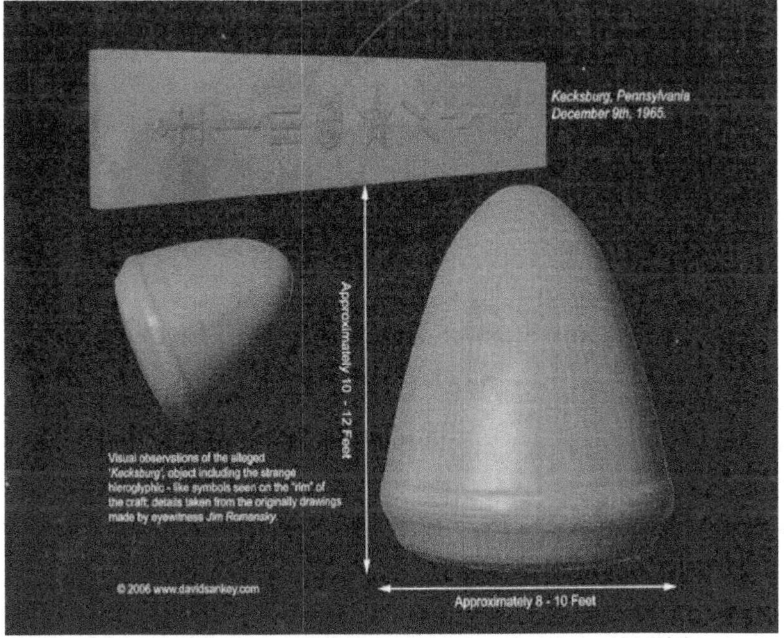

(Figure 11- A key witness describes a 5 pointed star with a circle in the center on the object which is used by our military)

(Figure 12- Cosmos 96 looks nothing like what was found)

Additional notes from the 1998 Stan Gordon Keckesburg DVD:

Here are some important witness comments:

1. Randy Overly- it glowed green
2. Bob Gatty- site may be radioactive.
3. John Hays- chased out of woods and told area may be radioactive.
4. Bill Weaver- 4 guys in moon suits carried a 4x4 box into the woods.
5. Ernie Hoffman- it was the size of 2 suitcases on the flatbed.

6. John Mays- 20-25 military on site; blue lights in woods.
7. Robert Blystone- Military was all over site.
8. Larry Snyder- Armed military barred access.
9. Lillian Hays- Military and civilian personnel used her house and phone. No calls registered on bill.
10. John Hays- Air Force and NASA at their home saw NASA patches on clothing.
11. Bill Bulebush- It made a turn. Saw Egyptian markings.
12. James Romanski- Saw Egyptian markings that looked like they were welded on.
13. Jerry Betters- drew the only notarized sketch of object on flatbed and it 100% matches the GE Mark 4.

After this article was published, detractors reported that December 7 was a sub-orbital launch that couldn't land in Kecksburg, yet the 1958 Pioneer 1 was sub-orbital and took 43 hours to come down. Others sited data on the MK1 and didn't even read this article. The Air Force lied that it was the meteor over Detroit that evening, lied that it only had three personnel there, and lied that they never tracked it on radar while also losing the evidence box. So why would you believe it was sub-orbital when the insertion of these three letters (sub) covered up this event. Any prior orbital launch could also have accounted for the event since the GE Mark 2 characteristics absolutely match the described event! There were also eight different Mark 2 type capsules and rest assured that some were secret projects. What I have learned, and known for a long time, is that there are no experts in the UFO field!

Owen tried to pursue with the C.D.C. his interest in whether there was an increase in Spinal Bifida after the crash due to radiation. Once he mentioned the UFO incident he received no cooperation. He was baffled by that. I told him no one is going to take him serious if he mentions UFOs. Owen did find out that a key witness who is now in his early 70's, has multiple cancers including on his hand which may have been caused by getting too close to the object.

In August of 2016, I was contacted by a man in Maine who said that a 21 year Army Officer who was at Roswell and in charge at Kecksburg gave the order to destroy all records of the Kecksburg case making any future documents suspect. This is why when the Sci-fi channel sued NASA there were no records to be found. This officer was Lt Colonel Gordon H. Rawson (1922-2013) of Paris, Maine. Rawson was told it was a Soviet satellite but he didn't want an international incident so he destroyed the records. We finally have confirmation that the Air Force lied about only having three Air Force personal on site. There is no mention of Kecksburg by Blue Book as they list 16 Pa cases among their 701 unexplained cases. Very odd that they didn't investigate Kecksburg.

This is a possible Soviet reusable VA re-entry vehicle which stood at nine feet:

There were also numerous NIKE Zeus missile launches to shoot down an MK2 as we started early anti-ballistic tests. Any one of these could've sent an MK2 off course towards Kecksburg.

We also discovered that some launches added a booster rocket and used Thiokol rubber fuel, a polysulfide rubber binder that gave improved performance and a smell of sulfur. It opened up the possibility of a second crash site, of the booster, in Mammoth Park.

UFO JOURNAL

December 2015 No. 572 $5

Has a top 5 UFO case been solved?

Was Kecksburg UFO a GE Mark 2 Reentry Vehicle?

by John Ventre, PA State Director
with Owen Eichler

On December 9, 1965, at 4:47 p.m. something navigated through our airspace and made a semi controlled landing in Kecksburg, Pennsylvania. For me, the entire story has been about how it made a left turn near Cleveland and a right turn near Kecksburg and slowed down before minimally "crash" landing in rural Kecksburg and avoiding population centers (like Flight 93). The legend has grown to include one witness who saw a scaly, three fingered hand come out of the top of the UFO, similar to the ending of the 1953 movie "War of the Worlds," to seeing an alien body on a gurney at Hangar 18 at Wright Patterson Air Force base alongside a cone-shaped craft.

I was contacted in February 2015 by Owen Eichler in regards to his theory that the December 9, 1965, Kecksburg UFO incident was potentially a crash and retrieval of a GE Mark 2 reentry vehicle (RV) launched on December 7, 1965. Owen said he has spent 10 years researching his theory and believes he is correct. The GE Mark 2 RV has never been mentioned as a possible candidate for Kecksburg. This object was a spy capsule that was kept secret until 1991. I posed a few questions that were significant to the case:

1. How did the object turn, slow down and perform a controlled landing? Owen said the GE reentry vehicle had four control jets and an internal weighting control system for stability and guidance using the Coanda effect to glide. Owen also said this was not a NASA project.
2. Why would the military show up in such force for a GE reentry vehicle? Owen said it was used for in-space identification of orbiting space craft and may have contained a Radio Isotope Thermal Generator (RTG) that needed to be recovered in order to control and prevent a radiation leak.

Figure 6 - Atlas rocket with Mark 2 Reentry Vehicle installed.

Continued on page 11

References:

1. Program 437, The Air Force's First Anti-Satellite Program, declassified May 6 1991. Maj Gen Paul T. Preuss, Deputy Chief of Staff, plans, HQ ADC, to ADCCS, et. al.. "Program 437 AP (U),' 10 Dec 65
2. Intelligent Revolution 1960: Retrieving the Corona Imagery that Helped Win the Cold War by Ingard Clausen and Edward A. Miller
3. Study of Reentry Vehicle Systems by the Department of Transportation/Office of Commercial Space Transportation 1990
4. Blunt Body Aerodynamics for Hypersonic Low Density Flows by James N. Moss, Christopher E. Glass, and Francis A. Greene
5. Wind Tunnel Investigations of Blunt Body Drag Reduction using Forebody Surface Roughness by Stephen A. Whitmore, Stephanie Sprague, and Jonathon W. Naughton January 2001
6. Intercontinental Ballistic Missiles by Maj. Jane Gibson and Maj. Kenneth G. Kemmerly.
7. International Journal of Engineering and Innovative Technology (IJEIT) Volume 3, Issue 3, September 2013
8. NASA Space Flight Risk Data Collection/Analysis Project Final Report May 11, 1994
9. PROGRAM 437: THE AIR FORCE'S FIRST ANTISATELLITE SYSTEM by Dr. Wayne R. Austerman May 1991
10. Shooting Down a "Star" *Program 437, the US Nuclear ASAT System and Present-Day Copycat Killers by* CLAYTON K. S. CHUN Lieutenant Colonel, USAF April 2000
11. Coming Home: Reentry and Recovery from Space by Roger D. Launius and Dennis R. Jenkins
12. Modeling of Ablation Phenomena in Space Applications by Daniele Bianche
13. www.spacelaunchreport.com

Chapter 33

The UFO Quiz

Here's a quiz with additional info:

1. When Truman Bethurum mentioned the planet Clarion, where did he originally say it was?
2. Who was Howard Menger?
3. What is the Coalition for Freedom of Information?
4. George Adamski also talked with an alien. Discuss his experiences.
5. Describe the Scoriton Mystery.
6. The first person to describe a UFO as a "saucer" was?
7. Who is Timothy Good?
8. Edward Ruppelt headed what organization?
9. What conclusions did this organization reach?
10. What was the fate of this organization?
11. Major Donald Keyhoe headed what organization?
12. What was the fate of this organization?
13. What conclusions did this organization reach?
14. In 1947 a UFO allegedly crashed near Roswell, New Mexico. What is the significance of this area?
15. One of the early investigators of the Roswell incident bills himself as a nuclear physicist. What is his name?
16. In 1999 a French think-tank published what report? What were its conclusions?

17. Who is Nick Pope?

18. In 1966 John G. Fuller published a book titled *The Interrupted Journey*. Who did it concern and what was it about?

19. What is Majic or Majestic 12?

20. Where is Bentwaters and what happened there?

21. A 1968 Report done by the University of Colorado had an official and an unofficial title. What were these titles?

22. What are the conclusions of this report?

23. Whitley Strieber is a New York author who became very famous for what book?

24. Explain the circumstances around the abduction of Travis Walton.

25. Explain the "UFO Curse." Who formulated this?

26. Who was James McDonald?

27. Budd Hopkins is an artist. What is his avocation?

28. Describe the "Cash-Landrum Case."

29. Who was Donald Howard Menzel? Where did his name surprisingly appear?

30. What is MUFON? Describe its structure? Who was its founder?

31. What alleged UFO evidence was found as an exact duplicate on eBay?

32. What is Project Serpo?

33. Describe the Bob Lazar story.

34. Richard Dolan is an historian who published what detailed and seminal work on UFOs?

35. Describe the Shag Harbor incident?

36. Who coined the phrase 'Swamp Gas' to explain UFOs?

37. Describe Jacques Vallee and discuss his theory of the origins of UFOs.

38. Describe the 1965 UFO incident at Kecksburg, Pennsylvania.

39. Who is Billy Meier?

40. What is 'The Varo Edition' of M.K. Jessup's book, 'The Case for the UFO'?

41. Who is Philip Corso and what are his allegations?

42. Both Jesse Marcel and Jesse Marcel, Jr. are famous names associated with Roswell. Why?

43. Describe Dr. Steven Greer's relationship with Mothra.

44. The Nellis Military Operations Area is otherwise known as?

45. Describe the Phoenix Lights incident, including the USAF explanation.

46. Describe the Lonnie Zamora incident.

47. Describe the Antonio Villas Boas case in Brazil in the fifties.

48. Bill Moore has authored several books on UFOs, but is controversial. Why?

49. Dr. Bruce Maccabee is considered an expert in what field?

50. Raymond Fowler's accounts of Betty Andreasson's abduction have a decidedly what slant?

51. Describe the idea behind the Drake Equation.

52. What is the Fermi Paradox?

53. Contrast the ETH and the IDH (sometimes called the EDH)

54. If you happened to take a picture of a UFO, what are the very next actions you should take?

55. What is the Robertson Panel & what were its conclusions?

56. What US President advocated Congressional hearings on UFOs?

57. What US astronaut personally saw UFOs and accused the government of cover-up?

58. What were the three code names for the Air Force study of UFOs—in the correct order?

59. Describe at least one UFO charlatan in detail

60. The "Cosmic Pulse of Life" was written by Trevor James Constable. What is his theory about the origins of UFOs?

61. Describe the Men in Black.

62. Who was Phillip Klass? What was his theory about UFOs?

63. Describe the "Big Sur Incident."

64. Who was Dr. John E. Mack?

65. What US President said he saw a UFO? What is the most common explanation for his sighting?

66. A UFO flap over an American city in the early fifties resulted in an unprecedented government response. What city was this and what did the government do?

67. Name at least one prominent UFO sighting prior to 1947.

68. Discuss the government response to the Stephenville, Texas sightings. What happened?

69. What do you think is the best UFO book ever written?

70. Who do you think is the Dean of Ufology today?

71. Name at least two serial ('periodical') UFO publications published today.
72. Who is the most prominent UFO bibliographer today and what has he published?
73. What is NARCAP?
74. A book called *My Saturnian Lover* was published by Marla Baxter in 1958. Who is this about?
75. Who was Thomas Mantell?
76. John G. Fuller wrote a book called 'Incident at Exeter.' Describe the incident.
77. Who is David Michael Jacobs?
78. Who is Michio Kaku? What has he contributed?
79. Linda Moulton Howe is famous for what?
80. Explain the CE-1, CE-2, CE-3, CE-4 classification scheme.
81. Discuss the Pascagoula, Mississippi abduction incident.
82. Explain the White Sands Incident.
83. What does the Biblical prophet Ezekiel have to do with UFOs?
84. Name at least three countries that have 'released' their files on UFOs.
85. Richard Doty claims what?
86. Explain the pros and cons of SETI.
87. What types of things are commonly misidentified as UFOs?
88. Name at least one organization dedicated to debunking UFOs.
89. What is 'Exopolitics' and the Disclosure Movement?
90. What is NUFORC? Bonus: Where, specifically, is it located?
91. David Biedney's technical expertise is in what field?

92. What crypto zoological creature is sometimes associated with UFOs?

93. Describe the JAL 1628 case over Alaska. Why is this noteworthy?

94. What is the most common explanation for UFO propulsion systems?

95. What is CUFOS? Who founded it?

96. Discuss the Alien Autopsy film by Ray Santilli.

97. What is unusual about the Belgium UFO flap in 1989-1990?

98. Describe the most common body types ascribed to aliens.

99. In 1954 President Eisenhower was in Palm Springs and went to the dentist. Where is it alleged that he REALLY went?

100. Describe the Gulf Breeze Incidents.

Answers:

1. Truman Bethurum was a 1950's era contactee who claimed to have been aboard a flying saucer from the planet Clarion, a place where everyone spoke perfect English, all were Christians, and all of whom attended church on Sundays. Bethurum's initial location for Clarion was "on the other side of the Moon," which is the correct answer. After having the impossibility of this location pointed out to him he then changed the location of Clarion to "the other side of the Sun" in the same orbit as Earth, therefore it could not be seen from this planet. He claimed he simply misunderstood the location at first. His first book is *Aboard a Flying Saucer; non-fiction—a true account of factual experience*. Los Angeles: DeVorss & Co., Publishers, 1954, 192pp. Pre-ISBN days.

2. Howard Menger was one of the 1950's era contactees. Unlike many contactees, he did not bring back a religious or apocalyptic message, but came back with stories of Atlantis and Lemuria, proper diet, and alien space music. He first encountered a 'girl from Venus' when he was a boy himself and recounts continued contacts throughout his life, including rides on spaceships to both Venus and the moon. His first and most famous book is *From Outer Space to You*, (Clarksburg, WV: Saucerian Books, 1959, 256pp. Pre-ISBN Days. Menger passed away in 2009).

3. The Coalition for Freedom of Information (CFI) is headed by journalist Leslie Kean and dedicated to "Achieving scientific, congressional and media credibility for the study of unexplained

aerial phenomena while working for the release of official information and physical evidence." One notable achievement of CFI is a successful lawsuit against NASA forcing the agency to release any documents on the Kecksburg, Pennsylvania case.

4. George Adamski's alien was named Orthon, who had long blonde hair. Orthon was from the planet Venus. Adamski claimed that Venus was fully inhabited with cities and farms. Of course, with a telescope all we can see of Venus is a cloud covered white orb. Adamski covered this by claiming when he took a ride in Orthon's space ship and that Earth looked in a similar fashion from only 50,000 miles out on space. This was before pictures of Earth from space proved conclusively that this was not so. Adamski's first book is *Flying Saucers Have Landed*. New York: British Book Centre, 1953, 232pp. Pre-ISBN days.

5. In 1965 in England Arthur Bryant allegedly had an encounter with a flying saucer. One of the three beings was a youth who spoke in an eastern European accent and called himself Yamski. Bryant also obtained some pieces allegedly from the P-51 fighter flown by Thomas Mantell. The story caused a sensation and a book was written by Eileen Buckle called *The Scoriton Mystery; Did Adamski return*? London: Neville Spearman, 1967, 302pp. Pre ISBN. Suggesting Yamski was the reincarnation of George Adamski. Bryant then died of a brain tumor. Upon interviewing his widow it turns out she knew the story because her late husband had written it as a science fiction novel.

6. Kenneth Arnold. His description of the craft themselves was NOT that they looked like flying saucers, but that their travel exhibited characteristics like a 'saucer skipping over water.' The craft themselves were sickle shaped with the blunt end leading and the sharper ends behind. Journalists picked up on his description and misused it by calling the craft flying saucers. This all happened near Mt. Rainer, Washington State, on June 24, 1947, while Arnold was flying a small plane over the Cascade Mountain Range. Arnold was looking for a crashed military airplane at the time. (Actually the correct answer is John Martin, see pg. 35 #22).
7. Timothy Good is a British Ufologist who has written a number of books on the subject. He is kind of a British Richard Dolan. His most comprehensive book is *Above Top Secret; the worldwide UFO cover-up*, New York: William Morrow & Co., 1988, 592pp. ISBN: 0-688-07860-5.
8. Edward Ruppelt, a highly decorated soldier from WW II (He was in the US Army. The Army Air Force split off into its own service after the war.), was director of the Air Force *Project Blue Book*. He also headed Project Grudge for a few months before its demise. Ruppelt was the first to standardize UFO reporting procedures. By all accounts he was as objective as possible in his approach, though there is much speculation that the project was a set-up by the Air Force. It does not follow that Ruppelt was aware of this, however. After his retirement from the Air Force Ruppelt wrote *The Report on Unidentified Flying Objects*, Garden City,

NY: Doubleday, 1956, 243pp, Pre-ISBN days where he talks of his experiences.

9. Project Blue Book's conclusions were really more complex than generally realized. It was more of a reporting agent than an analysis center. Its demise came about because of the Condon Report, which concluded that UFOs were unworthy of further study. On the one hand, Project Blue Book Special Report 14, an analysis by the Battelle Institute, concluded that 22% of the cases were listed as unknowns. On the other, the 'conclusions' were that UFOs were the result of mass hysteria, misidentifications, hoaxes, or produced by 'psychopathological persons.'

10. Project Blue Book was disbanded in 1969. The Air Force claims to have gotten out of the UFO business at that time.

11. NICAP: The National Investigations Committee on Aerial Phenomena began in 1956 to 1980. NICAP had several directors, but Keyhoe was arguably the most famous of them. The first link on the acronym points to the Wikipedia entry. The second points to an 'official' site funded by the Fund for UFO Research.

12. NICAP was a very straightforward organization that attempted to steer clear of the fringe elements if Ufology. Several members of its board had military ties, including an ex-Director of the CIA, Admiral Roscoe Hillenkoetter. Its major conclusion, if you will, was that the US government was holding back evidence and was engaged in a UFO cover up. Here is a History of NICAP by Richard Hall, who lived through all this.

13. NICAP disbanded in 1980 and its assets were purchased by CUFOS. The Wikipedia article cited above insists NICAP was a victim of its own incompetence and the waning interest in UFOs after the publication of the Condon Report. But many people, including Richard Hall, cited above, and Richard Dolan believe the demise of NICAP was intentional. The last Director, Alan Hall, was a retired CIA employee.

14. The significance of Roswell as an area is that at the time it was near the Roswell Army Air Force Base, which housed the 509th bomber group, the only air wing at the time capable of dropping atomic weapons. Speculation by Stanton Friedman and others is that the 'aliens' knew 'the kids got hold of the matches' (Friedman) and were checking out the situation when a reconnaissance craft crashed.

15. That's Stanton Friedman. He received a Master's degree in physics from the University of Chicago in 1956. He worked for a number of defense industry companies, but since 1967 has lectured exclusively in the UFO field. He was one of the first investigators of the Roswell, New Mexico crash and a principle supporter of the authenticity of the MJ-12 documents. He is strictly a 'nuts & bolts guy' who believes in the Extra-terrestrial Hypothesis.

16. This is the COMETA Report, done in France by Institute of Advanced Studies for National Defence, or IHEDN. Many high level defense people were involved in the report, but it is not an 'official' report in that it was neither commissioned nor funded by the government of France. After dealing with a number of

unexplained events the authors conclude that the Extra-Terrestrial Hypothesis is the most logical explanation for UFOs. They also are quite sure "The Superpower," i.e.: The US Government is withholding information and is engaged in a massive cover up. They urge all other countries to put pressure on the USA to divulge their secrets.

17. Nick Pope served in the British Ministry of Defence (MOD) as a civil service employee and spent several years as the MOD point of contact for UFO matters. Since his resignation from MOD he has become a frequent author and Ufologist with his own web site. His book, *Open Skies; closed minds* (New York: Overlook Hardcover, 1999, 270pp. ISBN: 978-0879519162) is a biography of his work within MOD.

18. Betty and Barney Hill. This is one of the first abduction cases which happened in 1961. This is one of those cases where the aliens stated their origin, Zeta Riticuli, and showed Betty Hill a star map that supposedly showed the stars from the viewpoint of Zeta Reticuli, this corroborating the aliens' story. A more recent treatment of this case can be found in *Captured; the Betty and Barney Hill UFO Experience* by Stanton Friedman and Betty's niece, Kathleen Marden. (Franklin Lakes, NJ: New Page Books, 2007, 320pp. ISBN: 978-1564149718.)

19. Majestic 12 is a code name for a group of high-level people who were brought together to deal with the 1947 Roswell, New Mexico crash and its aftermath. Opinions on the truth of this group

are highly controversial. Some people, such as Stanton Friedman, believe they are completely genuine. Others, such as Brad Sparks, maintain MJ-12 is a disinformation campaign put together by William Moore and James Doty, both of whom have been associated with such campaigns in the past. The documents themselves 'prove' (if they are genuine) a vast cover up. Members included Admiral Roscoe Hillenkoetter, also a member of the NICAP Board of Directors, and Howard Menzel, a noted UFO skeptic. The inference is that Menzel was engaged in a disinformation campaign of his own in debunking UFOs, but was secretly involved in the cover up. Friedman's latest book on the subject is *Top Secret/Majic; operation Majestic-12 and the United States Government's UFO Cover-up*. New York: Marlowe & Company, 1996, 282pp. ISBN: 1-56924-830-3.

20. Bentwaters refers to a Royal Air Force Base near Rendlesham Forest in Suffolk, England, where a UFO incident took place in December of 1980 which included a landing of a craft viewed by many airmen. A Lt. Col. Halt wrote a memo about the incident which was uncovered as well as a nearly indecipherable tape. As usual, there is controversy. Jenny Randles maintains there was nothing extraordinary about the sighting where Nick Pope believes it is a real event. Several books have been written about this, including *You can't tell the people; the definitive account of the Rendlesham Forest UFO Mystery* by *Georgini Bruni (*London: Macmillan, 2001, 200pp. ISBN: 978-0330390217.

21. The Condon Report is the popular name for the "Scientific Study of Unidentified Flying Objects" done by the University of Colorado under the direction of Dr. Edward Condon and under contract with the US Air Force.
22. The report concluded that UFOs were not worthy of further scientific study. As a result, the Air Force Project Blue Book was disbanded. It is, of course, a lightning rod for controversy, if for no other reason that Condon himself seems to have reached his conclusion before the study was finished. The "Low Memo" seemed to endorse the idea that the study was a fake. From the memo: "Our study would be conducted almost entirely by non-believers who, though they couldn't possibly prove a negative result, could and probably would add an impressive body of thick evidence that there is no reality to the observations. The trick would be, I think, to describe the project so that, to the public, it would appear a totally objective study but, to the scientific community, would present the image of a group of non-believers trying their best to be objective but having an almost zero expectation of finding a saucer."
23. The book is *Communion*. Strieber was a noted science fiction/horror writer prior to publishing this book, as well as several sequels, in which he claims repeated abductions by grey aliens, which he calls 'The Visitors.' Strieber has become somewhat of a celebrity in UFO circles, though some people claim in later years he has lost touch with reality. His web site, Unknown Country, is a platform for his current work. As for the books

themselves, there are some people convinced of his sincerity and others who think he remains a very good fiction writer.

24. Travis Walton was working on a reforestation crew in a national forest in Arizona when he was abducted in 1975. His work crew reportedly saw him hit with a flash of light from a UFO. Hey fled in panic. When they returned he was not to be found. A few days later he showed up in town making claims of abduction. The case is extremely controversial for a number of reasons. Philip Klass got involved in this one and suggested the real reason behind the 'abduction' was that the crew was behind in their contract work for the forest service. The story was made into a movie: *Fire in the Sky*. Walton's own book is *Fire in the Sky; the Walton Experience.* Marlowe & Company, 3rd edition, 1997, 330pp. ISBN: 978-1569247105

25. The "UFO Curse" was formulated by Philip Klass and was part of his Last Will & Testament: To Ufologists who publicly criticize me, or who even think unkind thoughts about me in private, I do hereby leave and bequeath: THE UFO CURSE: No matter how long you live, you will never know any more about UFOs than you know today. You will never know any more about what UFOs really are, or where they come from. You will never know any more about what the U.S. Government really knows about UFOs than you know today. As you lie on your own death-bed you will be as mystified about UFOs as you are today. And you will remember this curse.

26. James McDonald was a physicist from the University of Arizona who developed an interest in UFOs. He favored the ET Hypothesis and tried to get more scientists involved in the UFO field. He offered his services to the Condon Committee, but was refused, and when it became obvious where the Condon Committee was headed, he became an avowed critic. He was the one who leaked the Low Memo which detailed how the committee could pretend to study the subject, which resulted in Condon trying to get him fired. He also came at odds with Philip Klass. After his marriage broke up he apparently carefully planned his own suicide. He botched it, managing to blind himself, and then succeeded a few months later. A book on his life is *Firestorm: Dr. James E. McDonald's Fight for UFO Science*, by Ann Druffell. 2nd edition, Orem, Utah: Granite Publishing, 2003, 640pp. ISBN: 978-0926524583.

27. Yes, Hopkins is an artist whose medium is sculpture. His avocation is studying incidents of alien abduction by using hypnotic regression. He has written several books on the subject. He founded the Intruders Foundation "to provide sympathetic help, understanding and personal investigation for those reporting UFO abduction experiences." The 1992 movie Intruders is based on his work. Although he has never been accused of being anything but sincere, critics have accused him of leading witnesses during hypnotic regression and being out of his element even for attempting to do so In my own observations of Hopkins I have to say that he seems unusually accepting of anyone's stories even

when it appears to others that the story is an attention-getting device. I don't think he has ever met an abductions story he didn't like. Probably his most famous book is *Missing Time; a documented study of UFO abductions*. New York: Richard Merek Books, 1981, 258pp. ISBN: 0-399-90102-7.

28. The Cash-Landrum Case happened in 1980 to Betty Cash and Vickie Landrum near Dayton, Texas. Colby Landrum, Vickie's 7-year old grandson, was also in the car. They saw a diamond-shaped vehicle apparently having difficulty flying, surrounded by dozens of Chinook (i.e.: Military) helicopters. Cash got out of the car to stare at the object. Both women developed the symptoms of radiation exposure and both eventually died from cancer. A book on this incident is *The Cash-Landrum Incident,* by John Schuessler. Geo Graphics Printing Company, 1998, 323pp.

29. Donald Howard Menzel was one of the earliest UFO debunkers and a professor of astronomy at Harvard University, who authored several books debunking UFOs. His name, however, appears as one of the members of the covert Majestoc-12 group, suggesting he was part of an attempt to cover up UFO activities. This begs the question of the authenticity of the MJ-12 documents, of course. One of his books still available is *The UFO Enigma: The Definitive Explanation of the UFO Phenomenon*. New York: Doubleday, 1977, 297pp. ISBN: 978-0385035965.

30. MUFON stands for the Mutual UFO Network, founded by Walter Andrus. It appoints directors for each region, state, or even county and attempts to teach members the basics of UFO

investigation. In theory the structure is unusually hierarchical. One is assigned a position in the organization. I was a 'Research Fellow in Librarianship' when I was a member. It is one of the few places that actually attempts to offer courses on UFO research. It started in 1969 and is now the oldest continuously running UFO organization in the country.

31. The eBay UFO incident refers to the Billy Meier Ray Gun pictures. The exact same parts were found on an eBay listing for a toy gun made in China.

32. Project Serpo describes an alien/human exchange program where American astronauts traveled to an alien planet in the Zeta Reticuli star system, lived for a couple of years, and returned. There is a Serpo web site with vast amount of detail on the project. It is largely considered a hoax, particularly with the involvement of Richard Doty, who has been involved in several hoaxes, including Majestic-12 and Paul Bennewitz.

33. Bob Lazar is a self-proclaimed physicist who claims to have worked in alien craft at Area 51 in Nevada. He says he worked on reverse-engineering the propulsion systems. His talks contain an amazing amount of detail, but when you examine his claims, things start to fall apart. His claims for education, for example, cannot be verified. Instead of a Master's Degree from MIT, it appears Lazar took a course in electronics at Pierce Community College. He has been unable to show any degrees he claims he earned and attributes this to a government claim against him. It appears Lazar did work briefly for naval Intelligence. He was able to produce a

W-2 statement proving this, but it was for less than $1000, which cannot possibly be very much time. Tom Mahood keeps a Lazar Web Page analyzing his many claims and has a lot more detail than the wiki page.

34. Richard Dolan published *UFOs and the National Security State* which will wind up being three volumes of the most comprehensively researched and documented works in the English language. The first book has been out for many years: *Chronology of a cover-up, 1941-1973*. (Charlottesville, VA: Hampton Roads Publishing, 2nd edition, 2002, 477pp. ISBN: 1-57174-0) the second in the series, "The Cover-up exposed, 1973-1991 is expected in early 2009." The third volume will cover from 1991 to the present day and has no title yet.

35. The Shag Harbor Incident took place on the southeastern shore of Nova Scotia, Canada, in October, 1967. Witnesses heard what they thought was a plane crash during the night and observed lights out in the harbor. Rescue parties found nothing and authorities claimed all planes in the area were accounted for. However, the US and Canadian military apparently launched an operation to recover an object, which had since moved from Shag Harbor to the north. The link explains more about the incident. It has often been called the Canadian Roswell. Here is a link to an article by Don Ledger on the incident.

36. "Swamp gas" was the invention of Dr. J. Allen Hynek, 1910-1986, an astronomer who worked with the Air Force Projects Sign, Grudge, and Blue Book. There are quite a few 'explanations' of

the origin of the term, but we'll use Hynek's own explanation as the most definitive. "When In 1966 I suggested swamp gas as a possibility for the origin of a portion of the numerous Michigan sightings at Dexter and Hillsdale, in which *faint* lights over swampy areas were observed (the explanation was never intended to cover the entire spectrum of stories generated in that general area at the time), swamp gas became a household word and a standard humorous synonym for UFOs. UFOs, swamp gas, and I were lampooned in the press and were the subjects of many delightful cartoons (of which I have quite a collection.)" *–The UFO Experience*, pp195-196.

37. Jacques Vallee is a computer scientist and long-time UFO researcher. Although he originally championed the ETH, his later books show a changed position to the Inter-dimensional hypothesis, with a large dose of folklore and mythology thrown in. He is considered one the more erudite Ufologists. He left the UFO filed some time ago because of what he thought of as shoddy research in the field. He has published many books on UFOS. One is *Passport to Magonia: From Folklore to Flying Saucers*. Chicago: Henry Regnery Co, 1969, 372pp. Pre- ISBN days. This is listed here because it is the first book where Vallee strays from the ETH to a more circumspect view.

38. The Kecksburg Incident occurred in December, 1965 in Pennsylvania when witnesses saw an object strike the ground in the woods. Witnesses saw an acorn shaped object that had made a furrow in the woods before it came to a stop. The Army quickly

showed up in force and cordoned off the area. The object was removed on a flatbed truck in the middle of the night. Witnesses also reported hieroglyphic writing on the side of the craft and one witness reported a reptilian arm was seen coming out of a porthole of the craft after a General hit the craft causing a bell-ringing tone. Other witnesses claim the craft changed direction while in flight, indicating intelligent control.

39. Billy Meier is a one-armed Swiss contactee whose UFO photographs were originally considered stunning. The "UFO: Contact from the Pleiades" coffee table books show amazing pictures. He reports contact with one Semjase, from the Pleiades, who tells him the usual contactee stories. He has attracted a host of followers over the years and produced many photographs. However, they are all fakes. His pictures of Semjase came from the Donna Reed Show. His pictures of a 'ray gun' show parts available on eBay. His pictures from the Jurassic period, where he claimed to travel in time, came from a book. UFO models have been found in his barn. Recognizable parts from his 'wedding cake' UFO were found to be parts of a barrel. The entire thing is nonsense. The only surprising thing is that anyone believes him at all.

40. The Varo Edition refers to a special edition of Morris K. Jessup's book called *The Case for the UFO* where a copy of the book had been heavily annotated by several people critiquing the work apparently from a position of extraordinary knowledge on the truth about UFOs. According to Jessup, he was contacted by US Navy Intelligence, which had the original copy. He identified one

of the writers a Carlos Allende, whom Jessup had corresponded with regarding the Philadelphia Experiment. Apparently the Navy printed a small number of books with the Varo Publishing Company. The most common edition available today was reproduced by Gray Barker.

41. Philip Corso was a retired Lt. Col. in the Army who saw service during WW II and was a staff member for the National Security Council. Shortly before his death he published a book, *The Day After Roswell* where he claimed he was tasked with salting US Industry with UFO technology recovered from the 1947 Roswell UFO crash. Among the inventions he claimed came from the UFO were integrated circuits, lasers, fiber optics, etc. Corso also confirmed the existence of the Majestic-12 group. Critics of Corso argue that the history of the technologies he claims to have seeded show very well that these inventions were well along the way before Corso intervened. Hey also suggest Corso had a penchant for exaggeration. He claimed to have single-handedly saved Italy during WW II, for example. Corso himself was apparently upset over some of the book's contents, but his ill health and death prevented him from correcting the errors. His book is, *The Day After Roswell*. New York: Pocket Books, 1997, 341pp. ISBN: 0-671-00461-1.

42. Maj. Jesse Marcel was Intelligence Officer at Roswell and one of the first to encounter the debris from the disc that had crashed. On his initial inspection of the crash site he filled his car with some of the debris and made a stop at his home before proceeding to the

base. There he showed his son, Jesse Marcel, Jr., pieces of the debris. Marcel Sr. was later involved in the retraction of the initial report that the Air Force had recovered a crashed disk. After he left the service Marcel did not talk about the crash for many years, but when he did begin to talk, his story varied a bit and he apparently embellished some of it. However, the claim that he was a 'bad soldier' is not substantiated, especially in light of his commendations, linked to his name for this entry. Also, no one has been able to contradict his son's testimony about seeing the debris itself. Marcel wrote a book recently titled *The Roswell Legacy; the son of the first military officer at the 1947 crash site tells his father's story—and his own.* Helena, MT: Big Sky Press, 2007, 182pp. ISBN: 978-0-9795917-0-9.

43. Mothra was promoted by Dr. Steven Greer's web site as an etheric light being seen on one of his kumbaya camping trips to view UFOs, for which he charges $800. After derisive laughter was heard across the land, Mothra and his sidekicks were quickly taken off the web site with the hope they would disappear forever.

44. Area 51, near Las Vegas, Nevada. The U.S. Government now acknowledges that Area 51 is a top secret military base where advanced aerial craft are tested. The U-2, the Blackbird, and the F-117 are all examples of aircraft that have been tested and perfected there. The larger implication, of course, is that this is the area where the US has attempted to reverse-engineer flying saucers. A number of people (not just Bob Lazar) have testified this is the

case. In popular culture area 51 has become synonymous with UFOs and alien beings.

45. The Phoenix Lights incident happened on March 13, 1997. The initial sighting was seen by many people and consisted of a large triangular-shaped object over Phoenix itself. The second set of lights was identified by the USAF as flares dropped from an A-10 Warthog during exercises near the city. Governor Fife Symington held a press conference shortly after the event with one of his aids dressed up in an alien costume. He said it was to lighten the concern, but many so it as belittling the incident. Later on Symington claimed to have seen the triangular craft himself. A book of the same name (Hampton Roads Press, 2004, 248pp. ISBN: 978-1571743770, was published by Dr. Lynne Kitei.

46. Lonnie Zamora was a New Mexico policeman who reported an incident in 1964 where he saw a UFO land and occupants descend from the craft. The craft left behind physical traces in the form of fused sand that is apparently still there today. Zamora was on a recent edition of UFO Hunters where he described the scene. Ray Stanford wrote a complete accounting of the incident in Stanford's *'Socorro 'Saucer in a Pentagon Pantry'*, 1976, Blue Apple Books, ISBN 0-917092-00-7.

47. Antonio Villas Boas had one of the earliest abduction encounters in 1957 in Brazil when he was taken aboard a UFO. He was stripped naked and doused with a fluid that made him especially sexually excited. A young woman entered the room and had sexual intercourse with him. She pointed to her stomach and

then upwards before she left the room. He was given a tour of the spacecraft before he was escorted off and the ship left. Here is another account. Many of the earlier UFO books have an accounting of this story.

48. Bill Moore was active in UFO circles in the 80's and wrote such books as The Philadelphia Experiment and The Roswell Incident. He was also involved in the MJ-12 papers and was instrumental in making those public. However, Moore also admitted that he took place, along with Richard Doty, in a dis-information campaign. Specifically, he helped misinform Paul Bennewitz to such an extent that he went to a mental hospital after a nervous breakdown. It is widely believed that Bennewitz was 'neutralized' by the government because of his work exposing a cover-up. Moore explained his involvement in this disinformation campaign as an attempt to get closer to the real truth about UFOs, but his reputation was severely damaged by this admission and he gradually faded from the UFO scene.

49. Dr. Bruce Maccabee is a physicist who works for the US Navy and is considered an expert in photo analysis. His most recent UFO book is *UFO/FBI Connection: The Secret History of the Government's Cover-Up*. Llwellyn Publications, 2000, 216pp. ISBN: 978-1567184938.

50. Raymond Fowler has written five books on the Betty Andreasson Lucas abduction incidents: *The Andreasson Affair* (1979), *The Andreasson Affair, Phase II* (1982), *The Watchers*

(1990), *The Watchers II* (1995), and *The Andreasson Legacy*. Lucas's experiences are interpreted in a decidedly Christian slant.

51. The Drake Equation is an attempt to determine the likelihood of alien life using a speculative equation of parameters such as the number of stars with planets, the number of stars that could support life, the number that actually support life, etc.

52. The Fermi Paradox is the notion that if there is a high probability of advanced intelligent life in the universe, why do we not see them or hear from them?

53. The ETH is the 'Extra-Terrestrial Hypothesis' for the origin of UFOs which states that they come from other planets, other solar systems, etc. This is essentially the main 'Nuts & Bolts' idea that UFOs are real, physical craft embodying advanced engineering and propulsion concepts. The major criticism of this theory is that the limitation of the speed of light precludes inter-stellar travel. The IDH is the 'Inter-Dimensional Hypothesis' which holds that UFOs travel between and originate in other dimensions, meaning they do not need to travel large distances. The major criticism of this idea is that no one has really shown what these 'dimensions' could be.

54. Whether the camera is digital or film-based the major thing to do is nothing. Don't take the film or memory card out of the camera. Do not change the settings. Do not alter anything. Instead, seal the camera and get it to a reputable expert in photography. People such as J. Ritzmann, David Biedney, or Bruce Maccabee would be good choices.

55. The Robertson Panel was set up in 1952 at the behest of the CIA. This was immediately after the Washington DC UFO flap. It consisted of five physicists, astronomers, and radar experts with J. Allen Hynek as an 'Associate member.' After considering 23 cases (that's about 1% of what Blue Book had investigated up until then) in a whopping 12 hours of meetings the Panel concluded that UFOs were not a threat to the defense of the United States, but that continued questioning by the public was. Their conclusion was that the Air Force should embark on a 'public education' campaign to debunk UFOs. One of the immediate results was a downgrading of Project Blue Book in status.

56. This is kind of a trick question in that President Gerald Ford advocated Congressional hearings as a Representative from Michigan. He was prompted to do so after a flap in Michigan, the same one where J. Allen Hynek claimed some of the sightings could be explained by swamp gas.

57. There is actually more than one, Gordon Cooper had several encounters with UFOs, including one on the ground which was filmed and the film confiscated. The other astronaut was Dr. Edgar Mitchell, who has never seen a UFO, but says he has talked with people who have and that there is a government cover up.

58. Projects Sign, Grudge, and Blue Book. Sign started in late 1947 and lasted about a year. Grudge started in February, 1949 and lasted until late 1951. Blue Book lasted from 1952 until early 1970. The conclusions of Project Sign were that UFOs were likely extraterrestrial in origin, a conclusion that proved unacceptable to

the Air Force brass. Project Grudge started out with the premise that all UFO reports could be explained. Blue Book had essentially the same conclusions as Grudge, but here is that 'Blue Book Special Report #14,' a statistical analysis done by Battelle, which concluded 22% of the Blue Book cases remain unexplained.

59. Probably the easiest way to 'answer' this question is a link to ufowatchdog.com. This sight is no longer being updated, but it's 'Hall of Shame' has an extensive list of charlatans from which to choose, so much so that there are actually six halls to hold them all.

60. Trevor James Constable believes UFOs are living organisms populating our atmosphere. They can be seen by using an infrared camera. His most famous book on this issue is *The Cosmic Pulse of Life* (Borderland Sciences Research Foundation; Revised edition, 1990. 488pp. ISBN: 978-0945685074.)

61. The Men in Black were originally described by Gray Barker, who may have made the whole thing up, described them in his book, *They Knew Too Much About Flying Saucers*. (New York: Tower Books, 1967, 190pp. Pre-ISBN days) They are mysterious 'government agents' who show up after an incident and tell people to keep quiet. There is also a paranormal aspect to some of the reports. The Men don't act normally, seem stilted in speech and habits, and otherwise act strangely.

62. Phil Klass was probably the most colorful and strident debunker of all time. An editor for Aviation Week & Space

Technology, early on he took on UFOs and decided they were total nonsense. He did not criticize from afar but went to UFO Conferences and 'road the buses' with everyone else. He attacked people personally and got it back in return. His theory that UFOs were 'Plasma' has been widely derided. One of his many books is *UFOs; the public deceived.* Amherst, NY: Prometheus Books, 1986, 310pp. ISBN: 978-0879753221.

63. The Big Sur UFO incident involved the filming of an ICBM test at Vandenberg AFB which was filmed from a remote tracking station at Big Sur in California in 1964. Lt. Bob Jacobs was part of the film team. They successfully completed their mission and thought everything was fine. Then Jacobs was called into his commanding officer's office and shown the results, which consisted of a UFO intercepting the missile, shooting beams of light at it, and the warhead subsequently falling back into the atmosphere. The film was confiscated, the offending track removed. His boss, Maj. Mansmann, later confirmed the story. It is featured in Out of the Blue, by James Fox.

64. Dr. John E. Mack was a Harvard professor of Psychiatry (an M.D.) who studied abduction cases. He encountered stiff academic opposition to his studies, including an investigation of his activities, though he was eventually exonerated. One of his books: *Abduction: Human Encounters with Aliens*, New York: Scribner, 2008, 464pp. ISBN: 978-1416575801.

65. Jimmy Carter. It was Venus, end of story. He saw the object just after sunset in the Western sky at precisely the altitude that

Venus would have been. Venus can be no more than 60 degrees from the sun in the elliptic. It either precedes or follows the sun's path. The sighting was just after 7:00 pm, which would have made Venus the brightest object in the western sky still above the horizon. There is some controversy here because some reports show the sighting happened on October, 1969. However, given Carter's position as President of the Lion's Club at the time, this simply could not be correct because his term ran out the previous summer. Very likely the sighting happened in January of 1969. He reported it years after the fact.

66. Washington, DC in the summer of 1952. Although the Air Force suggested the sightings, which had been tracked on radar, were 'temperature inversions,' research has shown they scrambled jet fighters with the intent of shooting down the craft. The most recent book on the subject is *Shoot them down; the flying saucer air wars of 1952*. Frank C. Feschino, 392pp. ISBN: 978 0615155531. In the immediate aftermath of this flap the Robertson Panel was convened.

67. You have a lot of leeway here. The Foo Fighters, blobs of light that followed Allied planes during WWII would count. So would the Aurora Incident, which happened in 1897. There were a number of 'mystery air ship' sightings in the late 1800s and early 1900s. A book on these is *The Great Airship Mystery; a UFO of the 1890s*, by Daniel Cohen, New York: Dodd, Mead & Company, 1981, 212pp. ISBN: 0-396-07990-3. Ezekiel's Wheel (Ezekiel 1:15-21) is said to be a description of a UFO from the Bible.

68. The Stephenville, Texas sightings in early 2008 prompted national news organization to cover it in detail. Some people said they saw F-16 fighter jets pursuing the craft. After initially proclaiming there were no jets in the area during the time in question, the air force later said there were nine jets on a training mission and this accounted for the sightings.

69. Jerome Clark's multi-volume *UFO Encyclopedia (*2nd edition. Holmes, PA: Omnigraphics, 1998, 1218pp (2 vols), ISBN: 0-7808-0097-4.).

70 In a recent Paracast poll, the results were Stanton Friedman, 13 votes; Jacque Vallee, 8 votes; Richard Dolan, 6 votes; Bruce Maccabee, 2 votes. James Moseley, Don Ecker, and Gene & David together each received one vote. Paul Kimball, Nick Pope, and Timothy Good, though on the poll, received no votes. Write-ins include Dennis Balthazer, and Timothy Beckley.

71. *UFO Magazine* is one. Once edited by the Eckers and well-respected, it is now run by Bill Birnes, who will print pretty much anything. The Mufon Journal is published by the Mutual UFO Network. Back issues are here. *Flying Saucer Review* is a British publication. *Fate Magazine* covers UFOs as well as other paranormal and strange phenomena. *Saucer Smear* is still being published as an irregular newsletter.

72. There is only one, and that is George Eberhart, a senior editor at the American Library Association. His books*: A Geo Bibliography of Anomalies: Primary Access to Observations of UFOs, Ghosts, and Other Mysterious Phenomena by George M.*

Eberhart. Greenwood Press, 1980, 1114pp, ISBN: 978 0313213373, and *UFOs and the Extraterrestrial Contact Movement: A Bibliography.* Lanham, MD: Scarecrow Press, 1986, 1298pp. ISBN: 978-0810819191. The only problem here is that they cover only up to the mid-eighties, but they are formidable studies with a tremendous amount of information in them. The only other bibliography I know of is *The UFO Literature; a comprehensive abbot ate bibliography of works in English*, by Richard Michael Rasmussen, Jefferson, NC: McFarland & Company, 1985, 26pp. ISBN: 0-89950-136-2.

73. NARCAP: The National Aviation Reporting Center on Anomalous Phenomena was established late in 2000, and is dedicated to the advancement of aviation safety issues as they apply to Unidentified Aerial Phenomena (UAP). Their report on the O'Hare UFO Incident has become an instant classic. They are probably the most objective organization out there studying the phenomena today.

74. Baxter, Karla, aka Connie Weber Menger. *My Saturnian Lover.* New York: Vantage Press, 1958. This hard-to-find vanity press book is by contactee Howard Menger's wife, who claims he is the reincarnation of a being from Saturn. If you thought Menger's claims were strange (and an Adamski knock off) those of his wife are even stranger.

75. Thomas Mantell became famous when his pursuit of a UFO in his P-51 Mustang in 1948 led to his death. He climbed in pursuit to

over 20,000 feet and passed out due to lack of oxygen. The crash was prominent in many of the early books on UFOs.

76. John G. Fuller's *Incident at Exeter* (New York: G.P. Putnam's Sons, Publishers, 1966, 251pp, Pre-ISBN days) concerns a series of incidents in southeastern New Hampshire in 1965 where a UFO with pulsating lights was seen hovering in the woods or chasing cars. In the major incident two police officers were involved. The Air Force initially suggested the many witnesses had witnessed an air force exercise, but ultimately the Secretary of the Air Force admitted to the policemen involved that the case remained unexplained. Fuller's book wound up on the New York Times bestseller list.

77. David Michael Jacobs is an historian and professor of history at Temple University. He specializes in abduction cases. His PhD dissertation, *The UFO Controversy in America*, (Bloomington, IN: Indiana University Press, 1975, 362pp. ISBN: 978-0253190062) is still available. He endures the usual criticisms involving leading the patient in hypnosis.

78. Michio Kaku is a physicist and futurist who have done work analyzing the types of civilizations that could be extant in the Universe. His latest book: *Physics of the Impossible: A Scientific Exploration into the World of Phasers, Force Fields, Teleportation, and Time Travel*, (New York: Doubleday, 2008, 329pp, ISBN: 978-0385520690) discusses some of his theories.

79. Linda Moulton Howe was an award-winning journalist who rose to prominence in the UFO field initially for her work on cattle

mutilations. Her Earth Files web site, which is a pay site, has much of her work. She was also involved peripherally in the early MJ-12 documents, having been shown what appear to be prototypes by none other than Richard Doty. She has followed the crop circle phenomenon as well. Her support for the Caret Drones hoax and Doty trickery has tarnished her reputation. Her work on mutilations is *Alien Harvest: Further Evidence Linking Animal Mutilations and Human Abductions to Alien Life Forms*, self-published, 1989, 455pp, ISBN: 978-0962057014.

80. Close Encounters of the first kind equal a UFO sighting. Close encounters of the second kind involve leaving some sort of evidence behind, whether indentations, burn marks, or even physical material. Close encounters of the third kind involve contact with an 'alien' being. Close encounters of the fourth kind involve abductions of humans by aliens. This fourth set was not a part of the original three, which were developed by J. Allen Hynek. In the interests of completeness it must be mentioned that Dr. Steven Greer has postulated Close Encounters of the Fifth kind as 'equal' contact between aliens and humans.

81. Pascagoula Abduction concerned two shipyard workers: Calvin Parker and Charles Hickson, who claim they were abducted while fishing in 1973. One interesting aspect of the case is that when they contacted the police, the sheriff left them in a room together and secretly recorded them. They also demanded to take a polygraph test. A personal account was written by Charles Hickson

called *UFO Contact at Pascagoula*, 2nd edition, 1983, 284pp. ISBN: 978-0960855865. It is still available but expensive.

82. The White Sands Incident (Louisville, KY: Best Books, Inc., 1966, 120pp, Pre ISBN Days) was written by Daniel Fry, probably the first of the classic contactees. It described his rides in a spaceship and dealings with an alien named Alan in July, 1949. Subsequent to this encounter Fry founded a group called Understanding which published a newsletter of the same name.

83. Ezekiel's Wheel is a series of Bible verses: Ezekiel 1:4-28 which appear to describe a spacecraft.

84. Although everyone gets very excited when such a thing is announced, the released files from several countries have heretofore not produced any earth shattering secrets. Great Britain released many files in 2008. The French space agency, CNES, released their files in 2007. Brazil opened up its UFO files (can't find an online version). Even the United States released its Project Blue Book files, available several places on the Internet. Some of the unknown cases are here. Other countries which have released files include Denmark, and Canada.

85. Richard Doty has been involved in UFO disinformation campaigns for decades. It was Richard Doty who was involved, along with Bill Moore, in the Paul Bennewitz affair, helping to drive him over the edge. It was Richard Doty who showed Linda Moulton Howe MJ-12-like documents. It was Richard Doty who was instrumental in spreading the Serpo documents around. Richard Doty is even a consultant to the X-files TV show. He is

now a patrol Sergeant for the New Mexico State Police. He co-wrote a book with Richard Collins called *Exempt from Disclosure* (Vandalia, OH: Peregrine Communications, 2006, 192pp. ISBN: 0-9766426-3-8) that details some of his activities, perhaps.

86. SETI is the 'Search for Extra Terrestrial Intelligence.' In most iterations of SETI radio telescopes are set to listen on what is thought to be a common frequency, such as the wavelength for Hydrogen. The results are analyzed by computer to determine a non-random sequence in hopes of finding a transmission from another civilization. Some people in the UFO field and elsewhere feel that SETI is an extreme waste of time. Stan Friedman is of this opinion. Other people that active-SETI (sending transmissions rather than just listening), is dangerous because other civilizations may not be benign.

87. Some common misidentifications of UFOs include aircraft, secret or otherwise, bright planets or stars, satellites, reflections, birds, Sun dogs, balloons, car headlights, lights on towers, and street lamps.

88. Probably the most famous debunking organization is the Committee for Skeptical Inquiry (formerly CSICOP). Others include the James Randi Educational Foundation, The Skeptics Society, and the Center for Inquiry.

89. Exopolitics is a combination of Disclosure Movement with the idea that we need to take contact with the space brothers a notch upwards away from abductions and to a state of equal participation of all races. Promoted by people such as Steven Greer and Michael

Salla, and Stephen Bassett, their organizations offer courses on how to be an extra-terrestrial ambassador. Proponents of this approach tend to align themselves with conspiracy movements such as the Truthers (9/11 conspiracy enthusiasts), and a belief that the Obama administration will finally break the deadlock on Disclosure. The Disclosure Movement itself has a goal have all governments, but particularly that of the United States, to disclose all it knows about the UFO phenomenon and extra-terrestrial involvement.

90. NUFORC is the National UFO Reporting Center run by Peter Davenport. It is located on a decommissioned ICBM missile site in eastern Washington State between Davenport and Harrington.

91. David is especially well known for his expertise in Photoshop. His books include *Photoshop Channel Chops* (New Riders Publishing, 1998, 226pp, ISBN: 978-1562057237); Adobe *Photoshop; a visual guide for the Mac* (Addison Wesley professional, 1996, 160pp, ISBN: 978-0201489934); and *Adobe Photoshop Handbook 2.5* (2nd edition, Random House, 1993, 215pp, ISBN: 978-0679791287). He has exposed many UFO pictures as fakes.

92. Oddly enough, Bigfoot (Sasquatch). A book specifically on this subject was written by Jack Lapsertis: *The Psychic Sasquatch and their UFO connection.* (North Carolina: Blue Water Publishing, 1998, 225pp. ISBN: 978-0926524170.) Mr Lapsertis claims to be a Sasquatch 'contactee.' Reviews of the book are, ah, 'mixed.' Here is another accounting of such a connection.

93. Japan Airlines Flight 1628 was harassed by several UFOs over Alaska in November, 1986. The unusual issue is that radar on the ground and on the airplane itself also picked up the unidentified craft. The entire conversation between the aircraft, a 747, and both military and civilian air traffic was recorded and made public.
94. The most common popular explanation is some sort of anti-gravity device that does not require propulsion by thrust or wings that lift the craft into the air and rely on forward momentum (airplanes) or fixed rotors (helicopters) to keep the craft aloft.
95. CUFOS is the Center for UFO Studies founded by J. Allen Hynek. It published the *International UFO Reporter*, and also the *Journal of UFO Studies*, which is a scholarly journal in the field. CUFOS has one of the larger libraries of UFO books and archives available.
96. The Alien Autopsy film made a sensation when it was released in 1995 by Ray Santilli. He claimed it was taken shortly after the Roswell UFO crash in 1947. The setting contains period pieces that were available during that time frame, including the clock, instruments, and garb worn by those performing the autopsy on an alien creature. Although several people labeled the film a fake, they had trouble debunking it. Then in 2006 Santilli admitted faking it, but he said it was based on original film he did see, but that this film had deteriorated because of humidity and heat. That remains his story to this day.
97. The Belgium UFO flap in 1989 and 1990 was of triangular craft seen over Brussels and elsewhere in Belgium. The military

freely admitted he sightings and cooperated with civilian authorities and the press in revealing what they knew.

98. Probably the most common recent body type ascribed to aliens is of the 'Grey,' a bipedal humanoid characterized by spindly arms and legs, but a relatively large head with large slanted eyes. This has become an archetype or alien. Interestingly, it first gained prominence after Strieber's *Communion* was released. However this was an artist's rendition which did NOT match Strieber's description. In the early contactee days aliens were depicted as very human like, but perhaps a bit shorter than normal. Another body type is the "Nordics," who are depicted as unusually tall and thin, almost always with very blonde or light hair. A reptilian body type has also been described, still a humanoid, but with scales and characteristics reminiscent of dinosaurs. Those interested in some comic relief on this issue may want to consider *Barlowe's Guide to Extraterrestrials* by Wayne Douglas Barlowe. New York: Workman Publishing, 1979, 112pp. ISBN: 0-89480-500-2.

99. Instead of going to the dentist, the story is that Eisenhower visited with two Nordics at Edwards Air Force Base in 1954 and discussed world issues via telepathy. Salla, of Exopolitics fame, is one of the proponents of this theory.

100. The Gulf Breeze Incident was, in hindsight, a carefully choreographed series of sightings initially by one Ed Walters, a house builder in the area. He claimed sightings and visitations beginning in November, 1987. In an unusual move, Mufon proclaimed Walter's photos genuine and Both Budd Hopkins and

Dr. Bruce Maccabee contributed to Walters' book: *The Gulf Breeze Sightings; the most astounding multiple Sightings of UFOs in U.S. History*. (New York: William Morrow, 1990, 348pp. ISBN: 0-688-09087-7). This quickly became a media sensation and many other people reported seeing UFOs in the area. The story started falling apart when the new owner of Walters' old house found a model of a UFO in his attic. Then a teen age neighbor came forward with a story that Walters asked him to help in composing multiple-exposure photographs. Although the story still has its adherents, Mufon finally withdrew its support in 1990, shortly after Walters' book was published.

(Courtesy Michael Schuyler, 2009 and the Paracast)

Chapter 34

Conclusion

I love this picture!

"Three score and thirteen years ago, something drastically changed on earth"

-John Ventre (2015)

In Whitley Strieber's book Communion, he said that the entities weren't ET but demonic. He felt that the struggle was for his soul. Since the godfathers of Ufology, Hynek and Vallee concluded that UFOs were real but just not from outer space and astrobiologists claim there is no proven life in space, here's what I believe:

When I look at the monthly MUFON Journal recap of sightings, it is startling how many different sizes and shapes (24) these craft come in. Researchers also say there are 176 different types of ET. What if the craft and its occupants were shape shifters from another dimension? Kenneth Arnold made that very comment 15 years after his initial sighting that he believed the craft were living creatures. The sheer number of sightings would indicate a massage fleet is here. When you consider the ritualistic cattle mutilation phenomena and the never ending abduction phenomena, you can't possibly conclude that these are explorers from space. Their behavior is indistinguishable from demons. Another comment I hear from witnesses is that, "only they could see the UFO even though there were others looking up" or "it couldn't be filmed". That confirms that some of these cases are projections into the mind of the viewer by telepathy which is drastically different than a hallucination.

(MUFON CMS)

Shape of Object	Number of Reports	
Sphere	144	
Other	73	
Triangle	68	
Disc	67	
Star-like	57	
Circle	50	
Oval	30	
N/A	27	
Fireball	27	

Cylinder	25	
Unknown	23	
Square/Rectangular	21	
Boomerang	21	
Cigar	16	
Diamond	13	
Chevron	9	
Flash	9	
Blimp	8	
Cone	7	
Egg	4	
Teardrop	4	
Saturn-like	3	
Bullet/Missile	2	
Cross	1	

I can envision a scenario where the Yellowstone super volcano explodes due to the earth's core heating up and plunges the world into an environmental super crisis as the oceans begin to die and nothing will grow due to acid rain. The Vatican announces first contact and "They" are our brothers. UFOs show up to help. They neutralize the acid rain and clean up the environmental damage or can genetically upgrade us to adapt by altering our DNA and the image we were created in. They say they are our friends. A charismatic leader emerges. This leader along with multi-national corporations moves us toward a one world government, leader, religion and army. We willingly give up our Constitution and freedoms. We are deceived by the alien "Antichrist".

Stanton Friedman likes to say that "there is a Cosmic Watergate". I say there is a "Cosmic Deception". There is a concerted effort to attract our attention away from what is really going on.

For me, it was never about aliens or ghosts or God. For me, it was always about the origin of the species. Was it creation, evolution or the genetic engineering of us (intelligent design)? I started out researching end time prophecy in 1996 and have come full circle. I have concluded my 20 year journey and am quite comfortable with my conclusion that there are angels and demons and also ETs. The Universe is teaming with life but a portion of what we are experiencing in the modern era is the biblical conflict between Jesus and Lucifer. We are the pawns in this great game of chess that revolves around humanity. There are non-human entities out there who are players in this game or instruments to be used against us in a great Trojan horse deception. If these are simply ET scientists from outer space, then how many abductions do they need to extract samples? They could surely clone the first few samples. If they need minerals or raw materials, asteroids are loaded with them. There are way too many sightings and the craft and creatures too varied if they are simply mapping earth. No craft has ever been spotted approaching earth from deep space even though the Vatican is searching for one or more likely already knows the date and time of contact.

I firmly believe "They" were abundantly here in the before Christ days and openly showed themselves. Vedic text from 8000 years ago clearly describes Virmana or space ships and a war that erupted. There has clearly been a change in the pattern of contact commencing upon Christ's arrival and then again at the start of WWII. But again, who were "They"? Two years ago I was so certain that we were the product of an alternative history of alien intervention that went back 47,000 years because evolution doesn't add up and scientists are so smug regarding their theories (educated guesses). I was never quite comfortable with the ancient alien theory because we live on such a haunted planet where every culture, no matter how isolated or undeveloped, has similar spiritual and paranormal beliefs. I now realize, after applying theology to this equation, close encounters of the fourth kind (abductions) by Greys have been nothing more than the battle between Satan and the son of God where Satan will do everything possible to prevent Christ's return and deceive us and pull us away from the great truth. This includes the creation of soul-less hybrid humans that cannot be saved. And yet isn't it already upon us with Muslim terrorists, African butchery of their own and all violent criminal behavior, human trafficking and drug use? I've said for a long time that not all humans have souls. Human culture is not from God but of this world. Is it any different now than when Moses returned from Mount Sinai with the Ten Commandments? I surmised there weren't enough souls to go around or that some were the offspring of Godly Seth and some the offspring of evil Cain. Now I understand differently.

I also surmise that the Nordics are the "left behind" of their species and are under the control of the Greys who are fallen angels and demonic. The Nordics are often in the company of the Greys who do not seem autonomous. Let's hope this doesn't happen to us.

All programs have a beginning, middle and end. This modern program started around 1939 with the rise of Hitler and the advent of WWII. The middle has been the clandestine abductions where hybrids will replace pure humans in an invasion of the body snatchers scenario. How disturbing is it to hear from numerous abductees that the intruders plan to be here permanently with us and everyone will be happy in their place in the hybrid hierarchy? No freedom, no individuality. Many world leaders speak of the one world government which will be the culmination of their program and the end of us. You also can't overlook that 80% of serial killers have been after 1950, cattle mutilations after 1975 and exorcisms after 1990!

I would've never come to this conclusion without my research into the Grey alien abduction phenomena and the paranormal activity that has followed me since December 1988 when I almost switched my return flight from Europe to the doomed Pan Am flight 103. I needed to explain this which is beyond the scope of science. For others, this is strictly about government cover-up or aliens because they are not trying to explain the entire realm of the unexplained. You may think I'm just "flip flopping" my opinions but there is an evolution of knowledge that takes place and most experts do not research the history and entire field of UFOs and unfortunately get stuck on one theory for life.

We are experiencing two types of phenomena; nuts and bolts craft from outer space and copy cats from a hidden dimension. If we accept that UFOs are real but some are not from outer space and ask, "What is the String Theory for where do "They" and all that is unexplained but interlinked come from"? The answer would be inter-dimensional. There are too many real but unexplained paranormal events from ghosts to angels to glimpses of cryptids to ETs. What if they are all related to a dimension right around us, including Heaven and Hell, which some pass through by accident and others pass through by design? Inter-dimensional does not negate God. It may be the same thing; good and evil forces regardless of what you name them. Ultimately, it all comes down to faith. There will be no hiding or faking it when the time comes. Earth is at the intersection of dimensions and our sign post reads "Enter, we want to believe"!

Sadly, as I have bounced this realization off the many Ufologists I know. They all look at me like I'm nuts. None, and I mean none, believe this to be true. Being an Ufologist who believes in Jesus and Revelation is a lonely place. I believe I have experienced a mini "born again". It is safer to believe they travel in craft from light years away and are coming to stop nuclear war and clean up the environment. Only, it is not the truth. They have rarely and most likely never intervened for our benefit in modern times. The inability and unwillingness of science to explain UFOs after 75 years only supports an alternative theory. I am completely convinced there is a small group in the government that controls the information regarding this but the string theory of everything is that it all started in the Garden of Eden and it will all end there but with different results for us. In this field which is like quick sand and has no answers; fallen angels and ET are two separate but very real issues or the same issue. Knowing which is which and when is the question. . . . .

From Nick Pope with permission:

TOP SECRET
UK EYES ONLY

ALIEN INVASION WAR PLAN

1. First warning of an alien invasion is likely to come from the Hubble Space Telesc the Deep Space Network, or a radio telescope, e.g. Jodrell Bank. The Ballistic Missile E Warning System at RAF Fylingdales may also play a role in detection.

2. UK Threat Level will immediately be raised to CRITICAL.

3. The PM will form a War Cabinet, with membership to include the Home Secretary the Secretary of State for Defence, the Foreign Secretary, the Chief of the Defence Staff and the Government Chief Scientific Adviser.

4. Cabinet Office Briefing Room A (COBRA) will be activated and the Ministry of Defence (MoD) will exercise command of the joint military operation through the Perman Joint Headquarters at Northwood.

5. While the MoD has the operational lead, the Cabinet Office will co-ordinate the wi government response under the provisions of the Civil Contingencies Act 2004, supplemented by guidance contained in "Emergency Response and Recovery" and "Emergency Preparedness".

6. Any UK military response will probably form part of an international coalition, poss US-led, and involving NATO. Irrespective of what command and control arrangements a agreed, the UK must retain the right to invoke the National Veto.

7. Legal authority for military action would stem from the authority of the United Nati and the international community to resist an attack on soverign nations. While a UN Security Council Resolution authorising military action is desirable, the Attorney General should confirm such action is compliant with national and international law. All UK militar action must be in accordance with the Law of Armed Conflict and with domestic law.

8. All forces with air-to-air and ground-to-air capability may be deployed. The bulk of UK effort will comprise Eurofighter Typoon aircraft armed with Meteor missiles, and Type destroyers armed with Sea Viper missiles. The Defence Science and Technology Laboratory at Porton Down will be asked to develop a biological weapon, though if we a facing a machine intelligence, directed energy weapons and EMP weapons may be mor effective. The UK's strategic nuclear deterrant may be used as a weapon of last resort.

9. Extraterrestrial invaders will almost certainly possess weapons of mass destructio and technologies significantly in advance of our own. Key priorities must be to gather intelligence on alien technology, and to reverse-engineer it.

10. All information relating to this war plan is to be classified TOP SECRET.

Nick Pope
MJ12 (UK) (J9)

TOP SECRET
UK EYES ONLY

Chapter 35

Epilogue

This article appeared on the MUFON.com homepage in June 2015 and was gleaned from this book so I put it at the end even though it is a repeat:

I joined MUFON in 1998. I retired from UPS in 2012 and spend my time writing books, running multiple states for MUFON, appearing in a couple of TV series, playing racquetball and kick boxing. I'm my Rotary Club Pres. and volunteer for JDRF.

I have never seen a UFO and had no interest in the subject until I was almost 40 years old. I was a B-movie, comicon, horror movie and magazine fan as a kid. I had no interest in ET unless it was a cool movie creature like in Predator or Alien and there was a lot of action in the movie. I started to experience paranormal activity in my early thirties when I moved to Oklahoma weeks after almost getting on doomed Pan Am flight 103 returning from Europe. This inadvertently led me to wanting to write a sci-fi novel regarding end time prophecy which led me to the UFO question.

Along the way, my opinion has changed numerous times as to the nature of this elusive intrusive subject. My involvement with MUFON was nuts and bolts; "They" were ships from outer space. As I learned more about the phenomenon, my opinion changed to, "They" were inter-dimensional. I was searching for the string theory of everything unexplained. You can only form your opinion after reading many books with different viewpoints on the topic. My books have gone from religious to anti-religious to the genetic engineering of us to Tribulation.

For me, it was never about aliens or ghosts or God. For me, it was always about the origin of the species. Was it creation, evolution or the genetic engineering of us (intelligent design)? I started out researching end time prophecy in 1996 and have come full circle.

UFOs are real but are unexplainable by the close minded and by use of our primitive technology. Maybe if we weren't trying to shoot them down we would be closer to an answer, but until disclosure is made this will remain an observational science. Although most appear to be neutral, you cannot ignore the statements of abductees. I believe that we have always been in contact with them for as long as 50,000 years. Some say we may be codependent on each other; us for progress as they pull us forward and them for genetic material. I cannot support a theory of evolution that has missing links. I also firmly believe in God and a spirit world. There is also the possibility that they occupy part of our minds since many people feel a detachment between their minds and bodies but believe there is intervention from a guardian angel at times and that events are predetermined. We absolutely have free will which is the whole point. It seems as though this has something to do with everything; I believe it goes way beyond "interplanetary" as an explanation. I believe there is a connection between all paranormal including religion, dimensions and UFOs. Maybe we're just spirits on a human experience.

It is also obvious that the U.S. Air Force and C.I.A. have deliberately deceived the public in violation of the law and may be in communication with them. I also believe that our Defense Department is acting in our own best interests in this perverted act of protecting us and obtaining technology. The real Sword of Damocles that hangs over us is the scientific community's failure to investigate this phenomena and the media's failure to report on it seriously. Ufology has raised my consciousness and I no longer fear the unknown. I hope that humans are a unique and precious species in the Universe and not a resource for exploitation. I think the real threat of disclosure will be loyalty. Like a “Zeta” (Stockholm) Syndrome, many will side with the superior being, not their own kind.

But more importantly, how can we truly advance as a species until we know how we got here? How can we decide on our purpose until we know what the purpose of us is? If a superior Being created us, then we should all be in harmony with nature and non-violence and human equality. If we were genetically engineered then we should continue that engineering by enhancing our DNA to reach our pinnacle of perfection. I don’t think I want to be a new species. We would no longer be in the image of our creator and wouldn’t this in essence avert Satan’s destruction? If we evolved with no God then we should continue the Darwinian survival of the fittest pursuit of money and technology and be the best sinners possible since we are just animals and the end justifies the means. We should protect our planets resources from overpopulation by eugenically eliminating the weaker strains of humans from the genetic pool. Hasn’t evolution taught us to not believe in God but to put our faith in the infallibility of science and the coming ETs? This duplicity is our single most important question.

I have found the UFO question to be the most profound of my life and it has led me to where I need to be and was probably meant to end up. But like Bruce Lee’s JKD style of fighting, you must clear your mind of preconceived ideas and boundaries in order to see what is actually confronting you and how to react to it.

My next book, *The Ufologist: The Haunting of John Ventre*, will be on Demonology and I will explain the true nature of the Grey alien abduction and why Ancient Alien theory is wrong.

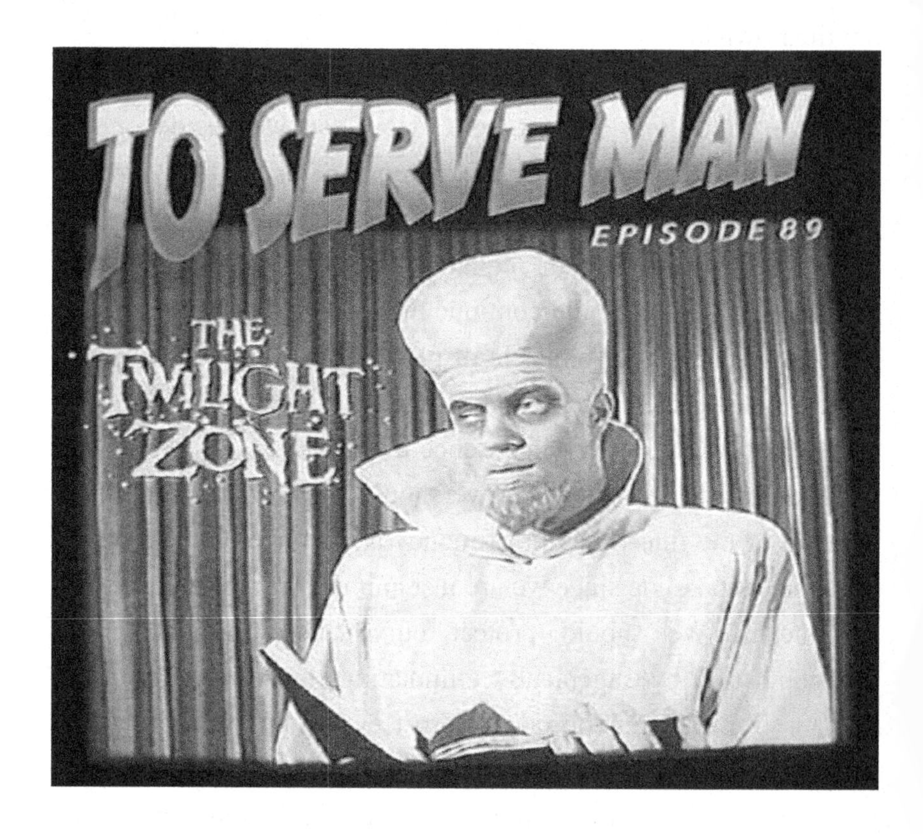

"And you were dead in your trespasses and sins, in which you formerly walked according to the course of this world, according to the prince of the power of the AIR (UFOs), of the spirit that is now working in the sons of disobedience." (Ephesians 2:1–2) **. . . also known as the Morningstar and can appear as an angel of light (Orbs)!**

Chapter 36

About the Author

"The truth is out there or has it always been in the Bible?"

John Ventre is an author, lecturer, and TV show host and occasional security consultant for the Gerson Lehrman Group. He is the retired Pennsylvania State Security and Public Affairs Director for UPS and was his company's liaison to his local Congressman and was elected to the Republican Committee. John used to also head up his company's crisis management team for three states. He ran for Westmoreland County Commissioner in 2019 and Republican Chair in 2020.

John was the Pa State Director for the Mutual UFO Network and was MUFONs first multi-state director managing seven states in the north east for ten years. John is the author of the novels: *12/21/2012 A Prophecy, The Day After 2012, UFOs over Pennsylvania, Apophis 2029 and An Alternative History of Mankind.* It was John's research into end time prophecy and ancient cultures that got him interested in UFOs in 1996. Many cultures spoke of star people or people from the sky which gave them advanced knowledge which interested John in UFOs. The more John researched, the more he found. John was a comicon; Famous Monsters of Filmland; Fate magazine reader in his younger days. John didn't choose Ufology; it chose him.

John was a member of the FBI's Infra-Gard group and the DHS Regional Business Coalition. John is also a lifetime member of the NRA. John has served on the Board of Directors for Juvenile Diabetes, the Westmoreland Economic Growth Connection and

Rotary. John is a United Way Tocqueville Society member for charitable giving and is his Rotary Club President. John is the co-inventor of the Thor Wood Splitter and owns the UFO themed Mexican restaurant trademark "Flying Salsa".

John appeared in the Discovery Channels *UFOs over Earth* series in 2008 and the History Channels *UFO Hunters* in 2009, the *Anderson Cooper* show in 2012, Destination America's *Alien Mysteries* and History's *Ancient Aliens* (cameo) in 2013 and H2's (History) *Hangar 1: The UFO Files* and PCTV21's *UFOs over Pittsburgh* in 2014 to 2017 and changed its name to *The String Theory of the Unexplained;* and *Close Encounters* for Discovery Science in 2015 and *UFO Conspiracy: Hunt for the Truth* in 2017. John has appeared on numerous radio shows and is a speaker at various UFO and Paranormal conferences such as the MUFON and Paradigm Symposium's, UFO Congress and Fortean Conference's. John has also lectured at Duquesne and Drexel Universities on UFOs along with the Wizard World Comicon in 2015. John gives twenty two different lecture presentations: End Time Prophecy, The Case for UFOs, UFOs in Art and History, The Chronology of UFOs, Anderson Cooper and the Case for UFOs, UFOs and the Media, An Alternative History, My Haunted Life, Kecksburg Solved, Eerie Pa and the 2008 Pa UFO Wave.

John has appeared in 3 movies: Kecksburg, Exorcism Prayer and Flatwoods.

John has come full circle with his research into alternative sciences and theories which have strongly led him back to Jesus, "The Ancient of Days". His biggest fear is that evolution does occur and the malevolent inter-dimensional entities have evolved faster than us and are now here to start the end of days.

I've adopted five Doberman's from shelters. Man's best friend and more loyal than any human could be:

Good Doggy- 1994-2004

Precious- 1990-1999

Mama Bear- 1999-2011

Poppa Bear- 2000-2012

Apophis- 2011-present

I was Apophis' sixth owner at ten months old. He was bred to be a guard dog. My next dog will be named Majestic since my dogs tend to live 12 years. . . . .

I wrote four books since I retired from UPS in 2012. This is my sixth and last UFO book that I intend to write on UFOs. I have other goals on my bucket list. I intend to run for an elected office.

Note: I wrote my seventh book in 2016 on Demonology based on a malevolent attack upon me while researching the true cause of alien abduction.

On the set of *Hangar 1*

"Quit making stuff up!"

(Used by permission©2016 CES www.grayzonecomics.com)

"Only through the eyes of death will I know the truth"

Kathy and Fred Lane presenting our Erie UFO Conference donation to JDRF May 2015

Warning

To young parents and new grandparents: do not ignore young children who just start to speak and in their first few years of intellect when they try to tell you of visitors. Whether it is of monsters or ghosts or aliens, there is something to it. Do not ignore it. Their spirits are closer to the truth and haven't been sealed in yet with disinformation as their brains are still in an alpha state. If any of my future grandchildren start speaking of such things, I will sit in a chair in their room overnight and watch just as the Watchers watch us. I will protect them in the physical realm as their guardian angel protects them in the spiritual realm. This is not something to be taken lightly or ignored. Do not send a young child back to their room to face these aberrations alone. The scariest words you can hear after death:

"I never knew you. Away from me"

- Matthew 7:21-23

Give this book as a Holiday gift

Similar to Pinochio, when you make stuff up, your hair grows:

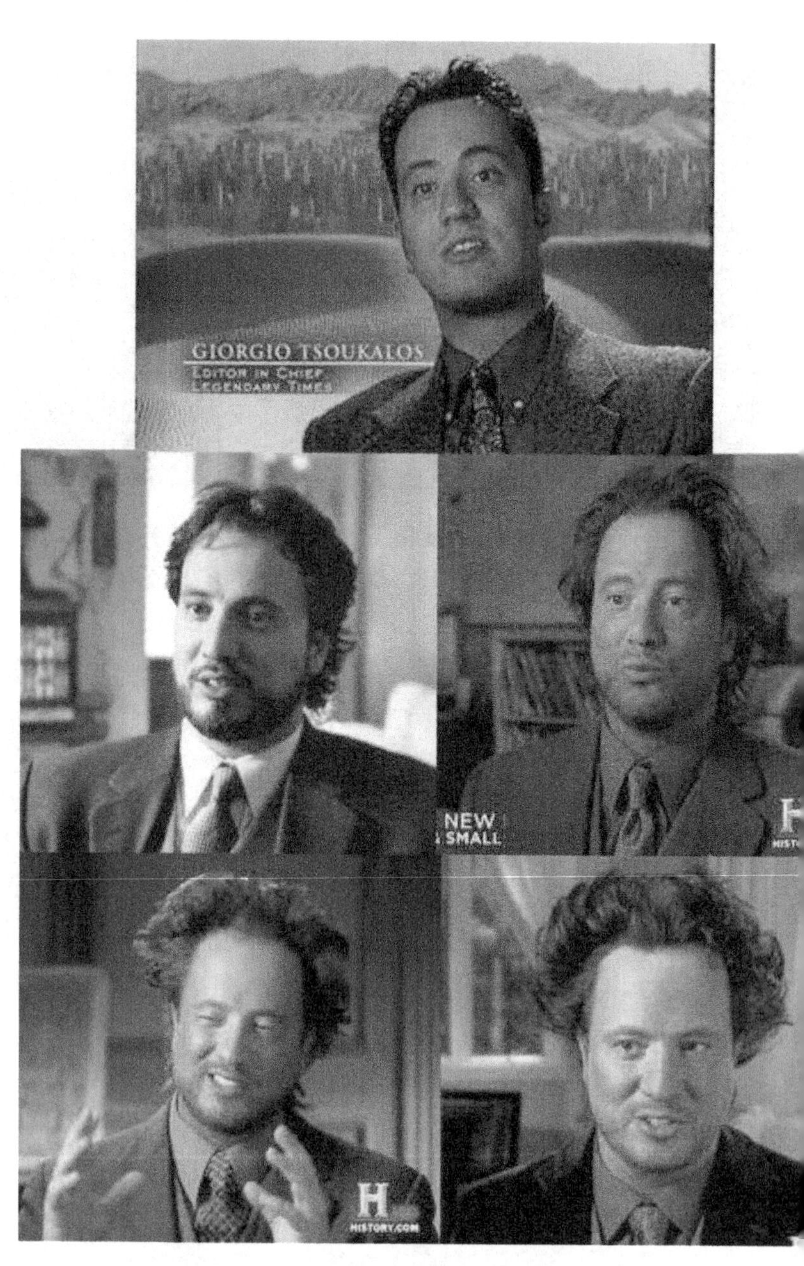

Similar to Pinocchio, his hair grew with every lie. . .

Although the election is 8 months from this publishing, my pick to save America from socialism is:

Trump is the equal and opposite reaction to Obama

Made in the USA
Middletown, DE
17 October 2021